The Bilingual Muse

SRLT

The Bilingual Muse

Self-Translation among Russian Poets

Adrian Wanner

NORTHWESTERN UNIVERSITY PRESS / EVANSTON, ILLINOIS

Northwestern University Press
www.nupress.northwestern.edu

This book is freely available in an open access edition thanks to TOME (Toward
an Open Monograph Ecosystem)—a collaboration of the Association of American
Universities, the Association of University Presses, and the Association of Research
Libraries—and the generous support of the Pennsylvania State University. Learn
more at the TOME website, available at openmonographs.org.

DOI: 10.21985/n2-8cfb-pa17

Printed in the United States of America

10   9   8   7   6   5   4   3   2   1

Library of Congress Cataloging-in-Publication Data
Names: Wanner, Adrian, 1960– author.
Title: The bilingual muse : self translation among Russian poets / Adrian Wanner.
Other titles: Studies in Russian literature and theory.
Description: Evanston, Illinois : Northwestern University Press, 2020. | Series:
    Northwestern University Press Studies in Russian literature and theory | Includes
    bibliographical references and index.
Identifiers: LCCN 2019042529 | ISBN 9780810141230 (paperback) |
    ISBN9780810141247 (cloth) | ISBN 9780810141254 (ebook)
Subjects: LCSH: Russian poetry—19th century—History and criticism. | Russian
    poetry—20th century—History and criticism. | Self-translation. | Russian
    poetry—Translations—History and criticism. | Multilingualism and literature.
Classification: LCC PG2985 .W36 2020 | DDC 891.7109—dc23
LC record available at https://lccn.loc.gov/2019042529

Contents

Acknowledgments

The impulse for writing this book came from an invitation to give a keynote at a conference in Uppsala in June 2014. The theme of the conference, which was organized by Julie Hansen and Susanna Witt, was translation and translingualism in Russian contexts. Searching for a topic, I settled on self-translation among Russian-American poets. This subject had the advantage of engaging the two conference themes of translation and translingualism. I had worked on translation and translingualism before, but never in combination with each other, and an additional advantage of this choice was that it allowed me to indulge my love for poetry. Over the years that followed, the project continued to grow and eventually morphed into a more comprehensive study of Russian poets of the past 200 years who translated their own works not only into English, but also into German, French, and Italian, the languages I grew up with in Switzerland.

In hindsight, the Uppsala conference has acquired the status of an almost legendary event. Many of the participants have become regular presenters in the translation panels that have sprung up at the conventions of the Association of Slavic, East European and Eurasian Studies and the American Association of Teachers of Slavic and East European Languages. A related phenomenon, which has begun to overlap with the former group, are the panel streams on translingualism at the meetings of the American Comparative Literature Association organized by Steven Kellman and Natasha Lvovich, who also hosted, together with Ilan Stavans, a symposium entitled "Writing in the Stepmother Tongue" at Amherst College in October 2015. All of these events gave me inspiration for my project. During a sabbatical leave in 2016–17, I presented aspects of this book at conferences and symposia in New York, Oslo, Uppsala, Tartu, and Utrecht. A workshop on the Russian Literary Diaspora organized by Maria Rubins at University College London in May 2018 provided a welcome opportunity for additional helpful feedback.

I am grateful to my numerous colleagues for inspirational conversations. In particular, I thank Julie Hansen, Natasha Lvovich, Maria Rubins, and David Bethea, who read earlier versions of portions of this book and provided useful comments. I am also indebted to Miriam Finkelstein, who invited me to a stimulating symposium on multilingual Slavic poetry at the University of Innsbruck in June 2017. I thank Kevin Platt, Pamela Davidson, Zakhar Ishov, and Eugenia Kelbert for helpful suggestions. Hilde Hoogenboom, many decades ago, introduced me to the work of Elizaveta Kul'man while we were both graduate students at Columbia University, and Ilya Vinitsky engaged with me in a spirited exchange of e-mails devoted to Kul'man in the summer of 2018. Natalia Bochkareva, Alexandra Berlina, and Anna Lushenkova Foscolo provided assistance with locating hard-to-find materials, and Rainer Stillers in Berlin kindly allowed me to benefit from his expertise in Italian poetry.

Earlier versions of chapters 4 and 6 have appeared in *Slavic and East European Journal* ("Poems and Problems: Vladimir Nabokov's Dilemma of Poetic Self-Translation," *Slavic and East European Journal* 61, no. 1 [2017]: 70–91) and in *Translation Studies* ("The Poetics of Displacement: Self-Translation among Contemporary Russian-American Poets," *Translation Studies* 11, no. 2 [2018]: 122–38). I thank Irene Masing Delic, the former editor of *Slavic and East European Journal*, and the two anonymous reviewers for their careful and detailed engagement with my article. I am also indebted to the two readers of *Translation Studies* and the two peer evaluators of Northwestern University Press for their constructive feedback.

The poem "October Tune," which appears on page 148, is from *Collected Poems in English* by Joseph Brodsky, copyright © 2000 by the Estate of Joseph Brodsky; reprinted by permission of Farrar, Straus and Giroux and by Carcanet Press Limited.

I thank Andrey Gritsman and Katia Kapovich for their kind permission to cite their self-translated poems in Russian and English. I owe a special gratitude to Andrey for inviting me to speak at a bilingual evening of Russian-American poetry in New York in January 2018 and for visiting my translation seminar at Penn State in April 2018, giving the students the unique opportunity to discuss works of self-translated bilingual poetry with their author. My Penn State colleague Patrick McGrady, the Charles V. Hallman Curator at the Palmer Museum of Art, has shared with me his insights about Kandinsky, while Irina Mikaelian, Yelena Zotova, and Alexandra Shapiro have provided me with helpful comments about the finer points of their native Russian language. The debt I owe my most faithful reader, Cathy Wanner, for her moral support and everything else, is beyond words.

The Bilingual Muse

"The Trick of Doubling Oneself"

WHAT HAPPENS WHEN poets translate their own work into a foreign language? Can such a thing even be done with any success? If poetry, according to Robert Frost's much-quoted dictum, is what is lost in translation,[1] the attempt to rewrite one's own poems in another language seems doubly doomed to failure. The intimate connection of poetry to the sound, rhythm, and morphology of its linguistic medium makes the translation of poems an elusive enterprise. Moreover, the aesthetic viability of poetic creation outside the mother tongue has been met with widespread skepticism since the romantic period. A poetic self-translator, then, seeks to accomplish simultaneously two feats that are generally considered extremely challenging, if not impossible—translating poetic texts, and writing poetry in a foreign language.

Not everybody would agree, of course, that these are insurmountable hurdles or even serious impediments to poetic self-translation. The assumptions underlying the putative hardship of translingual creativity are conditioned by cultural and psychological factors. Popular opinion notwithstanding, poetic self-translation is actually a less marginal activity than what one may think. Contrary to what has been claimed, the phenomenon cannot be reduced to just "a few very rare exceptions."[2] As Rainier Grutman has pointed out, no fewer than eight Nobel Prize laureates in literature, roughly one out of every thirteen, have been self-translators. Five of them—Frédéric Mistral, Rabindranath Tagore, Karl Gjellerup, Czesław Milosz, and Joseph Brodsky—were poets.[3] This fact has not received much attention because the "monolingual paradigm," to use a term coined by Yasemin Yildiz, still predominates in literary criticism. According to this paradigm, "individuals and social formations are imagined to possess one 'true' language only, their 'mother tongue,' and through this possession to be organically linked to an exclusive, clearly demarcated ethnicity, culture, and nation."[4] In such a view, poetic writing outside the mother tongue and self-translation into a non-native language appear as eccentric anomalies that fall through the cracks of a taxonomy where, despite evidence to the contrary, "mononational

1

constructions of modern and contemporary poetry" are still largely posited as the norm.[5]

In this book I analyze the bilingual oeuvre of seven Russian-born poets—some very prominent, some less so—who self-translated their poems from their native Russian into English, French, German, or Italian. For a variety of historical, geographical, and political reasons, Russia has provided a particularly fertile environment for multilingual writing and self-translation. As an entity uneasily hovering between empire and nation-state, the country has given rise to both ideologies of translatability and untranslatability. In his monograph on translation and the making of modern Russian literature, Brian Baer argues that the privileging of the mother tongue and the proclaimed impossibility of translation have served to promote an agenda of nationalist exclusiveness. By contrast, multiethnic and multilingual empires have had a theoretical and practical investment in the idea of translatability.[6] Given the exalted role that poetry has enjoyed in the ecology of Russian culture since the late eighteenth century, the country offers a privileged site to consider self-translation and the vagaries that affect poetic texts when their authors propel them outside the national language.

POETRY BEYOND THE MOTHER TONGUE

Poetry occupies a distinct status in debates about translingualism and the monolingual paradigm. It is a commonly held belief that writing great prose in an acquired language is hard, but achievable—after all, Joseph Conrad, Vladimir Nabokov, and Samuel Beckett are here to prove it—but that "genuine" poetry can only be written in the mother tongue. Some of this thinking goes back to German romantic notions of the national soul rooted in the native idiom, of which poetic masterpieces provide the highest and most exemplary illustration. In his seminal lecture "On the Different Methods of Translating" delivered to the Prussian Academy of Sciences in 1813, Friedrich Schleiermacher, the German theologian and founder of hermeneutics, argued that it could not be a legitimate goal of a translation "to show the work as it would be had the author himself written it originally in the reader's tongue," because he regarded original creation outside the mother tongue as a chimera, if not a crime. In Schleiermacher's opinion, "if the aim of this activity were truly to write equally as well and as originally in the foreign tongue as in one's own, then I would not hesitate to declare this a wicked and magical art like the trick of doubling oneself, an attempt not only to mock the laws of nature but also to bewilder."[7] Richard Wagner, in his screed against "Judaism in Music," asserted that "to make poetry in a foreign tongue has hitherto been impossible, even to geniuses of highest rank."[8] We may dismiss such statements as an expression of nationalist or anti-Semitic prejudice, but similar views have also been voiced by far different people, for example the eminent cosmopolitan intellectual Sir Isaiah Berlin. In a conversation about Joseph Brodsky's English-language poetry (of which he disapproved), Berlin said the following:

> A poet can only write in his own language, the language of his childhood. Not a single poet has ever created anything worthwhile in a foreign language. . . . Poetry only speaks in the native language.

This categorical assertion was followed by a remarkable personal admission:

> Genuinely, I only love Russian poetry. I know English poetry, I studied in England, I went to English school, I know it from childhood, all of that. Of course there are remarkable things. But this cannot be compared to my attitude towards Russian poetry. . . . I read Pushkin or whomever, even minor poets . . . not good poets at all . . . it speaks to me about something. English poetry does not speak to me.[9]

Similar opinions have also been expressed by other multilingual intellectuals or poets such as Tsvetan Todorov and Czesław Milosz.[10] If appreciating a poem written in a foreign language already poses problems, *composing* poetry in a non-native tongue seems even more challenging. As David Ian Hanauer has put it, "it is commonly perceived that second language writers who by definition have acquired and learnt this second language do not and probably cannot write poetry."[11] This is not necessarily only a question of verbal or technical competence. In her comprehensive study of the bilingual mind, the psycholinguist Aneta Pavlenko argues that "at the heart of the L2 poetry 'problem' is not the lack of linguistic mastery but the lack of an emotional and physical connection: the same linguistic estrangement that enables self-exploration through L2 prose weakens emotional self-expression through L2 poetry."[12] To back up her argument, Pavlenko refers to the example of Marc Chagall, who was not only a painter, but also a poet. Despite living in France after age twenty-four and being a fluent French speaker, Chagall wrote poetry only in Yiddish and Russian, the languages of his childhood and adolescence. As Pavlenko argues, the French language, acquired in adulthood, "did not provide emotional access and relief" and was therefore unsuitable for poetic expression.[13]

Pavlenko's theory is predicated on the romantic notion of poetry as a vehicle of emotional self-expression. But surely this is not the only way to experience or to define poetry. T. S. Eliot, for example, took a very different tack when he famously wrote that "poetry is not a turning loose of emotion, but an escape from emotion; it is not the expression of personality, but an escape from personality."[14] As a counter-example to Chagall, one could mention another twentieth-century Russian painter who was also a poet: Wassily Kandinsky. Kandinsky wrote poetry in three languages: his native Russian, German, and French. Remarkably, he began writing in French only after his forced relocation from Germany to France in 1933 when he was already in his seventies. Rather than providing emotional relief, the switch to French afforded Kandinsky an opportunity to experiment in a new linguistic medium, just like his switch from painting to poetry had been a form of artistic border-crossing.

The most basic feature that distinguishes poetry from prose is a specific use of language based on formal constraints. Why should it not be possible to develop an appreciation or capacity for poetic creation in a non-native language—aside from the fact, of course, that for most people writing verse is more difficult than writing prose? (This is also true for poetic creativity in the native tongue.) One could even argue that it might be easier to write poetry than prose in a foreign language. The constraints attached to poetic discourse make it a more artificial form of expression. In that sense, writing verse differs from writing prose in the same way that using a foreign language differs from self-expression in the native idiom, adding an element of artifice and conscious linguistic effort. The physical effect of producing a "foreign" sound, rather than disconcerting, can also be exhilarating. Not all people share Isaiah Berlin's emotional blockage with regard to poetry written in a non-native idiom. A perfect command of the language might not even be required to appreciate foreign-language poetry. Joseph Brodsky developed a lifelong love for John Donne and W. H. Auden during his exile in the Russian north at a time when his knowledge of English was still rudimentary at best.

As Brodsky's example shows, the assumption that poetry can only be appreciated in the native tongue is open to challenge. Choosing a foreign language as a medium of poetic expression may carry certain risks, but it also offers creative opportunities. If we assume that language shapes thinking, expanding one's linguistic repertoire entails a widening of potential poetic creativity. Writing poetry "with an accent," so to speak, can open new expressive pathways that are closed to a monolingual speaker trapped in the conventions of the native idiom. Furthermore, one could argue that the "de-automatized," slowed-down approach necessitated by a less familiar linguistic medium corresponds to a mode of reading that is ideally suited for poetry. As David Ian Hanauer puts it:

> The relatively slow decoding and semantic activation processes of second language readers leads to a situation in which the L2 reader always has some cognizance of the actual surface features of the text that they are reading. . . .

In fact, as early as the beginning of the 20th century, Russian Formalists argued that poetry reading involved texts that were linguistically constructed so as to specifically overcome the automaticity of first language reading. Ironically, perhaps, these statements seem to suggest that poetry reading turns first language readers into second language readers; or to put it in a different way, poetry reading for first and second language readers may be a similar process.[15]

Composing poetry in a non-native language or in multiple languages is less rare than one might think. As Leonard Forster has shown in his pioneering monograph *The Poet's Tongues* (1970), multilingual poetry was a widespread practice in medieval and early modern Europe, when authors routinely switched between Latin and a vernacular language, and increasingly also between individual vernacular languages. Poetic creativity in non-native languages can also be found among more recent poets, such as Stefan George, Rainer Maria Rilke, and members of the twentieth-century European avant-garde. As Forster shows, before the concept of language was essentialized by Johann Gottfried Herder and the German romantics, poets switched quite easily from one idiom to another without much concern for "language loyalty." Such an approach was possible because, as Forster points out, "poetry operated with a relatively restricted range of subject matter, formulae and topoi, which were international and formed part of a general European cultural heritage."[16] Similarly, switching languages became a more common practice again in twentieth-century avant-garde and conceptualist poetry, where language is treated as simply a kind of raw material rather than invested with metaphysical significance. Viktor Shklovsky's modernist concept of *ostranenie* (defamiliarization) validated "foreignness" as a positive aesthetic quality. In fact, seen from a historical perspective, as Shklovsky pointed out, poetic language was often quite literally foreign: "Just as Sumerian might have been regarded as a 'poetic language' by an Assyrian, so Latin was considered poetic by many in medieval Europe. Similarly, Arabic was thought poetic by a Persian and Old Bulgarian was regarded likewise by a Russian."[17]

While much of the early modern poetic writing in non-native languages amounted, in Forster's words, to mere "five-finger exercises," it could occasionally acquire a more serious significance. Commenting on the poetry that John Milton wrote in Italian, Forster makes a telling observation: "It sometimes happens that the poet can express his feelings more freely in the foreign language than his own. It is as if the use of the foreign language removes certain inhibitions; the formal exercise suddenly acquires 'soul.'"[18] We seem to be back in Pavlenko's domain of poetry as emotional self-expression, but with a reverse argument. For some poets, it appears, the expression of feelings is facilitated, rather than impeded, by the foreign-language medium. Poetry in a foreign language can even have a particular kind of seductive appeal. Theodor Adorno used an eroticized metaphor when he likened the attractiveness of foreign words to "the craving for foreign and if possible exotic girls; what lures is a kind of exogamy of language, which would like to escape from the sphere of what is always the same, the spell of what one is and knows anyway."[19] To be sure, such infatuations may be superficial and naive and lead to eventual disappointment. But surely, if we want to stay for a moment with Adorno's simile, exogamy can also result in a lifelong happy marriage.

THE CHALLENGE OF SELF-TRANSLATION

If there are no a priori reasons that would preclude a poet from composing verse in a foreign language, the stakes are raised considerably when it comes to the issue of self-translation. The problem now is not only to create a poetic text in a non-native idiom, but to reproduce an artistic concept that has already received a concrete shape in the native tongue by re-creating it in a different linguistic medium. Given the rootedness of poetry in sound and form and the identity of author and translator, the practice of poetic self-translation raises a host of questions: Is the self-translated version a variant of the original text? Should one speak of two parallel poems, or two originals? How does the passage from one language to another affect the poem's form and content? How "faithful" should a self-translator be—or does this term even make sense when the functions of author and translator coincide? In other words, can an author "betray" himself or herself in translation? And what does "faithfulness" mean anyway?[20]

Self-translation has only relatively recently developed into a serious topic of inquiry in the context of translation studies, but it is now commanding considerable and increasing scholarly attention. We can get a sense of the changed fortune of this concept if we compare the different editions of the *Routledge Encyclopedia of Translation Studies*. The first edition, published in 1998, did contain an entry on "auto-translation," but the author, Rainier Grutman, complained that translation specialists "have paid little attention to the phenomenon, perhaps because they thought it to be more akin to bilingualism than to translation proper."[21] However, in the second edition of the same encyclopedia, published eleven years later, Grutman was able to report that "once thought to be a marginal phenomenon, [self-translation] has of late received considerable attention in the more culturally inclined provinces of translation studies."[22] Over the past decade, there has been a steady stream of monographs,[23] edited volumes,[24] and specialized journal issues devoted to self-translation.[25] By 2012, the investigation of self-translation had become, in the words of Simona Anselmi, "a newly established and rapidly growing subfield within translation studies."[26] A bibliography of academic research on self-translation, which is maintained and regularly updated by Eva Gentes at Heinrich-Heine University in Düsseldorf, has reached the impressive length of 201 pages in its latest iteration, containing over 1,000 entries of published items and over 200 entries of unpublished items.[27]

In spite of the ever-growing volume of research devoted to self-translation, many issues remain unresolved. One difficulty in coming to terms with this phenomenon is the challenge it presents to received notions of translation theory and textual authority. As Jan Hokenson and Marcella Munson have pointed out, self-translation "escapes the binary categories of text theory and diverges radically from literary norms: here the translator *is* the author, the translation is an original, the foreign is the domestic, and vice versa."[28] In collapsing the roles of author and translator, self-translations tend to acquire in the eyes of the reading public a more authoritative status, given that the writer-translator, compared to an extraneous translator, is supposed to be closer to the original text. At the same time, somewhat paradoxically, it is assumed that the author-translator, as the intellectual owner of the text, "can allow himself bold shifts from the source text which, had it been done by another translator, probably would not have passed as an adequate translation."[29]

Both of these premises are open to challenge. One could object that privileging the author as the translator of his or her own work means falling prey to a rather naive intentional fallacy. The underlying notion of the crucial role of authorial intention stems, as Sara Kippur has pointed out, from a "pre-death-of-the-author era" which turns the author into a privileged agent for the communication of "something that only an author can know and that only he can reproduce."[30] The translation scholar Susan Bassnett, in her rejoinder to a 2013 special issue of the journal *Orbis Litterarum* devoted to self-translation, dismissed the idea that a self-translator is privileged in comparison with other translators as "bizarre." As she argues, "if all translation is a form of rewriting, then whether that rewriting is done by the person who produced a first version of a text or by someone else is surely not important."[31] While Bassnett raises a valid point, there is nevertheless a clear difference between self-translation and extraneous translation from the point of view of reception. The identity of author and translator endows a self-translated text, rightly or wrongly, with a kind of authority and permanence that a regular translation lacks. If the author himself or herself has translated a text, it is unlikely that someone else will do it again.

Another question is whether the "bold shifts" to which a self-translator is presumably entitled and inclined always occur in practice. Empirically, it is not clear that self-translations are necessarily "freer" than other translations.[32] As we will see, Vladimir Nabokov's ethos of literalism in the translation of poetic texts became a dilemma when he rewrote his Russian poems in English. In the context of translating poetry, the meaning of "faithfulness" is far from evident—does it pertain to semantics or to form, or to both? Joseph Brodsky took a diametrically opposed approach to Nabokov's by foregrounding the preservation of meter and rhyme in his self-translated poems. And yet both Nabokov and Brodsky claimed to be faithful translators and condemned alternative methods for betraying or distorting the original text.

How different, then, are self-translations from "ordinary" translations? As Rainier Grutman and Trish Van Bolderen have pointed out, extreme caution is advised when generalizing about self-translated texts as a "product" with definable and predictable characteristics:

> While the process of self-translation seems to possess several features that define it as an original practice or at least a particular category of translation (chief among those features are the potential for bidirectionality and simultaneity, as well as privileged access to private sources and the—albeit reconstructed—memory of original intention), it is much harder to pinpoint what sets self-translated texts apart as products. More research is needed before we can make general statements concerning the complex relationships between self-translations and original versions and especially to other, sometimes called "heterographical," translations.[33]

Even if we grant the self-translator "privileged access" to private sources and memories, such access can be perceived as a burden rather than a blessing. The Cuban-American academic and poet Gustavo Pérez Firmat claims that "the bilingual muse is a melancholy muse; it divides and does not conquer." As a consequence of this predicament, according to Pérez Firmat, "of all the varieties of translation, perhaps none is more faithless than self-translation. Although the technical challenges are the same, it adds a dimension of personal and creative reassessment missing from second-party translation. The author who translated his or her own work knows it too well, rather than well enough. . . . Equally important, biscriptive writers have a unique, *untranslatable* relation with each of their languages."[34] Ilan Stavans, who grew up in Mexico speaking Yiddish and Spanish before moving to Israel and later to the United States, expresses similar misgivings about his multilingual identity and the possibility of self-translation. In his words: "A language is always more than a code of communication. Languages come packaged with cultural memories and literary traditions. Those of us who have a choice of languages are fortunate, but our situation is complicated. The chief benefit is a sense of freedom, of infinite possibility. The chief drawback is a sense

of being up in the air, of belonging nowhere in particular."[35] The feeling of
having different "selves" is a common perception among bilingual or multilingual individuals.[36] As far as Stavans is concerned, he prefers to work with
extraneous translators rather than trying to reconcile his different linguistic
incarnations on his own.

Self-translation is frequently perceived as a wrenching and un-
settling experience for the author-translator. Beckett complained about
the "wastes and wilds of self-translation,"[37] while Nabokov compared it
to "sorting through one's own innards, then trying them on for size like a
pair of gloves."[38] The fact that both authors nevertheless engaged in self-
translation—Beckett almost compulsively so—has led Anthony Cordingley
to suggest that such behavior may constitute a particular form of masoch-
ism.[39] Why is self-translation such a punishing activity? Is it because it de-
prives us of the pleasure, inherent in the act of translation, of discovering
and appropriating the "other," confronting us instead with our own tedious
self? As the Romanian scholar Costin Popescu has argued: "When an author
translates his own work, he is robbed of the fascination of discovery—he
can only discover what he himself has constructed."[40] On the other hand,
of course, one could argue that self-translation facilitates a peculiar kind of
self-discovery by bringing about a confrontation between one's different linguistic selves.

As the examples of Pérez Firmat and Stavans show, not every bilingual
or multilingual author is also a self-translator. In his seminal monograph
on literary translingualism, Steven Kellman distinguishes between "monolingual translinguals," that is, authors who write exclusively in an acquired
idiom, and "ambilinguals" who write in two or more languages.[41] "Ambi-
lingualism" seems to be a necessary, but by no means a sufficient condition
for self-translation. Perhaps unsurprisingly, "monolingual translinguals" are
extremely unlikely to engage in this activity. This does not mean that their
work cannot be suffused by an awareness of their own "foreignness" in the
language that serves as their vehicle of literary creation. A good example is
the contemporary Russian-American poet Eugene Ostashevsky, who writes
in English, but whose poetics is informed by a reflection of clashing linguistic
and cultural codes.[42]

It should be noted that the term "self-translation" is in itself ambigu-
ous, depending on whether we see the "self" as the subject or the object of
the translational process. If seen as the subject, the self is the agent of textual
production. If the self is perceived as the object, self-translation literally involves a "translation of the self." Seen from that angle, any literary writing in
a non-native language could be considered a self-translation of sorts, as has
been argued by Mary Besemeres.[43] Self-translation, then, is a worthy object
of study not only because of the challenges it poses to established notions of

translation theory, but also because of the unique questions about bilingual and bicultural identity that it raises.

SELF-TRANSLATION IN RUSSIA

Russia has proven to be a particularly fertile environment for self-translation. As Brian Baer has pointed out, the notion of translation lies at the core of Russia's self-definition as a multilingual and multiethnic empire, in which "imperial realities produced an enormous number of bilinguals and a culture marked by hybridity."[44] From its very inception, Russian literary culture was determined by translations and adaptation of Byzantine models in the context of a diglossia between the imported Church Slavonic and the native East Slavic language. Starting in the eighteenth century, Russian aristocratic elites chose French as their preferred linguistic medium, creating a corpus of "Russian literature in French." The multilingual character of the Russian Empire carried over into the Soviet period. With non-Russophone writers translating their own work into the lingua franca of the empire, the Soviet Union presented an exemplary case for the colonial working of self-translation. This phenomenon has not received much attention from Slavic scholars thus far—partially, no doubt, because of a lack of linguistic expertise, given that not many Slavists, in addition to Russian, also know such languages as Uzbek, Azeri, or Estonian.

Soviet scholarship on the topic of self-translation, as far as it exists, has tended to follow the "people's friendship" paradigm. This can be shown in the treatment given to Chinghiz Aitmatov (1928–2008), perhaps the most prominent self-translating Soviet novelist, who wrote both in his native Kirghiz and Russian and self-translated his work between the two languages. An article about Aitmatov published in 1984 in the journal *Druzhba narodov* (*Peoples' Friendship*) claims that Russian, as the language of international contact and communication, serves as the ideal vehicle for the idea of interethnic harmony.[45] Of course, Aitmatov did have good reasons to self-translate his work into Russian, for doing so gave him access to a much wider domestic and international audience. In fact, the translations of his works into third languages have almost invariably been done from the Russian version rather than from the Kirghiz original. The flip side of a self-translation into a dominant language, however, is that it tends to eclipse the version written in the "minor" language. If we have a "second original" in a more accessible language endowed with the authority of authorial intent, why do we need to bother with the "first original" at all? A logical next step for the author is to dispense with the "first original" altogether and to proceed directly to writing in the dominant language, thus engaging in what Rebecca Walkowitz has called "preemptive translation."[46] The Soviet Union facilitated a rather strange genre that could be dubbed "pseudo-self-translation." A number of Soviet "minority" poets produced Russian cribs of works that they allegedly had written in their native tongue, but which in reality were composed directly in Russian. Some bilingual poets who had an excellent command of Russian verse, such as the Latvian Anatols Imermanis (1914–1998), were forced to publish their Russian poems under the disguise of an authorial translation from a nonexistent source.[47] With its simulation of a bilingual text, pseudo-self-translation conformed better to the myth of people's friendship than the outright replacement of the native tongue with the dominant language.

The rhetoric of Soviet interethnic harmony concealed a significant linguistic power differential, which, via self-translation, or pseudo-self-translation, often led to a virtual or actual erasure of the minority text. Of course, this situation is not unique to the Soviet Union; it occurs in any "asymmetrical" translation between a "minor" and "major" language. This conundrum has led the poet Christopher Whyte, for example, to condemn his own practice of self-translating his poetry from Gaelic into English.[48] Perhaps it was for similar reasons that Gennadii Aigi (1934–2006), a prominent Russian poet of Chuvash origin, abandoned the practice of self-translation. Aigi began his poetic career in his native Chuvash language and wrote Russian cribs of his Chuvash poems before switching entirely to Russian. He was also a prolific translator from French and other languages into Chuvash. However, instead of self-translating his poetry between Chuvash and Russian, Aigi imbued his mature Russian texts with a latent "translingual" quality that ultimately aimed at creating a universal poetic idiom untethered from any incarnation in a specific linguistic medium.[49]

The postcolonial legacy of Russian and Soviet self-translation, which also includes the interesting situation of contemporary bilingual writers in the newly independent former Soviet republics, remains a lacuna of Russian translation studies. The present book is concerned with a somewhat different phenomenon, though: it deals with poets who self-translated not from a minority language into the lingua franca of the empire, but from Russian into other major European languages. Since German, Italian, French, and English are idioms of comparable literary prestige with Russian, one could argue that self-translated texts between these languages do not marginalize the original; rather, both versions continue to exist on a relatively equal footing in their own respective linguistic orbits. We may call such self-translations "symmetrical," following Rainier Grutman's suggestion.[50] We have to remain aware, of course, that for Russian émigrés during the Soviet period, who found themselves cut off from readers in the homeland, Russian and the languages of their respective host countries did not have an equal status. If these authors continued to write in Russian, their audience was limited to a dwindling circle of fellow émigrés, while other languages offered, at least potentially, the possibility of wider recognition and financial reward. In that sense, the "symmetrical" bilingualism of Vladimir Nabokov was different from that of Samuel Beckett, who had a choice of publishing his work in France or England. Since the late 1980s, it has become possible again for Russian authors living abroad to remain connected with audiences in the homeland. This means that the use of a particular language has become more of a free choice than a decision prompted by economic incentives.

Unlike Kirghiz, Latvian, or Chuvash, languages like German, Italian, French, and English were not autochthonous idioms of the colonial space occupied by the Russian Empire. It is true, of course, that French served as the preferred means of communication among elites in tsarist Russia as a result of self-colonization, and there was also a significant population of ethnic Germans living in Russia. Three of the authors discussed in this book—Elizaveta Kul'man, Wassily Kandinsky, and Marina Tsvetaeva—spoke German since childhood because they were partially of German descent and learned the language from a parent or grandparent. As a member of a Russian upper-class family, Vladimir Nabokov was brought up trilingually in Russian, French, and English. However, in spite of their early multilingualism, most of these authors only became active as self-translators after they left Russia. Their self-translations thus relate mainly to what Grutman calls "exogenous" rather than "endogenous" bilingualism.[51] This variant of bilingualism usually occurs as a consequence of migration or exile.

This is not to say that migration is a necessary condition for the emergence of multilingual poetry. The first poet discussed in this book, Elizaveta Kul'man, never left her native St. Petersburg. This did not prevent her from creating an immense poetic oeuvre in multiple languages. Kul'man was a multilingual poet and self-translator by choice rather than by circumstance or necessity. In all other cases, however, the decision to write in languages other than Russian was brought about by the experience of exile or emigration. The history of Russia in the twentieth century was particularly propitious for the flowering of exogenous bilingual and self-translated literature. But external constraints are hardly sufficient to explain a poet's decision to expand beyond the native language. Poets may self-translate not only to gain a different audience but also to create a new artistic experience. This is especially true for the present situation, when, thanks to international travel, electronic communication, and the global reach of social media, authors living outside the territory of the mother tongue have a choice to remain moored in the native idiom or to cross the linguistic boundary and engage in an exploration of their own bilingual identity.[52]

POETIC SELF-TRANSLATION: EXPLORING A
TERRA INCOGNITA

The only self-translating Russian poet who has received more than cursory attention thus far is Joseph Brodsky. Brodsky's prominent status as a Nobel Prize winner and American poet laureate guaranteed his self-translations a wider visibility, but they could not ensure a positive response. Critical reactions to Brodsky's Anglophone poetic oeuvre, as opposed to his English-language essays, which received high praise, have been mixed, to say the least. However, after much neglect, Brodsky's self-translations have become a subject of serious academic study in recent years. They are the topic of no fewer than four doctoral dissertations as well as an excellent monograph by Alexandra Berlina, which provides close readings of the Russian and English versions of multiple poems.[53]

With the six other self-translating Russian poets discussed in this book, we enter more or less a terra incognita. In some cases, this may seem surprising. After all, Nabokov is no less famous than Brodsky as a bilingual Russian-American author, yet his self-translated poetry has received almost no attention. One reason for this oversight may be the belief that Nabokov's poetic oeuvre is inferior to his novelistic work. However, the same cannot be said about Marina Tsvetaeva, who is one of the most celebrated Russian poets of the twentieth century. Yet the French self-translation of her long narrative poem *Mólodets* (*The Swain*), published many decades after her death, suffers from a similar kind of neglect, possibly out of an unstated assumption that poetry written in a non-native language cannot possibly be as "good" as the one composed in the mother tongue. Wassily Kandinsky, a towering figure in twentieth-century European art, suffers from a double handicap when it comes to the appreciation of his poetry. Since he is primarily known as a painter, his literary work may be deemed amateurish, and, given his Russian origin, his use of German and French may be dismissed as inauthentic or incompetent. The scholars who have paid attention to Kandinsky's poetry have been mainly art historians, and not literary critics. Finally, Elizaveta Kul'man is not widely known even among Slavic specialists. Likewise, the contemporary Russian-American poets Andrey Gritsman and Katia Kapovich cannot be called canonical figures in the same way as Brodsky. In part this is a consequence of the more restricted "niche market" that poetry occupies in contemporary American culture. Usually published by small presses rather than by major publishing conglomerates, it is considered a genre mainly enjoyed by a coterie of specialists and aficionados.

My aim in this book is not necessarily to draw attention to "neglected masterpieces" of translingual poetic writing (even though I do think that

Tsvetaeva's brilliant French rendition of her fairy-tale poem *Mólodets* deserves more attention than it has hitherto received). Rather, I intend to investigate how the switch between languages affects poetic creativity. This can only be done with a close reading of concrete texts. Dwelling on such technical matters as meter, rhythm, rhyme, and the minutiae of sound may seem old-fashioned in an age that has largely lost a taste for formal poetry, but, given the nature of poetic discourse, it seems to me a necessary approach if we hope to gain insights about the workings of the bilingual muse. Following the refraction of a poetic text through the prism of disparate linguistic media offers its own aesthetic appeal. There may be a cognitive gain involved as well. Mikhail Epstein has offered the provocative suggestion that "stereotextuality," that is, the effect produced by the parallel existence of a text in two different idioms, is perhaps a necessary condition for its full understanding. In his words: "Can an idea be adequately presented in a single language? Or do we need a minimum of two languages (as with two eyes and two ears) to convey the volume of a thought or symbol?"[54] Seemingly "saying the same thing twice" in two different languages also becomes a test case for larger questions of cultural allegiance and bilingual identity. Comparing both versions (or, in the case of Elizaveta Kul'man, all three versions) of a self-translated poem offers a compelling tool for this kind of research. Juxtaposing the parallel texts in different languages creates a rather unique translational situation where, contrary to Friedrich Schleiermacher, we do seem to see "the work as it would be had the author himself written it originally in the reader's tongue."

Inasmuch as any translation of a poem is also an interpretation, the identity of author and translator makes the self-translated version a kind of self-exegesis and self-commentary. In other words, self-translation is, or can be, an extremely self-conscious form of writing. As Will Noonan has noted with regard to the bilingual oeuvre of Samuel Beckett, "considered in terms of an alternative trope, that of commentary, self-translation can also be thought of as a type of reflexive metacommentary in which the self-translated work reflects on the prior version of the text, and by doing so foregrounds the workings of both source and target languages."[55]

As a kind of multilingual palimpsest, the self-translated poetic text offers insights into the functioning of poetic creativity in different languages, the conundrum of translation, and the vagaries of bilingual identity. At the same time, it also raises the problem of reception and reader response. Do we read and judge a self-translated text differently from a monolingual creation? Who is the intended, or the ideal, reader of such texts? Does such an audience even exist? Is it growing today? These are the kinds of questions that we will keep in the back of our mind and to which I will return in the conclusion of this book.

The poets will be discussed in more or less chronological order. The first chapter, devoted to Elizaveta Kul'man, takes us back to the early nineteenth century. Kul'man was a child prodigy who knew eleven languages and wrote poetry in several of them. Her main legacy is a vast corpus of pseudoclassical parallel poems written in Russian, German, and Italian. Even though she was a contemporary of Pushkin and the German romantics, Kul'man exhibits a pre-romantic attitude towards language. Writing in multiple idioms came quite naturally to her. Since she did not seem to identify language as the ultimate marker of her identity, she had no fear of "betraying" her native culture by a switch to a foreign tongue. If anything, she probably would have considered multilingualism as a defining feature of her personality. Her omnivorous acquisition of ever more languages was only cut short by her premature death at age seventeen.

With Wassily Kandinsky, who is discussed in chapter 2, we enter a new, modernist phase of multilingualism. Clearly, Kandinsky was not bound to the "language loyalty" inculcated by romantic theories. In that respect, his attitude comes close to that of Kul'man's pre-romantic attitude. There is one other aspect linking Kandinsky to Kul'man: both were practitioners of what has become known as simultaneous or "synchronous" self-translation, that is, they created parallel linguistic versions of their texts from the very inception. Aurelia Klimkiewicz defines this phenomenon as "the simultaneous process of writing and self-translating, blurring the boundaries between original and self-translated text," as opposed to "asynchronous self-translation (consecutive self-translation of the existing original)."[56] The most prominent practitioner of this approach in the twentieth century was Samuel Beckett. By working on the French and English variants of his texts simultaneously, as Rainier Grutman argues, Beckett was able to create a "dynamic link between both versions that effectively bridges the linguistic divide."[57] In a similar manner, Kandinsky drafted some of his prose poems in Russian before translating them into German, and he drafted others first in German before translating them into Russian. In addition, he added an intersemiotic "bridge-building" component to the interlingual transfer by arranging his texts in an album that correlated a sequence of prose poems with a sequence of woodcuts.

Marina Tsvetaeva, who is discussed in chapter 3, is not generally known as a multilingual poet. It is true that she wrote little original poetry in languages other than her native Russian, even though foreign words and expressions, especially German ones, as well as bilingual puns, frequently appear in her Russian-language texts.[58] Tsvetaeva's translingual magnum opus is her self-translation of the long narrative poem *Mólodets* into French verse, which makes her perhaps the most remarkable poetic self-translator in Russian literary history. With the virtuosity of its rhythm, rhymes, and wordplay, the use of archaic, folk, and Church Slavonic elements, and Tsvetaeva's own idiosyncratic neologisms and elliptic compression, *Mólodets* presents daunting challenges to a translator. Almost miraculously, many of these features are preserved in the French translation, which retains the hallmarks of Tsvetaeva's personal style. At the same time, the self-translation becomes a form of self-exegesis by making explicit what is unspoken or only hinted at in the Russian original. In that sense, the French version can be used as an interpretive tool to arrive at a better understanding of the Russian version. Furthermore, in rewriting the poem in a different language seven years after its original composition, Tsvetaeva added a layer of self-awareness and self-reflection. In particular, while reworking her poem in French, Tsvetaeva became more attentive to issues of gender and of her own exilic condition as a Russian living in France.

Chapter 4 analyzes the self-translated poetry in Vladimir Nabokov's bilingual volume *Poems and Problems* (1970). Even though he continued to claim allegiance to the literalist doctrine championed in his translation of Pushkin's *Eugene Onegin*, Nabokov deviated considerably from this theory when his own poetry was at stake. The choice of "killing" the original text and replacing it with a hypertrophied commentary, as he did with *Eugene Onegin*, was not a viable solution for Nabokov when it came to the translation of his own work. Instead, he strove to preserve as much of the form as possible as long as he did only minimal violence to the semantics of the original. The urge for revision of his earlier poetry came into conflict with his self-imposed ethos of translational fidelity, according to which any improvement or paraphrase would amount to falsification. This dilemma forced Nabokov to come up with his own idiosyncratic solutions to the problem of poetic translation. A comparative analysis of the Russian and English versions demonstrates how Nabokov attempted to exploit seeming deficiencies in his English prosody as a creative way to express specific concepts present in the Russian original.

Joseph Brodsky, discussed in chapter 5, was in many respects Nabokov's antipode. While both Nabokov and Brodsky rejected "smooth" translations, they had opposite ideas about what constitutes faithfulness in the rendering of a poetic text. In contrast to Nabokov's semantic absolutism, Brodsky championed a kind of formal absolutism. His insistence on the preservation of meter and rhyme in translation set him on a collision course with the Anglophone poetry establishment and led to strained relations with some of the prominent poets who had volunteered to translate his poetry, but who felt piqued when Brodsky proceeded to alter their translations beyond recognition. His dissatisfaction with extraneous translators eventually prompted Brodsky to take the translation of his poems into his own hands. One motivating factor clearly was the urge to demonstrate that his theory was able to produce convincing results. Unlike Nabokov, who largely abandoned his rigid theory when translating his own poems (albeit without openly admitting it), Brodsky brooked no compromise. In some respects, his "take no prisoners" approach, which infuses English prosody with Russian elements, resembles Tsvetaeva's self-translational technique. This is probably no accident, given that Tsvetaeva was the poet whom Brodsky admired more than any other.

The sixth and final chapter explores the practice of self-translation by two contemporary Russian-American poets, Andrey Gritsman and Katia Kapovich. Both of them take a looser approach to self-translation than Nabokov and Brodsky did, leading to what one could call a poetics of displacement. For both Gritsman and Kapovich, translating their own work becomes a means of exploring the mutation of the self through time, migration, and changing linguistic and cultural environments. A significant difference between the two authors concerns the way in which they present their poems. Gritsman invites a comparison between source and target text and the gaps between them in a bilingual *en face* edition. In contrast, Kapovich camouflages her self-translated poems as English originals. In spite of the different staging and performance of self-translation, both poets—by stressing difference rather than similarity in translation—turn their self-translated texts into a metacommentary on their own shifting transnational identities. In taking a long view, we notice that the self-translational practice of contemporary poets mirrors parallel developments in translation theory, where the idea of translation as a necessarily deficient "copy" has given way to a more dynamic model of creative rewriting and the infinite profusion and refraction of potential meanings.

Elizaveta Kul'man: The Most Polyglot of Russian Poets

ELIZAVETA BORISOVNA KUL'MAN (1808–1825) has the distinction of being the most formidable poetic self-translator that Russia ever produced. The unusual and extreme case of her multilingual poetry does not lend itself to easy generalizations, but it raises issues of translingual creativity and linguistic identity that will also be at the heart of more recent twentieth- and twenty-first-century developments in transnational poetic writing. Kul'man is a unique figure in the history of Russian literature, or more precisely, the history of Russian, German, and Italian literature. A child prodigy with phenomenal linguistic gifts, she stands out both for her polyglot prowess and for her outsized literary productivity. At the time of her premature death at age seventeen, Kul'man left behind an unpublished oeuvre in multiple languages of more than 100,000 verse lines. Her tombstone in the Smolenskoe Cemetery in St. Petersburg, adorned with quotes in Ancient and Modern Greek, Latin, Church Slavonic, Russian, German, French, English, Italian, Spanish, and Portuguese, bore the inscription "Prima Russicarum operam dedit idiomati graeco, undecim novit linguas, loquebatur octo, quamquam puella poetria eminens" ("The first Russian woman who learned Greek, knew eleven languages, spoke eight, even though a girl, an eminent poet").[1] Thanks to the efforts of Kul'man's tutor, Karl Friedrich von Grossheinrich (1783–1860), the Imperial Russian Academy brought out several posthumous editions of her works in the 1830s and 1840s, including a trilingual collection of her Russian, German, and Italian poetry and her translations of Anacreon. Starting in the 1840s, Kul'man's collected works in German were published in multiple editions in Germany, while her Italian poetry appeared in Milan. The composer Robert Schumann, who set several of her poems to music, was so taken with Kul'man that he kept a copy of her portrait in his study.[2]

Despite the posthumous fame that she enjoyed during the second half of the nineteenth century, Kul'man is nowadays a more or less forgotten poet.

Nearly everything we know about her is mediated through her tutor, mentor, editor, and biographer Grossheinrich, who published an extensive biographical sketch of his pupil as a foreword to her German collected works, and, in Russian translation, in the popular journal *Biblioteka dlia chteniia* (*Library for Reading*) in 1849.[3] All other accounts of Kul'man's life derive from Grossheinrich's testimony, including Aleksandr Nikitenko's biography appended to the Russian Academy edition of her works.[4] As Hilde Hoogenboom has shown, Grossheinrich and Nikitenko created two competing biographical narratives. While the former emphasized Kul'man's prodigious intellect and classicist leanings, the latter highlighted her status as a tragic romantic figure cut down by a cruel fate.[5]

Grossheinrich was certainly not a disinterested biographer but Kul'man's "discoverer," educator, mentor, and promoter. His biography of her is in part calculated to showcase his own crucial role in the development of a person he considered a poetic and linguistic genius. Writing about himself in the third person, Grossheinrich projects a persona akin to the tutor of Rousseau's Emile.[6] Since it is the only existing source for Kul'man's life, it is impossible to independently verify the factual accuracy of Grossheinrich's account.[7] With this proviso in mind, his testimony nevertheless deserves attention for the information that it provides about the circumstances of Kul'man's upbringing, the development of her multilingualism, and the origins of her poetry. Given that Kul'man is little known even among specialists, I will discuss her life in some detail before addressing the issues raised by her multilingual poetry.

POVERTY AND LINGUISTIC PRODIGY

Kul'man did not come from a privileged background. References to her destitute material circumstances form a recurrent topic in her poetry. Her German poem "Meine Lebensart" ("My Way of Life") begins with the lines: "In der ganzen Stadt ist keine / Hütte kleiner als die meine" ("In the entire city no hut is smaller than mine").[8] Kul'man's father, a descendant of seventeenth-century Alsatian immigrants to Russia, was a mid-level army officer and war veteran who had retired from military duty to become a civil servant in St. Petersburg. Kul'man's mother was of Russian-German descent and spoke fluent German. Elizaveta was the youngest of nine children. Her seven older brothers all engaged in military careers and became victims of the Napoleonic Wars—four were killed outright, two died from illnesses contracted during the war, and one was maimed in battle.[9] Kul'man's father died shortly after her birth in 1808. Elizaveta was raised by her mother in a hut on Vasiliev Island (the dwelling referenced in "Meine Lebensart"), dependent on the largesse of a distant relative who paid the modest rent for their lodging.

According to Grossheinrich's account, signs of an unusual linguistic talent became noticeable very early in Kul'man's life. At the age of eighteen months, she still had no teeth, but she already was able to talk fluently. Her bilingual mother, according to Grossheinrich, "strove tirelessly to teach her the Russian, and later the German language, as purely as possible."[10] We do not know when exactly her mother began to speak with her daughter in German. Elizaveta certainly seems to have been fluent in both Russian and German by age five, when Grossheinrich, a former friend of Kul'man's father, entered the girl's life. A lawyer by training, he had come to Russia from Germany a few years earlier to serve as a tutor for the children of a Russian aristocrat. In view of young Elizaveta's apparent talent, Grossheinrich volunteered to teach the child pro bono in his spare time, which he continued to do for the remainder of Kul'man's short life.

From Grossheinrich's discussion of his pedagogical approach, it becomes apparent that, at least initially, he tried to avoid pushing his pupil to achievements that he did not consider age-appropriate (which seems quite different from the modern-day obsession with unleashing the potential of "Baby Einsteins" as early as possible). Thus, Grossheinrich intentionally kept all books from young Elizaveta in order not to stimulate a "boundless thirst for knowledge" that he deemed harmful for her age (17). The first book with which Kul'man came in contact at age five was *Baumgartens Welt in Bildern* (*Baumgarten's World in Pictures*), a four-volume illustrated guide to animals and minerals, with legends in German, French, English, Italian, and Latin. Elizaveta learned the names first in German, and then in all the other languages as well, repeating the sounds spoken to her by Grossheinrich. Despite the girl's entreaties, however, he was reluctant to teach her the alphabet, since he considered her still too young for such endeavors. When he finally gave in, Kul'man acquired the ability to read German within three weeks.

Probably stimulated by her own bilingualism and the discovery of the existence of multiple more idioms thanks to the *Welt in Bildern*, young Elizaveta made it a game to imitate the voices and intonation of speakers of foreign languages that she chanced to overhear. Apparently she had a perfect ear for phonetics and language melody. Grossheinrich reports that she managed to fool people into believing that she spoke fluent French, English, and Italian by quickly enumerating a series of animal names in the respective language with perfect, native-like pronunciation and intonation (18). Nevertheless, it was decided that for the time being she should not be taught other languages besides Russian and German, since Grossheinrich reasoned that "learning three or four languages at the same time must necessarily have a bad influence on a child, so that no firm notion of the peculiarities of each language can form in her mind" (18). By age six, Elizaveta knew the entire content of the *Welt in Bildern* by heart (the only book she was allowed to see!), and she spoke and read fluent German and Russian. When she turned seven, Grossheinrich decided to teach her how to write (a year earlier than he had originally planned), first in German and then in Russian. This was followed by lessons in grammar.

An important milestone occurred at age nine, when Kul'man was introduced to poetry. The texts chosen by Grossheinrich to initiate his pupil into the poetic "realm of harmony and beauty" (33) were the fables of Gellert and the idylls of Gessner.[11] At the same time with this introduction to literature, Elizaveta began to study French. Grossheinrich made it clear that French should not be considered "the language of a single nation," but a "world language." Voicing a polyglot's contempt for monolingual insularity (and perhaps also a German nationalist perspective), he elaborated that the French were "lucky" inasmuch as their native idiom allowed them to communicate with the entire world, but limited in that they usually "only understand their own language" (33). Even though Elizaveta's mother knew some French, she refrained from practicing the language with her daughter out of fear that she could ruin the child's pronunciation with her foreign accent. Since Grossheinrich was able to see his pupil only on weekends, Elizaveta was left to learn French mainly on her own, which she did by reading French books, mostly travelogues, a fashionable genre at the end of the eighteenth century. Inspired by the German poetry that she had been given to read, she also began to write her own poems without being prompted to do so by her tutor.

It was at this moment that the nine-year-old Elizaveta expressed the wish to learn Italian. Following a by now familiar pattern, Grossheinrich at first reacted with skepticism, reasoning that Elizaveta should perfect her first three languages before tackling a fourth one, but he finally gave in. His method of language instruction could be described as grammar-translation on steroids. With every new language that he taught Elizaveta, Grossheinrich followed the same procedure. He first provided his pupil with a handwritten grammar that listed all the regular morphological endings. At the same time Elizaveta received a book written in the new idiom, the content of which was already familiar because she had read it before in a language known to her. She was given the task of reading the foreign book on her own and memorizing all the new vocabulary. Grossheinrich reports that with this method, Kul'man was able to become fluent in a new living language within three months (with Latin and Greek it took a few months longer). As soon as she had reached the appropriate level, Elizaveta began to translate from the newly learned language into the languages she already knew, and vice versa.

While any new language was a source of pleasure and excitement for Kul'man, none seems to have stimulated her as much as Italian.

Grossheinrich writes that "as soon as Elisabeth had three or four lessons in Italian, she declared to her teacher that she probably would learn no other language with such assiduousness as Italian, because this latter seemed to her to surpass all others in gracefulness and euphony" (38). For her tenth birthday, Grossheinrich gave his pupil a copy of Tasso's *Gerusalemme liberata* (*Jerusalem Delivered*). Elizaveta was moved to tears by this gift and promised that she would learn the entire book by heart, which indeed she did. At the same time, having read all of Gessner, she received a new batch of German poetry from her teacher, consisting of "Haller, Gotter, Kleist, Gleim, and Jakobi" (40).[12]

Six months after learning Italian, Kul'man expressed the wish to learn English. This time, she did have the opportunity for oral practice, since her mother's landlord happened to be an Englishman who loved to engage Elizaveta in conversation. Following his customary method of language instruction, Grossheinrich provided his pupil with a two-volume edition of Milton, an English translation of Gessner's idylls, and a London edition of Petrarch. He encouraged Elizaveta to read Gessner in English, but he advised her to avoid for the time being Milton's *Paradise Lost*, for which he deemed her not yet mature enough.

In the meantime, a change had occurred in Kul'man's living situation. The relative who paid the rent for her modest lodging on Vasiliev Island had died, which left mother and daughter essentially homeless. At that moment, they were rescued by Petr Meder, the director of the Mining College and a former colleague of Kul'man's father, who installed them in an empty room in the apartment of the College priest P. S. Abramov. Abramov taught Elizaveta Old Church Slavonic, the only language (aside from Russian and German) that she learned from someone other than Grossheinrich. Elizaveta became friends with Meder's daughters and was able to join them in studying drawing, dance, music, botany, mineralogy, physics, and mathematics. She also had access to Meder's substantial library.

Abramov was an enthusiastic Latinist who usually conversed with Grossheinrich in Latin. This gave the by now twelve-year-old Elizaveta the idea to learn that language as well in order to surprise Abramov on his birthday with a congratulatory message composed in Latin. Grossheinrich obliged Elizaveta's request to instruct her in Latin, and shortly thereafter he agreed to teach her Ancient Greek as well. After only a few months of study, she could read the New Testament in the original, followed by the writings of Anacreon. By age thirteen, she had made a prose translation of Anacreon into five languages, and a metric one into her three "favorite languages" of Russian, German, and Italian. Grossheinrich explains that he gave Anacreon's writings to his pupil because of the relative simplicity of the language and the "shortness of his songs" (49), but there can be no doubt that Kul'man developed a particular affinity for this poet. The "anacreontic" form of unrhymed iambic trimeter with feminine endings became prevalent in her own poetic writings.[13] For the rest of her life, Kul'man continued to translate Anacreon into multiple idioms. The manuscript division of the Russian National Library in St. Petersburg contains, in Grossheinrich's handwritten copy, Kul'man's translations of Anacreon's odes into Russian, German, French, Italian, English, Spanish, Portuguese, and Modern Greek.[14] Around 1822–23, Grossheinrich sent a selection of Kul'man's Russian and German translations of Anacreon to the Empress Elizaveta Alekseevna, who rewarded the young poet with a diamond necklace. Probably when she became aware of Kul'man's precarious material circumstances, the empress also granted her a modest annual stipend of 200 rubles.

Knowing eight languages at age twelve still did not leave Kul'man satisfied. It only whetted her appetite for more, especially when she heard about the Italian cardinal and famed hyperpolyglot Giuseppe Mezzofanti (1774–1849), who allegedly was fluent in thirty-eight languages. This stimulated an ambition in Kul'man to achieve a similar feat. Grossheinrich knew three more languages that he hadn't taught yet to his pupil: Spanish, Portuguese, and Modern Greek. Abandoning his earlier determination not to overload Elizaveta with too much simultaneous linguistic information, he agreed to teach her all three languages at the same time. Kul'man mastered them in three months and decided to devote henceforth one hour every day to each of the newly acquired idioms. At the same time, she expressed a desire to branch out beyond the European language family by learning Arabic and Persian. Having no knowledge of these languages, Grossheinrich offered to take classes at the university and to teach Elizaveta what he had learned (the thought that Kul'man could herself study these languages at the university was too outlandish to even be considered).

Sadly, the plans for further language learning were cut short by Kul'man's deteriorating health. In 1824 she had caught cold while attending her brother's wedding. As a consequence of the catastrophic flood of St. Petersburg in November of that year, the cold turned into consumption. Kul'man's life could probably have been saved with a cure in a milder climate, as she pointed out herself in one of her German poems:

> Ich würde bald genesen,
> Dies ist des Arztes Wort,
> Verlebt' ich nur acht Monden
> Im warmen Süden dort.[15]

> I would soon recover,
> This is the doctor's word,
> If only I could spend eight months
> There, in the warm south.

However, given her poverty, traveling abroad was out of the question. After a protracted illness, Kul'man died on November 19, 1825, at age seventeen.

REACTIONS TO KUL'MAN'S LEGACY

At the moment of Kul'man's untimely death, none of her literary works had yet appeared in print. Her oeuvre was of truly enormous proportions. It consisted of a trilingual body of verse translations from Anacreon as well as hundreds of original poems in a pseudoclassical style, all of them in Russian, German, and Italian versions; many more poems written only in German; and several fairy tales in Russian and German verse. In addition, Kul'man left behind numerous translations. According to Grossheinrich's inventory, these included German versions of Vladislav Ozerov's and Vittorio Alfieri's tragedies, Tomás de Iriarte's fables translated from Spanish, excerpts from Luís de Camões's *Lusiads* and thirty odes by Francisco Manoel de Nascimento translated from Portuguese, excerpts from Milton's *Paradise Lost* and *Paradise Regained*, several poems by Pietro Metastasio, a Russian translation of Alfieri's *Saul*, and a translation of Modern Greek folk songs completed shortly before Kul'man's death (110).

Grossheinrich devoted the rest of his life to the mission of making the world aware of his former pupil. He remained in Russia until his death in 1860, never got married and, at his own wish, was buried next to his student. While few people had ever heard of Kul'man at the moment of her death in 1825, she did become better known in the following decades, especially after the appearance of Nikitenko's and Grossheinrich's biographies made the story of her life more widely known. In general, the narrative of a young genius who suffered a life of material deprivation with stoic equanimity and was cut down prematurely by a tragic fate had a greater appeal to the Russian public than Kul'man's actual poetry. Opinions about the quality of her literary work were mixed. Vissarion Belinsky, the leading radical critic of the time, in his 1841 review of Kul'man's collected works published by the Russian Academy, called her a "wondrous and beautiful phenomenon of life," but "no poet whatsoever."[16] The Decembrist poet and friend of Pushkin, Vil'gel'm Kiukhel'beker, had a more positive opinion, even though he, too, valued Kul'man's persona higher than her poetry. In a diary entry from January 28, 1835, he wrote that "[Kul'man's] verses are better than all the women's poetry [*damskie stikhi*] that I had the opportunity to read in Russian, but she herself is even better than her poetry." He regretted that he never met Kul'man in person because he "would no doubt have fallen in love with her."[17] A day later Kiukhel'beker composed a lengthy ode, in which he presented an exalted vision of Kul'man as an unearthly being appearing among the giants of world literature.[18]

Kul'man fared somewhat better among German critics. None other than Goethe, if we are to believe Grossheinrich, expressed a flattering opinion of her poetic gifts. In his biography, Grossheinrich reports that, using an acquaintance from his university days as an intermediary, he sent a selection of thirty German, six Italian, and four French poems by the thirteen-year-old Kul'man to Goethe in Weimar. The acquaintance wrote back that Goethe was very intrigued by these poems and commissioned him to "tell the young poet in my name, in Goethe's name, that I prophesy for her in the future an honorable rank in literature, she may write in any of the languages known to her" (53). Grossheinrich revealed this verdict to Kul'man at her name day party. The same compendium of poems was also sent to the German romantic writer Jean Paul. His response only reached Kul'man when she was already mortally ill. Jean Paul, too, allegedly admired Kul'man's poetry, telling Grossheinrich's correspondent that "we Southern people thus far have shown little interest in Nordic literature, but I have a premonition that this little, brightly shining star of the North will force us sooner or later to turn our eyes toward it" (93). A third luminary of German culture, who, according to Grossheinrich, expressed admiration for Kul'man was Johann Heinrich Voss, the classicist and celebrated translator of Homer. Allegedly Voss praised Kul'man for penetrating so deeply into the spirit of ancient Greece that her poems in the antique style read like "a masterful translation of the works of a poet from one of the most splendid periods of Greek literature," adding that "it is difficult to understand how such a young woman could reach such a deep and extensive knowledge of art and antiquity" (107).

Robert Schumann's interest in Kul'man has already been mentioned. While the praise of Goethe, Jean Paul, and Voss are hearsay, there is solid evidence for Schumann's admiration. He interlaced his Kul'man songs with comments expressing his fascination with the poet and her unusual life. It becomes apparent that for Schumann, Kul'man's appeal lay in her romantic status as an enigmatic child-genius whose poetry was penetrated by a premonition of her own untimely death. He calls Kul'man "one of those wonder-talented beings that only rarely, after large intervals, make their appearance in this world. The highest insights of wisdom, expressed with masterful poetic perfection, are communicated here through the mouth of a child." Schumann's manuscript ends with the words: "Thus she parted from us, light as an angel, passing from one shore to the other, but leaving behind in far-shining streaks the traces of a heavenly apparition."[19]

Overall, Kul'man did acquire a somewhat greater notoriety in Germany than in her country of birth. In part, this may simply be attributable to the larger dimensions of her German oeuvre—more than 600 of her poems exist only in German.[20] Moreover, the German poems differ from the trilingual pseudoclassical Russian-German-Italian corpus by focusing on more modern and personal themes. Some of them address Kul'man's poverty, her dreams of poetic fame, and, heartbreakingly, the defeat of her ambitions by her illness and impending death. However, even though her collected works in German went through eight editions in the course of the nineteenth century and a selection of her German poems was reprinted in 1981, Kul'man is now as much a forgotten figure in the German-speaking world as she is in her Russian homeland. Only very recently has she begun to attract the interest of feminist scholars who are looking at her work through the lens of gender studies.[21] A rather curious subgenre of Kul'man criticism has emerged among musicologists and Schumann biographers. The consensus in that field, at least until recently, was to dismiss her poetry as second- or third-rate, and to explain Schumann's infatuation with Kul'man as, at best, naive and misguided, or, at worst, a sign of the composer's impending mental illness.[22]

In Russia, Kul'man's poetry also elicited negative reactions. Increasingly, her shortcomings as a poet were blamed on Grossheinrich, whose role in her biography changed from hero to villain. According to this new narrative, Kul'man's pedantic German tutor forced her to write in an arid, pseudoclassicist style rather than letting her talent develop freely and naturally. After the October Revolution, the animosity against Grossheinrich acquired an additional political dimension. In an article published in 1937, the Soviet critic S. N. Durylin argued that Grossheinrich pursued a reactionary agenda—by "tearing Kul'man away from reality and depriving her of being nourished by the saps of modernity" he intended to keep his pupil "within the limits of seventeenth- and eighteenth-century aristocratic courtly command-culture" characterized by an "imitative glorification of tsars and heroes." Thus, according to Durylin, it was no accident that the Russian court rewarded Kul'man for her work, and that Grossheinrich, when trying to get Kul'man's poetry published, turned to Admiral Shishkov, a well-known "pillar of literary reaction."[23]

Some of the animosity against Kul'man's tutor probably had its origin in wounded national pride: Grossheinrich was resented for turning someone into a "German" who would or should have been rightfully a Russian poet. A biography of Kul'man published in 1886 presents her tutor as a foreigner who was completely ignorant of and indifferent to Russian culture. The author argues that "Russia was alien to [Grossheinrich]; his sympathy belonged to Germany, and the only thing that kept him here was the possibility of good earnings. He knew many foreign languages and literatures, but totally ignored Russian literature and language. Only later did he begin to study it under the direction of his pupil."[24] This account seems questionable in several respects. First of all, from his biography one does not gain the impression that Grossheinrich was particularly well-remunerated. Second, and more importantly, while it is likely that he arrived in St. Petersburg with little knowledge of Russian, it is highly unlikely that, as a person of considerable linguistic curiosity and ability, he would not have striven to learn the language of the country where he happened to be living. In fact, Grossheinrich's correspondence with Shishkov shows that, at least by the 1830s, he was able to express himself in Russian with native-like ease.

Nevertheless, it is true that Grossheinrich initially instructed Kul'man to write her poems in German before translating them into Russian and Italian. The reason, as he explains in his biography, was purely pragmatic: his own knowledge of Russian was insufficient for giving his pupil feedback about poetic diction, and with Kul'man knowing both languages equally well, he felt that it made no difference whether she wrote in Russian or German. It is interesting to note, however, that he later changed his opinion on this account. When Kul'man had become more mature, he advised her to write her poems first in Russian before translating them into other languages. This is not because Grossheinrich's own Russian had significantly improved—he conceded that he would still not dare to make technical judgments about Russian verse. Rather, he was of the opinion that Kul'man, even though she had the ambition to become a significant poet in three languages, nevertheless "belonged most of all to her [Russian] fatherland" (85). As he elaborated: "However well you know these two languages [i.e., German and Italian], I am sure that you think in Russian, i.e., that the first expression in which you dress your poetic thought is Russian. You will do best, then, to write down every poem in the language in which you thought it" (85).

As we can see, in spite of his own multilingualism, Grossheinrich subscribed to the Herderian notion of a tight confluence between native language and national identity, which, in Kul'man's case, he determined to be Russian. The fact that she had two mother tongues (quite literally—after all, her mother was a Russian-German bilingual) did not deter Grossheinrich from assigning Kul'man a clear national identity based on her "fatherland." This unequivocal determination based on patriarchal notions of national belonging is problematic, to say the least, but it seems to invalidate the accusations leveled against Grossheinrich by Russian nationalists. Rather than trying to turn his pupil into a German, he tried to convince her of her own Russianness.

Another reproach against Grossheinrich is perhaps more pertinent. As has been noted before, the choice of authors he presented to Kul'man as role models for poetic writing was decidedly old-fashioned and outdated by the standards of his time. As far as German poetry was concerned, Grossheinrich seems to have valued the likes of Gessner and Gleim higher than Goethe and Schiller as pedagogical tools (even though, ironically, he did seek Goethe's verdict about the merits of Kul'man's poetry). Kul'man herself, in one of her German poems, likens Goethe to Niagara Falls, in comparison to whom all other poets are mere "little cascades,"[25] but it is unclear how much of Goethe's work she actually read. There is no indication, for example, that she was familiar with *Faust*.[26] Similarly glaring lacunae also exist in Kul'man's exposure to English literature—apparently she was ignorant of Shakespeare, and of contemporary romantic poetry. The same picture emerges with regard to Russian literature. Given Grossheinrich's relative ignorance in that domain, one has to assume that Kul'man's education in Russian letters was mainly entrusted to the priest P. S. Abramov, who also taught her Church Slavonic. In his 1832 letter to A. S. Shishkov, the president of the Russian Academy, Grossheinrich writes that Kul'man was familiar with "Lomonosov, Kheraskov, Ozerov, Derzhavin" as well as Shishkov's own poetic prose translation of *Gerusalemme liberata*.[27] Focusing on eighteenth-century figures rather than the contemporary literary scene may have been a tactical move to gain the sympathy of the notorious "archaizer" Shishkov.

Nevertheless, one cannot help wondering whether Kul'man was aware of Pushkin (who was Shishkov's antagonist and nemesis). The first four chapters of *Eugene Onegin* appeared in 1823–25 while Kul'man was still alive, but there is no indication that she read them, or any other of Pushkin's works. Possibly, this ignorance was a consequence of her low socioeconomic background. R. Iu. Danilevskii notes that "in the half-educated milieu of middle-brow St. Petersburg the young Pushkin was not particularly well-known."[28] Moreover, the "thick journals" publishing Pushkin's work would have been unaffordable to someone living in poverty.[29] We know that Grossheinrich was aware of Pushkin, or at least he became so after Kul'man's death. In a move reminiscent of his earlier attempt to secure a verdict about Kul'man's poetry from Goethe, he reports in his biography that he showed three of Kul'man's fairy tales to Pushkin in the summer of 1836 in order to receive a judgment on them from "Russia's greatest poet." Pushkin allegedly only found one flaw—he regretted the absence of rhymes (108). We do know for a fact that Pushkin kept a copy of the 1833 Russian Academy edition of Kul'man's works in his personal library, but he does not seem to have been particularly interested: the only pages cut open are from the biographical introduction and the Anacreon translations. He seems to have read none of Kul'man's own poems.[30]

While one may regret Grossheinrich's archaic tastes in literature and his failure to expose his pupil to more contemporary writings, there can be no doubt that Kul'man enthusiastically embraced the pseudoclassicist style in which her teacher encouraged her to write. Whether she would have become a better poet without the shackles allegedly imposed on her by her German tutor must remain an open question. In any event, Grossheinrich deserves considerable credit for recognizing and nurturing Kul'man's linguistic talent. His own knowledge of languages surpassed by far what would have been customary for an educated European of that time. He must have recognized in his pupil a kindred soul. In that sense, it was no doubt a fortunate coincidence that Kul'man's tutor and mentor happened to be himself a formidable linguist and polyglot.[31]

Opinions about the literary merit of Kul'man's poetry vary considerably, as we have seen. While much of what she wrote may indeed be naive or clichéd, we should not forget that we are dealing after all with the writings of a gifted child and adolescent. What Kul'man would have written at a more mature age remains anybody's guess. What is incontestable is her linguistic talent. There can be no doubt that she must have been blessed with a truly phenomenal memory and an extraordinary gift for languages. In that respect it is interesting to note that Goethe, if indeed his verdict is authentic, stressed precisely the multilingual aspect of Kul'man's gift, encouraging her to write in "any of the languages known to her." Kul'man's polyglot poetics and self-translational practice have remained a largely unexplored aspect of her work.

SELF-TRANSLATION AND THE CREATION OF A MULTILINGUAL OEUVRE

The fact that Kul'man resorted to translation as a privileged form of self-expression was not unusual for a Russian woman of her time. As Wendy Rosslyn has shown in her study of Russian female translators in the eighteenth and early nineteenth centuries, women used translation as a preferred entryway to the world of letters, given that "the task of entering Russian literary life was easier for woman translators than for women poets. Translation was considered less prestigious than original writing and therefore less presumptuous, and it minimized the grounds for accusations of vanity and self-display."[32] This had to do with the fact, as Sherry Simon has noted, that "translators and women have historically been the weaker figures in their respective hierarchies: translators are handmaidens to authors, women inferior to men."[33] However, Kul'man differs in two respects from the translators discussed in Rosslyn's study: unlike them, she did not hail from the upper echelons of society, and she blurred the distinction between translation and original writing more radically. While she did engage in bona fide translation work, the majority of her oeuvre consists of pseudo-translations, that is, of texts which, while presented as translations, are really original creations.[34] Furthermore, by self-translating these texts into other languages, Kul'man undercuts the notion of translation as a subservient genre. In translating herself rather than another person, she abandons the usual auxiliary status of the translator as a handmaiden of the original poet and emerges as the author of multiple "parallel originals."[35]

What is remarkable about Kul'man is not only her ability to write poetry in multiple languages, but her creation of a vast corpus of linked texts in three languages simultaneously. The edition of Kul'man's poetry published by the Russian Academy contains over a thousand pages. Most of this space is taken up by her "Piiticheskie opyty"/"Poetische Versuche"/"Saggi poetici," a vast trilingual compendium in three parts. Part 1 contains the translations of twenty-five of Anacreon's odes into Russian and German and a cycle called "Wreath," a series of Greek myths in Russian, German, and Italian verse relating to the metamorphosis of various people into flowers. Part 2, "The Poems of Corinna, or a Monument to Eliza" is inspired by the legend of Pindar's defeat by Corinna during the Olympic poetry competitions. Grossheinrich suggested to Kul'man that she create a body of poetry in Corinna's name in the same way that Macpherson had invented Ossian's poetry. Part 3, entitled "Monument to Berenice," is dedicated to the mother of Ptolemy I and contains poems written in the name of multiple Greek poets of the Hellenistic period.

Kul'man's identification with Corinna deserves particular attention. The German scholar Andrea Geffers has argued that Kul'man, while seemingly accepting the norms of feminine literary production, symbolically criticized the limitations imposed on women's creativity. As Geffers shows, Kul'man's quest for fame, expressed in her impersonation of a female poet who defeated her male competitors, transcends the traditional norms of submissive female behavior.[36] By the same token, one could argue that Kul'man's extensive self-translations transcend the subordinate, and therefore feminized, status assigned to translators. The Russian, German, and Italian versions of her poems are linked horizontally as mutual translations of each other while at the same time posing as translations of a fictitious Greek Ur-text (or, in the case of Anacreon, they actually are translations of an existing Greek source). Kul'man's collection thus combines translation, self-translation, and pseudotranslation into a unified whole. Given this multiple translational mirror effect, it becomes difficult to determine what, if anything, should be considered the "original."

As has been mentioned before, Grossheinrich encouraged Kul'man to write her poems in Russian first before translating them into German and Italian. In reality, though, it appears that she worked on the three versions simultaneously. Grossheinrich reports in his biography that "the translations into German and Italian kept in general the same pace as the Russian originals, and were always finished at the same time or at most a few days later" (102–3). This approach makes Kul'man an early practitioner of what has been called "synchronous self-translation." The most prominent example of a synchronous self-translator in the twentieth century is Samuel Beckett. As will be shown in the next chapter, the painter Wassily Kandinsky also engaged in this activity. Not only did Kul'man make a similar effort long before Kandinsky and Beckett, but she also appears to be the only example of a synchronous self-translator who worked not in two, but in three languages.

Kul'man left two statements about her personal approach to translation. As an epilogue to her collection of Anacreon in Russian, she included a poem that begins with the following two stanzas:

> Исполнились мои желания,
> Достигла цели юных лет!
> Нежнейшие цветы Геллады
> На Русских вижу я полях!
>
> Я, вынув их рукой дрожащей
> Из теплыя земли родной,
> Как мать дитя свое, лобзая,
> На север их перенесла.[37]

> My desires have been fulfilled,
> I have reached the goal of my young years!
> The most tender flowers of Hellas
> I see in Russian fields!
>
> Having picked them with a trembling hand
> From their warm native soil,
> As a mother [picks up] her child, kissing it,
> I transplanted them to the North.

As Wendy Rosslyn has pointed out, Kul'man's simile is unusual for using feminine imagery to present the figure of the translator. As we can see, she envisions her role as that of a mother and gardener who "gives birth to the translated text, and thus is partly its author, and nurtures it through the transplantation/translation process until it takes on an independent existence."[38]

A second, more extensive source for Kul'man's views on translation is provided by a letter quoted in Grossheinrich's biography, where she writes:

> If I were asked why I keep such conscientious fidelity in translating, my answer would be the following: I look at each work that I translate as if it were my own, but existing for the time being only in my imagination, and I have to find words in order to communicate it to the reader exactly as I imagine it. With me there can never be any talk of the great difference between the languages from which and into which I translate, because I envision the author's thoughts not in their embodiment, i.e., in words, but in their spirit [*Geistigkeit*], if I am allowed to use that word. As a consequence of this approach,

I always find, almost without my own involvement, for each notion, i.e., for each word of the author, the corresponding word in the language into which I translate, and therefore my translations usually have the double advantage of first, being literal, and second, nevertheless containing nothing that would offend the ear of the reader. (108)

As R. Iu. Danilevskii has noted, Kul'man's statement combines an Enlightenment belief in the transferability of an immutable content from one language to another with a proto-romantic attention to the poetic imagination of the translator.[39] It becomes obvious that Kul'man's stance consisted in a strong personal identification with the author of the translated text. In the process of self-translation, the hypothetical position of looking at the translated work "as if it were my own" becomes an actual statement of fact. At the same time, Kul'man endorses the idea that poetry is essentially translatable, given that the outward differences between individual linguistic codes recede behind a fundamental "spiritual" sameness. In this respect, as we will see, Kul'man's stance anticipates the later opinion of Marina Tsvetaeva about multilingual creation and poetic translation. Kul'man claims to achieve a feat in (self-) translation that almost amounts to squaring the circle, namely, to preserve both the "spirit" and the "letter" of the translated text. How exactly the spirit and the letter relate to each other is not something that she seems to have given much thought to, though. Her optimistic belief in the translatability of poetry rests on the somewhat naive assumption that individual languages function essentially like interchangeable codes.

If we compare the parallel Russian, German, and Italian versions of Kul'man's poems, we notice indeed that the wording remains usually quite close. This closeness is facilitated in part by the stilted, classicist style and the focus on a restricted set of literary topoi. Also, since these texts are all written in unrhymed verse in accordance with their "antique" character, there is a reduced need for syntactic and semantic alterations to accommodate formal equivalence.[40] The vast majority of the Russian and German poems are written in iambic trimeter with feminine endings, while the Italian version has a corresponding verse-length of seven syllables.

Nevertheless, we can find discrepancies between the Russian, German, and Italian versions that go beyond syntactic detail and metrical adjustment. In some cases, the Italian text is significantly longer. The poem "Gelikon"/"Der Helikon"/"L'Elicona" is four times as long in Italian as it is in Russian and German.[41] Grossheinrich, in his notes to the German edition, writes that an etching of the Egyptian city of Edfu inspired Kul'man to expand the poem, but only in the Italian version.[42] Of particular interest is the description of a grotto with a tombstone bearing the inscription "Alla memoria di Etta, / Dalle Camene amata, / Che nel fiore degli anni / Crudo fato rapi" ("To the memory of Etta, / Beloved by the Muses / Whom in the bloom of her years / A cruel fate cut down").[43] According to Grossheinrich, Kul'man was already mortally ill when she wrote these lines. Being fully aware of her impending death, she nevertheless pretended to believe in her convalescence in order to spare the feelings of her mother, who eagerly followed her daughter's writings in Russian and German, but was unable to do so in Italian. Kul'man therefore created this poetic vision of her own tombstone (with "Etta" standing in for "Elizaveta") only in the Italian version of the poem.[44]

Aside from the tactical consideration of inserting a coded message intelligible to her teacher, but not to her mother, Kul'man's emotional attachment to the Italian language may have been another reason why she chose this idiom, rather than her native Russian or German, to write her own epitaph. Kul'man's status as a trilingual poet raises the question of whether the languages at her disposal were of equal value to her as tools of literary expression. As we have seen, Grossheinrich tried to convince her that Russian was her primary and most "natural" language. It was indeed the first language that she learned, even though she added German at an early age. It is unclear which language predominated in daily-life communication with her mother. Presumably they used both idioms, given her mother's preoccupation with teaching her daughter "pure" Russian and German. Kul'man did call Russian her "mother tongue" in a letter to Grossheinrich, and in a dedicatory poem to the Russian empress and a hymn devoted to Anacreon, she referred to the Russian language as "otechestvennye zvuki" ("sounds of the fatherland") and as her "iazyk prirodnyi" ("natural language"). These expressions have no equivalent in the German versions of the poems.[45] There can be no doubt that Kul'man saw herself as a Russian patriot and that she accepted the patriarchal notion of Russia as her "fatherland." However, this does not necessarily mean that Russian was the language in which she thought and wrote most "naturally." We should remember that many members of the Russian upper class at that time expressed themselves more easily in French than in Russian. Also, the preferred language for poetic creation does not necessarily have to coincide with the language used in daily life. It could thus very well be that Kul'man, as a poet, was equally at home, or perhaps more at home, in languages other than her native Russian.

THE MOON IN THREE LANGUAGES

We will explore Kul'man's linguistic identity and trilingual poetics in more detail by following the metamorphosis of one particular poem through its incarnation in Russian, German, and Italian. "To the Moon" is part of the collection "Monuments to Berenice." Like most poems in Kul'man's trilingual corpus, the text is presented as a pseudo-translation of an imaginary Greek original. In the present case, the poem is attributed to the Greek poet Philemon. Grossheinrich, who considers "To the Moon" as one of Kul'man's masterpieces, reports that it was included in a collection of exemplary Russian poems for public instruction.[46]

К луне

Светлая дочь и любимица Неба,
Трон занимая эфирный чредой
С огненным братом, свергающим токи
Злата кипящего с горных высот;

Ты проливаешь из полныя чаши
Иль из серебряных ясных рогов,
Струи прохладны, дающие силу
Смертным, усталым от знойного дня.

Взор их везде следит за тобою,
Ходишь ли ты по лазурным полям,
Где растет под стопами твоими
Светлый сонм разноогненных звезд;

Или медлительным шагом проходишь
Длинный чертогов облачных ряд.
Царь-соловей, твоего не любящий
Брата, тебе воспевает хвалы.

Ты с умилением внемлешь напеву;
Смотришь порой, коль он весел, сквозь туч;
Или скрываешься в темном их недре,
Коль выражает печаль он свою.

Ты во всяком виде прелестна;
Но прелестней, когда ты стоишь
В западе, рядом с вечерней звездою,
В блеске младости нежной твоей.

Вы, двум душам великим подобны,
Там сияете — радость земных —
Без тщеславия, в дружном союзе,
Обе довольные сами собой.[47]

To the Moon

Bright daughter and favorite of the Sky,
Occupying the ethereal throne in turn
With the fiery brother, who hurls down streams
Of seething gold from mountainous heights;

You pour from a full cup
Or from silvery bright horns
Cool streams that give strength
To mortals tired from the hot day.

Their gaze follows you everywhere,
Whether you walk across azure fields
Where underneath your steps
A bright swarm of stars grows with various fires;

Or you wander with a slow pace
Through a long row of cloudy chambers.
Tsar-nightingale, not loving your brother,
Sings the praise of your glory.

You listen with tenderness to the song;
Once in a while, if he is cheerful, you peer through the clouds;
Or you hide in their dark depths
If he expresses his sadness.

In any form you are enchanting;
But most enchanting when you stand
In the west next to the evening star
In the splendor of your tender youth.

You, resembling two great souls,
Are shining there—a joy to the mortals—
Without vanity, in a friendly union,
Both pleased with themselves.

The German and Italian versions of the poem read as follows:

An den Mond

Glänzende Tochter und Liebling des Himmels,
Die den Thron des Aethers du teilst
Mit dem feurigen Bruder, der Ströme
Siedenden Goldes den Höhen entgeusst;

Selbst vergeudest aus voller Schale
Oder aus blendendem silbernem Horn
Sanfte Kühlung du, um nach des Tages
Mühen der Sterblichen Kraft zu erneu'n.

Ueberall folgt dir ihr dankendes Auge,
Sei's dass du das lasurne Gefild
Heiter durchwallest, wo farbige Sterne
Tausendweis deinen Spuren entblühn;

Oder mit zögerndem Schritte die Säle
Deines Wolkenpalastes durchirrst,
Horchend dem Liede des Sängers der Nächte,
Der, der Sonne feind, dich nun erhebt.

Tönt sein Gesang in fröhlichen Weisen
Lächelnd blickst aus Wolken du dann;
Tönet er Gram, so ziehst du dich trauernd
In des Palastes Tiefen zurück.

Schön bist du Mond, in allen Gestalten,
Aber am schönsten, wenn freundlich du
Neben dem Abendstern strahlest im Westen,
In der Jugend blendendem Glanz.

Beide gleicht ihr zwei grossen Seelen,
Die Bewundrung, der Trost der Welt:
Frei von Ehrsucht, und frei von Neide,
Glänzen sie, ihres Verdiensts sich bewusst.[48]

Alla Luna

O figlia primogenita del cielo,
Che alterna ascendi sull' etereo trono
Col fratello di fuoco, che torrenti
Lancia di liquid' auro a se d'interno;

Tu dall'aurata coppa o dalle argentee
Corna ritorte spandi dolce lume,
Che ai miseri mortali, dal soverchio
Lavoro esausti, dà ristoro e forza;

Te dovunque ti segue il nostro sguardo,
Sia che passeggi negli azzurri campi,
Ove germoglian sotto i passi tuoi
Stelle infinite, di color diverse;

Sia che traversi d'ambulante reggia
Le smaltate di perle aeree stanze,
Allor che l'usignuol, del Sol nemico,
Per celebrarti alza la chiara voce.

Prestando orecchio all' armoniose note,
Miri, s'ei canta lieto, tra le nubi,
O rimani nel seno loro ascosa,
S'egli in mesta armonia suo duolo esprime.

Tu vezzosa mai sempre in ogni aspetto,
O Luna! ma vieppiù tale ne sembri,
Quando giovin nel lucido ponente
Splendi alla stella vespertina accanto:

E come due bell' alme generose,
Sostegno e gioia dell' umana vita,
Non rivali splendete in cielo amiche,
Ambo contente della luce vostra.[49]

Grossheinrich reports that Kul'man had nurtured a special predilection for the moon from her earliest childhood (10). While the moon appears in many of her poems, "K lune"/"An den Mond"/"Alla luna" is the only treatment of this topic in three languages. The poem also stands out within the corpus of Kul'man's poetry for its choice of meter. Rather unusually for Kul'man, it is written in dactylic tetrameters with alternating feminine and masculine endings. Both in the Russian and the German versions there are occasional missing syllables. This looseness of form may be intended to evoke the variegated flow of Homer's epic dactyls, but it can result in clumsy lines, such as the rhythmically awkward "Der, der Sonne feind, dich nun erhebt." The Italian version is written in hendecasyllabics, that is, lines of eleven syllables (a standard meter in Italian poetry), with consistent feminine endings. With its fluid regularity, the Italian verse shows none of the clumsiness of the Russian and German dactyls.

Perhaps the most intriguing cross-linguistic issue, when comparing the Russian, German, and Italian versions of the poem, concerns the role of gender. The moon is clearly imagined as a feminine persona—hence the choice of the grammatically feminine word "luna" in Russian (as opposed to the masculine "mesiats," which designates the full moon). This feminine moon is in a state of competition with her "brother," the sun, but she entertains friendly relations with the evening star, another feminine presence in the text. The German version undermines this gender constellation, given that "der Mond" and "der Abendstern" are both grammatically masculine and "die Sonne" is feminine. Rather oddly, the German poem is written never-theless as if the opposite were true, creating a disjunction between seman-tics and grammatical gender.[50] In the German version, the femininity of the grammatically masculine moon and the masculinity of the grammatically feminine sun are indicated by kinship terms (the moon is called a "daughter" and the sun a "brother"), while the evening star is simply masculine without any attempt to "feminize" it. This creates a different gender dynamics than in the Russian and Italian versions, where the moon and evening star are presented as female friends. In one instance, Kul'man did insert a "gender correction" in the German text. The nightingale serenading the female moon is masculine in Russian ("solovei") and Italian ("usignuol"). The correspond-ing German noun ("die Nachtigall") would be feminine, but rather than nam-ing the bird, Kul'man replaced it in the German version with the masculine paraphrase "Sänger der Nächte" ("singer of the nights") in order to maintain the scenario of heterosexual courtship.

Given the difficulties of matching semantics and grammar in German, we have to assume that the poem was originally conceived in Russian. Or did the inspiration come from the Italian? Interestingly, the gender constellation of the poem works best in that language. Not only are the moon ("luna," using the same word as in Russian) and the evening star ("stella vespertina") grammatically feminine, but the sun (not named directly in the poem) is masculine in Italian. This makes the designation "fiery brother" more natural in Italian than in Russian, where the sun is grammatically neuter (in German, as already mentioned, the sun is feminine, which turns its status as "brother" into a grammatical oxymoron). Since the poem is presented as a pseudo-translation from Greek, it may be worth mentioning that the sun and the moon are masculine and feminine in Greek as well, which means that the Italian version comes closest to the gender constellation of the imaginary Greek "original." Moreover, the sense of female solidarity between the moon and the evening star is expressed most succinctly with the Italian word "ami-che" ("[female] friends"). In Russian the plural of the word "friend" cannot be marked for gender. In German, while technically possible ("Freundin-nen"), it would sound rather awkward.

While there are no major semantic deviations between the three ver-sions, they do differ in a multitude of details. By comparison, the Italian text has more of a "life of its own," that is, it contains more elements which exist in that version alone and cannot be found in the other two languages. In Italian the moon is called the "first-born" daughter of the sky, while it is the "favor-ite" daughter in Russian and German. The sun radiates not from above, but from its inner core (which seems more astronomically sound), while the moon pours out its light from a "golden" cup rather than a "full" cup. The "mortals" in stanza two seem more miserable in the Italian version—they are "exhausted from excessive labor," while they are suffering mainly from the heat in Russian and German. The cloudy chambers of the moon are "coated with pearls" only in Italian. The song of the nightingale is called "harmonious" (twice) in Italian, but not in Russian or German. The moon and the evening star are "generous souls," as opposed to "great souls" in Russian and German. In one instance, we can observe a sort of amplification in the passage from Russian to German to Italian: the "swarm" of stars in Russian turns into "thousands" of stars in German, and "infinite" stars in Italian. The final line also differs in the three versions: in Russian the moon and evening star appear smugly "pleased with themselves," in German, rather ponderously, they are "conscious of their own merit," while in Italian they are "pleased with [their] light."

In general, the poem seems more compelling in its Italian incarnation than in Russian or German. This is true for many of the poems in Kul'man's trilingual corpus. To a modern reader, and no doubt even to a reader of her own time, Kul'man's Russian style makes an archaic impression. The numerous Slavonicisms typical of eighteenth-century poetry appear awkward and ponderous in the context of the Pushkin period. Her German, while slightly more modern than her Russian, also feels somewhat outdated. This is no doubt the consequence of a schooling in German literature that focused almost exclusively on eighteenth-century models. By contrast, Kul'man's Italian seems more contemporary and elegant. At first sight, this may appear surprising, given that her Italian role models—Dante, Petrarch, Tasso—were even more ancient than the eighteenth-century Russian and German poets that she had been encouraged to emulate. However, we have to remember that Italy reached its poetic pinnacle centuries earlier than Russia and Germany. In that sense, Kul'man's study of classic Italian literature may have provided her with a better instrument for poetic creation than the antiquated brand of Russian and German poetry that was imparted to her by her teachers Abramov and Grossheinrich.

THE CHOICE OF LINGUISTIC ALTERITY

There is another reason why Italian had a different status for Kul'man than Russian and German. We should not forget that Russian and German were both her mother tongues, while Italian was a *chosen* language. The special attraction that Italian had for her may lie precisely in its foreignness: it was an idiom that her mother did *not* know, and, unlike French, it was not a language routinely spoken by upper-class Russian society. In consequence, Italian offered to Kul'man an alternative identity from her Russian-German roots. Together with all the other languages that she learned, it provided an escape hatch from her impoverished life on the fringes of Russian society and helped to fulfill her frustrated longing for cultural expansion and travel. Similar to ancient Greece, Italy turned into an idealized locus of Kul'man's imagination and yearnings.

The trilingual edition published by the Russian Academy contains two dedications directed specifically to Kul'man's German and Italian readers. Written only in German and Italian, these poems seem to have been composed shortly before her death. The German dedication addresses the women of Germany with a plea to "remember once in a while / the poor girl from the north, / who, without knowing you / adores you, and in the spring / of her years is dying."[51] The Italian poem, written in an even more emotional tone, begins with a declaration of love:

> Italia, Italia mia!
> Oh! la più bella terra
> Del vasto mondo intero;
> E a me (dopo la patria,
> Di cui l'amore innato
> Col core insieme cresce)
> Cara vieppiù d'ogni altra![52]

> Italy, my Italy!
> Oh! the most beautiful country
> In the whole wide world;
> And to me (after the fatherland,
> of which the inborn love
> grows together with the heart)
> dearer than any other!

After summarizing the crucial role that Italian poets and the Italian language played in her life, Kul'man ends her poem with the words:

> Italia idolatrata,
> Ti scrissi queste righe.
> Dolce mia vita, addio!
> Addio, Italia mia![53]

> Idolized Italy,
> I wrote these lines for you.
> My sweet life, farewell!
> Farewell, my Italy!

It looks almost as if Kul'man had to forcefully remind herself of the love that, as a loyal subject of the tsar, she owed her Russian fatherland, while her real attachment belonged to a country that was neither her fatherland nor her motherland.

Kul'man's example demonstrates that a strong emotional connection can very well exist to a non-native language, and that this language can become a preferred instrument of poetic expression in spite of, or perhaps because of, its foreignness. It is probably no accident that, aesthetically and stylistically, Kul'man's poetic oeuvre is rooted in the eighteenth century rather than the romantic period. As a poet, she was still unencumbered by Herderian notions of "language loyalty" and was thus able to create in multiple linguistic spheres simultaneously. By the same token, the massive trilingual edition of her works published by the Imperial Russian Academy in the 1830s speaks to an official tolerance and acceptance of multilingualism that was to vanish with the increasing spread of a patriotic ideal equating the national language with the national soul.

For the rest of the nineteenth century, in spite of the Russian-French bilingualism of the Russian upper class, poetic self-translation remained a marginal phenomenon. Pushkin did write a few French poems in his youth, but it never would have occurred to him to self-translate his Russian poems into other languages. The only major Russian poets of the nineteenth century who did engage in this activity, although on a rather modest scale, were Vasilii Zhukovskii (1783–1852) and Evgenii Baratynskii (1800–1844). Zhukovskii translated a total of thirteen of his Russian poems as well as a fairy tale into German. Most of his German self-translations were written after his permanent relocation to Germany in 1841, where several of his German works appeared in print during the final years of his life. Baratynskii translated twenty of his poems into French in order to make them accessible to his Parisian friends and acquaintances. Neither Zhukovskii nor Baratynskii preserved the form of the Russian originals in their translations, preferring to create "free" prose versions. Zhukovskii resorted to a sort of elevated poetic diction, while Baratynskii tried to compensate for the absence of meter and rhyme with rhetorical amplifications and a heightened emotional tone. Apparently, though, he remained dissatisfied with the results and refused to get his translations published.[54] Afanasii Fet (1820–1892), another major nineteenth-century poet, was, like Kul'man, a Russian-German bilingual who would have been perfectly capable of writing in either language. Yet the only available example of a self-translation by Fet is a rather humdrum circumstantial poem written on the occasion of a relative's silver marriage celebration.[55]

The practice of poetic self-translation only returned after a long hiatus, when the monolingual paradigm imposed by romantic ideology had run its course. The spirit of linguistic experimentation inspired by the advent of modernism led, a hundred years after Kul'man, to a renewed exit from the mother tongue, a trend reinforced by the massive uptick in emigration in the early twentieth century. Unlike Kul'man, who never left her native city and became a world traveler only in her imagination and through her multilingual practice, this new generation of cosmopolitan poets, whether by choice or necessity, engaged in actual travel and often ended up in permanent dislocation from the native land. An example of this modernist border-crossing is provided by the trilingual poetry of the painter Wassily Kandinsky, to whom we will now turn.

Wassily Kandinsky's Trilingual Poetry

NOT MANY PEOPLE are aware that Wassily Kandinsky (1866–1944), one of the most celebrated artists of the twentieth century and an originator of abstract art, was also a poet. Even fewer have paid attention to the fact that Kandinsky was a *multilingual* poet and self-translator working in three languages: his native Russian, German, and French. Even though Kandinsky wrote poetry throughout his life, the peak of his literary activity falls into the watershed years of his career before World War I when he transitioned from representational to abstract painting. It was during that time, as Kandinsky later put it in his 1938 essay "Mes gravures sur bois" ("My Woodcuts"), that he felt most compelled to engage in a "change of instruments" by putting the palette aside and using in its place the typewriter. As he explained, "I use the word 'instrument' because the force that prompts me to work always remains the same, that is to say, an 'inner pressure.' And it is this pressure that often asks me to change instruments."[1] Kandinsky's biographer Jelena Hahl-Koch has argued that crossing over from painting into poetry played a crucial role in Kandinsky's artistic evolution. It gave him the necessary freedom to grow as an artist, since, according to Hahl-Koch, Kandinsky "felt himself less constrained in a field in which he was not a professional, and therefore was able to 'play' and experiment."[2] It is important to note that Kandinsky created his experiments not only in a medium in which he was not a professional, but also partially in languages in which he was not a native speaker. Changing instruments, for Kandinsky, could also mean switching languages.

Kandinsky's trilingual poetic oeuvre has received only sporadic attention thus far. One reason for this neglect may be the fact that his poems are not easily accessible. Even though Kandinsky wrote poetry his entire life, not much of it was published during his lifetime. His most significant poetic publication is the album *Klänge* (*Sounds*), a collection of thirty-eight German prose poems, which appeared in Munich in 1912. Later in his life, Kandinsky published occasional poems in various journals. Starting in the 1990s, many more previously unpublished poems began to "seep out" somewhat haphazardly from Kandinsky's two main archives, kept at the Gabriele Münter and Johannes Eichner Foundation in Munich and the Musée National d'Art Moderne (Centre Pompidou) in Paris. Most of the existing Russian versions of the *Klänge* texts, based on the manuscripts at the Centre Pompidou, were published in Moscow in 1994.[3] In 2011, the Russian art historian Boris Sokolov drew attention to the existence of a multitude of additional prose poems in Russian and German that Kandinsky wrote in 1914 as a sort of sequel to *Klänge*.[4] The German variants of seven of these texts were included in a 2007 edition of Kandinsky's writings, together with a number of other previously unpublished works.[5] This edition served as the source for an anthology of Kandinsky's German poems that came out in Berlin in 2016.[6] Kandinsky's Russian poetry, by contrast, has never appeared in book form and remains largely unknown. With very few exceptions, even the Kandinsky specialists in Russia have shown little interest in his Russian-language writings.[7]

Many of Kandinsky's poems exist in two versions—Russian and German—as a result of self-translation. The absence of a satisfactory edition makes the study of these parallel texts a somewhat cumbersome enterprise. The people who transcribed Kandinsky's Russian and German manuscripts do not seem to have consulted with each other, perhaps because they lacked a common language. As a general practice, the editors bringing out Kandinsky's poems focused on the work written in one language without paying any attention to the existence of a "double" in a different idiom. This is a regrettable omission. For one thing, consulting the self-translated variant would have helped to avoid some of the mistakes that occurred in the deciphering of Kandinsky's not always very legible handwriting.[8]

Kandinsky had not always been a multilingual writer, of course. His first poems were written exclusively in his native Russian. The same holds true for his theoretical and theatrical writings.[9] At the beginning of his career, Kandinsky drafted most of his works in Russian before self-translating and reworking them in German. Even in his earliest Russian essays, however, we find German expressions such as "Überschneidung" (intersection) and "Gegensatz" (contrast) inserted into the Russian text.[10] The stage compositions of 1908–09 exist in both a Russian and German version, as does the famous treatise *On the Spiritual in Art*.[11] After 1912, Kandinsky tended to write directly in German. His memoirs *Rückblicke* (*Backward Glances*) of 1913 were first written in German without a Russian draft and were only later self-translated into Russian. In his poetic writings, Kandinsky also evolved gradually from his Russian beginnings to a Russian-German bilingualism in which the German language came to play an increasingly important role. After his final departure from the Soviet Union, Kandinsky became essentially a monolingual German-language writer, before evolving towards a German-French bilingualism after 1933.

We might be inclined to look at Kandinsky's multilingual practice as simply a pragmatic accommodation to the different linguistic milieus that he happened to inhabit in the course of his life. He was a voluntary Russian expatriate in Bavaria from 1896 to 1914, a refugee from the Soviet Union in Weimar Germany from 1921 to 1933, and a refugee from Nazi Germany in Paris after 1933. The need to adapt himself to new environments is hardly a sufficient explanation for Kandinsky's multilingual poetry, however. Marc Chagall, who lived in France much longer than Kandinsky, only used Yiddish and Russian for his poetic writings and never switched to French. For Kandinsky, the linguistic border-crossing clearly responded to a creative need that would have remained unfulfilled by remaining within the monolingual orbit of his mother tongue.

KANDINSKY'S FIRST STEPS AS A TRANSLINGUAL POET

Kandinsky began to write poetry at an early age. In his memoirs *Rückblicke* he mentions that "like many children and young people, I tried to write poems, which sooner or later I tore up."[12] Nothing of these juvenilia seems to have survived. The earliest known poems can be found in the notebooks dating from Kandinsky's ethnographic expedition to the Vologda region in 1889, which are preserved in his Paris archive and were published for the first time in 2007.[13] The same edition also contains three more early Russian poems of uncertain date.[14] Thoroughly conventional in style and form, these texts reflect the late romantic and symbolist literary environment in which Kandinsky had grown up.[15] Displaying a melancholic mood, they depict a provincial funeral, a nature scene in late autumn, and a self-admonition to remain silent that seems inspired by Fedor Tiutchev's famous poem "Silentium."

The self-reflective poem "Poeziia" ("Poetry") deserves particular attention, since it formulates the program that Kandinsky set for himself as a budding poet:

> Цветы поэзии рассеяны в природе.
> Умей их собирать в невянущий венок.
> И будь хоть скован ты, но будешь на свободе,
> И, будь хотя один, не будешь одинок.

> The flowers of poetry are scattered in nature.
> Know how to collect them in an unfading wreath.
> And, even in fetters, you will be free,
> And, even alone, you will not be lonely.

Kandinsky later included a German self-translation of this poem in his manuscript *Riesen* (*Giants*, 1908–09), the first version of what eventually would become his stage composition *Der gelbe Klang* (*The Yellow Sound*):

> Die Blumen der Dichtung sind über die Welt gestreut
> Sammle sie in einen ewigen Kranz
> In der Wüste wirst du nicht einsam sein
> Im Gefängnis frei[16]

> The flowers of poetry are scattered over the world
> Collect them into an eternal wreath
> In the desert you will not be lonely
> In prison free

While the Russian original of the poem has received no attention, the German version has become a focus of scholarly scrutiny in connection with Kandinsky's stage compositions. Naoko Kobayashi-Bredenstein interprets this text as a manifesto of Kandinsky's synthetic art, in which he intends to achieve a "harmonic relation between different religions, peoples, and cultures." The fact that the flowers of art and religion bloom even in the desert, according to this interpretation, signals the "immortality of the spirit." At the same time, the allusion to prison and desert suggests the "arduous path of the artists and believers."[17] Locating a possible source for the poem in Goethe's *Torquato Tasso*, Kobayashi-Bredenstein is unaware that Kandinsky is quoting his own Russian poem in a German self-translation. The purported internationalist message that she detects in this text works better in the German than in the Russian version, which features "nature" instead of "world." The same holds true for the image of the desert, which, while not incompatible with the concept of being alone, only exists in the German translation. As can be seen, Kandinsky's self-translation from Russian to German implied subtle forms of rewriting and reinterpretation. The fact that he translated the poem into German prose without attempting to preserve the iambic hexameter and "AbAb" rhymes of the Russian original shows that, at least at the time of the composition of *Riesen*, he was not yet confident enough in his command of German versification to attempt a metrical and rhymed version. As we will see, this was to change when Kandinsky worked further on his stage compositions.

The earliest poems that Kandinsky composed directly in German were addressed to the painter Gabriele Münter, his former student with whom he had fallen in love in 1902, and who by 1903 had become his de facto wife (Kandinsky was at that time still married to his first wife, Anna). In a letter to Münter on October 27, 1902, Kandinsky mentions a German poem written in July of that year in which he expressed his state of bliss.[18] In September 1903 he sent Münter a poem in a quite different mood:

> Die weiße Wolke, der schwarze Wald!
> Ich wart' auf dich. O komm doch bald.
> So weit ich sehe, so weit nach vorn,
> Das glänzend gold'ne, reife Korn.
>
> Du kommst ja nicht. O welcher Schmerz!
> Es zittert und blutet mein armes Herz.
> Ich wart' auf dich. O komm doch bald.
> Ich bin allein im schwarzen Wald.[19]

> The white cloud, the black wood!
> I wait for you. O come soon.
> As far as I see, so far ahead
> The radiantly golden ripe grain.
>
> But you do not come. O what pain!
> My poor heart trembles and bleeds.
> I wait for you. O come soon.
> I am alone in the black wood.

It looks as if Kandinsky's strained emotional state made him search for a form of self-expression that went beyond ordinary prose. In his correspondence with Münter, Kandinsky mentioned that he had composed a few beautiful poems in Russian, but he expressed dissatisfaction with his ability to write poetry in German.[20] The problem did not really lie in a poor command of the German language. Kandinsky's poem, rather than a linguistically awkward text written "with a foreign accent," looks like the effusion of a sentimental German with a penchant for banal rhyming (the notorious pair "Schmerz"— "Herz" ["pain"—"heart"] is probably the most shopworn rhyme in the German language). With its emphasis on visual impressions and stark coloristic contrasts, the poem has a certain painterly quality. Kandinsky himself, in his letter to Münter, commented that it would perhaps make a good subject for a "drawing on black cardboard."[21]

He actually completed this picture, a gouache on dark grey board, which he gave the title *Weisse Wolke* (*White Cloud*).[22] The painting depicts a blue rider on a white horse following a path winding through blooming trees toward a vanishing point between hills, which is obscured by a thickly painted white cloud. The black wood of the poem is nowhere to be seen (except, perhaps, in the dark background), while the golden corn has metamorphosed into a few colored dots in the crown of the central blooming tree. The bleeding heart of the poem is indirectly represented by a few red dots near the stem of the tree, which look like droplets of blood amidst the white flowers covering the meadow. The color blue, which is not mentioned in the poem, plays an important role in the painting. It predominates in the crown of the blooming trees and also traces the movement of the road and the curve of the hills.

Overall, the painting makes a more optimistic impression than the poem. With its subtle interplay between lines and dots and carefully crafted coloration, it is certainly a much more compelling work of art than the text that served as its inspiration. In Kandinsky's defense, it has to be said that he never intended to publish his poem. It was a private message sent to Münter shortly after the consummation of their relationship. Münter's biographer Gisela Kleine speculates that Kandinsky's intention may have been to restore a sense of romantic distance that had become shattered through physical intimacy.[23] Given that Münter knew no Russian, Kandinsky had no choice but to write his poem in German if he wanted her to understand its message.

"Die weisse Wolke" is one of several poems, or "little songs," that Kandinsky wrote for Münter, all of them in a similar tone and of similar quality.[24] The playlet *Abend* (*Evening*), a more extended literary text in German, dating from the time when Kandinsky and Münter resided in France in 1906–07, was also essentially conceived as a private communication between the two lovers.[25] Quite different in tone from the earlier quoted poem, this humorous and slightly erotic dialogue between two cats, "Minette" and "Wasska," shows Kandinsky from an unexpectedly light-hearted and even bawdy side (for a Russian speaker, the name "Minette" evokes the slang term for oral sex).

How good was Kandinsky's command of German? Even though he grew up in Russia and never received any formal schooling in German, the language was not unfamiliar to him, given that his maternal grandmother was a Baltic German. In his memoirs Kandinsky mentions that he spoke frequent German during his childhood.[26] An important influence was his maternal aunt, Elizaveta Tikheeva, who became a sort of replacement mother for him when Kandinsky remained in the care of his father after the divorce of his parents in 1871. Tikheeva used to tell him German fairy tales.[27] If German was not Kandinsky's mother tongue, it was thus nevertheless his "grandmother tongue," his "aunt tongue," and—perhaps most crucially—his "wife tongue." Technically speaking, Gabriele Münter, who was Kandinsky's companion from 1902 to 1916, was not his wife, since he never formally married her, but he considered his relationship with Münter to be a "Gewissensehe" ("marriage of conscience").[28] One surmises that Münter reinforced the positive emotional connotation of the German language that had been implanted in Kandinsky by female members of his family during his childhood. One of the terms of endearment he used for Münter was "mein deutsches Ellchen" ("my German Ellchen"—"Ellchen" being a folksy diminutive of "Gabriele").[29] In a letter to Münter on November 16, 1904, he wrote: "The Russians take me for an alien and have no need for me. The Germans are good to me (at least better than the Russians). I grew up half German, my first language, my first books were German, my engine [*Motor*] is Germany. . . . I have a good feeling toward Germany. And, finally . . . my Ellchen is a German."[30]

However, even though he ended up living in Germany for a total of almost thirty years, and in spite of his familiarity with the language since early childhood, Kandinsky did not pass for a native speaker of German. When Münter mentioned his Russian accent in a 1910 letter, Kandinsky reacted with vexation. He said he would never consent to change his pronunciation and claimed that some people even found the sound of his "l" particularly "pretty."[31] The publishers and editors of Kandinsky's German writings often criticized his style, which they found "foreign"-sounding and in need of revision. At the same time—as is bound to happen with emigrants who have spent a long time away from their country of origin—Kandinsky's Russian was also criticized for its "foreign" or "German" quality. Boris Sokolov argues that Kandinsky's theoretical writings are composed in a "strange Russian language" replete with Germanisms.[32] Kandinsky was unable to publish the Russian version of *On the Spiritual in Art* in the modernist journal *Apollon* because he refused to make the stylistic changes demanded by the editor, Sergei Makovskii. In a letter to Münter from St. Petersburg, Kandinsky wrote on October 30, 1910: "Makovskii wanted to publish my brochure, but, here too, my language is an obstacle. But I don't want to change anything. I find this stupid [*So was finde ich dumm*]."[33]

As we can see from this quote, the occasional "strangeness" of Kandinsky's language, be it in German or Russian, could be an intentional effect rather than simply the result of stylistic clumsiness or foreign linguistic interference. The unusual, even ungrammatical passages in Kandinsky's poetic writings in German cannot be attributed to the fact that Kandinsky, as a Russian native speaker, had an insufficient knowledge of the language. His more utilitarian prose and correspondence show an entirely correct command of German syntax and grammar. And yet, in his German prose poems we find "strange" passages such as the following: "Es sich entreißt dem schwarzen Traum. Der Tod das Leben will" ("It itself tears from the black dream. Death life wants").[34] Kandinsky certainly knew German well enough not to commit such elementary syntactical mistakes (the correct word order would be "Es entreißt sich . . . Der Tod will das Leben"). In fact, the manuscript reveals that Kandinsky first wrote the passage in correct German before altering the syntax.[35] The reason for this change has probably to do with metric considerations—"Es sích entréißt dem schwárzen Tráum.

Der Tód das Lében will" scans as an iambic line. The parallel passage in the Russian version of the text—"Ot chernogo sna vyrvalos'. Khochet Smert' Zhizn'"—shows no regular rhythmic pattern.[36] The syntax of the second sentence is also somewhat unusual, however. It looks as if Kandinsky is trying to "hammer in" his point with two stressed monosyllabic words. As we can see, rhythmic elements are a key consideration in Kandinsky's writings, but he violates the grammar and syntax of German more radically than that of his native Russian in order to achieve specific rhythmic effects. One could speculate that it was easier for Kandinsky to conduct such experiments in German, since he was "deforming" a language in which, as a foreigner, he enjoyed a certain freedom.

Kandinsky's increasing use of German as a literary language was thus not only determined by pragmatic factors—the fact that he lived in Germany and was addressing a German audience—but also by artistic considerations. Precisely because of its "foreignness," German could at times serve as a more attractive medium of creative expression. Moreover, German was the prevalent medium of Kandinsky's spoken, daily-life communication and was unencumbered by any history of formal writing. Jelena Hahl-Koch, who made a word-for-word comparison between the German original of Kandinsky's *Rückblicke* and the Russian self-translation that came out in Moscow in 1918, notes that the Russian language of his memoirs is "closer to the conventional written norm, and therefore more dry and complicated," whereas the German is "more shaped by the spoken word, and for that reason makes a more unconventional and lively impression."[37]

While Kandinsky's beginnings as a German poet may have been rather inauspicious, he gradually did become more comfortable with writing German verse. From a purely private matter between him and Gabriele Münter, his German poetic writings began to turn into a more professional affair. This development can be followed by taking a closer look at the poems in Kandinsky's theatrical compositions, to which we will now turn.

THE SELF-TRANSLATED POETRY IN KANDINSKY'S STAGE COMPOSITIONS

Partially inspired by Richard Wagner's idea of the *Gesamtkunstwerk*, Kandinsky pursued his own quest for a new synthetic form of "monumental art" with the stage compositions that he began writing in 1908. In addition to Wagner, other formative influences include the symbolist dramas of Maurice Maeterlinck, the theatrical theories of Edward Gordon Craig, theosophical and anthroposophical doctrines, and the iconography and narratives of Christian eschatology. Kandinsky's theatrical pieces combine colored lights, music, and dance into an abstract spectacle without a conventional plot and are largely devoid of dialogue or monologue. While they have attracted a host of different interpretations,[38] almost no attention has been paid to the fact that nearly all of Kandinsky's theatrical texts exist in a Russian and a German variant. *Der gelbe Klang* (*The Yellow Sound*), Kandinsky's best-known stage composition, was first conceived in German under the title *Riesen* (*Giants*), followed by a Russian version called *Zheltyi zvuk* (*Yellow Sound*), which remained unpublished until the 1990s.[39] A reworked German version bearing the same title, *Der gelbe Klang*, was included in the almanac *Der blaue Reiter* in 1912.[40] Attempts to stage the play remained unrealized because of the outbreak of World War I. In addition to *The Yellow Sound*, Kandinsky wrote several more "color dramas" that remained unpublished during his lifetime and have only come to light relatively recently. They include the pieces *Green Sound* (*Grüner Klang/ Zelenyi zvuk*) and *Black and White* (*Schwarz und Weiss/Chernoe i beloe*), which also date from 1908–09. In both cases, the Russian version preceded the German translation. A short piece called *Black Figure* (*Schwarze Figur*) exists only in German. A later piece called *Purple* (*Violett*), which differs considerably in style from the earlier compositions, was written in 1914 and later reworked and partially published in 1926 during Kandinsky's Bauhaus years. In that instance the German text, which is more extensive, appears to be the primary version.[41]

For the most part, the text of Kandinsky's theatrical compositions consists of stage directions (for lack of a better term) rather than spoken dialogue. However, his three early pieces from 1908–09 contain several inserted lyrical passages written in traditional metered and rhymed verse.[42] Comparing the Russian and German variants gives us an impression of Kandinsky's struggle with poetic form and the difficulties he faced when transposing his texts between the two languages.

The Yellow Sound opens with a hymn performed by a concealed chorus while the stage is illuminated in dark blue light. Since no such song exists in the earlier *Riesen* manuscript, we have to assume that the Russian version appearing in *Zheltyi zvuk* is the original text:

> Твердые сны . . . Разговоры утесов . . .
> Глыбы недвижные странных вопросов . . .
> Неба движение . . . Таяние скал . . .
> Кверху растущий невидимый вал . . .
> Слезы и смех. Средь проклятий молитвы.
> Радость в слиянии. Черные битвы.
> Мрак непрогляднейший в солнечный день.
> Ярко светящая в полночи тень.[43]

Hard dreams . . . Conversations of rocks . . .
Motionless clumps of strange questions . . .
Movement of the sky . . . Melting of cliffs . . .
Upwards growing an invisible wall . . .
Tears and laughter. Prayers amidst curses.
Joy in fusion. Black battles.
Most impenetrable darkness in a sunny day.
A brightly shining shadow at midnight.

With its impressionist vagueness and diffuse mysticism, this choral hymn is reminiscent of early twentieth-century symbolism. The lack of verbs evokes the "nominal" style cultivated in Russia by Afanasii Fet and Konstantin Bal'mont. The paradoxical, oxymoronic semantics have been interpreted as an expression of synesthetic harmony and balance, or, conversely, an evocation of the primordial chaos before Creation.[44] The dactylic tetrameter, with a caesura in the middle of each line, evokes the chorus of an antique tragedy. Opposing concepts are expressed in chiastically arranged lines.[45]

In German, this song takes the following form:

Steinharte Träume . . . Und sprechende Felsen . . .
Schollen mit Rätseln erfüllender Fragen . . .
Des Himmels Bewegung . . . Und Schmelzen . . . der Steine . . .
Nach oben hochwachsend unsichtbarer . . . Wall . . .
Tränen und Lachen . . . Bei Fluchen Gebete . . .
Der Einigung Freude und schwärzeste Schlachten.
Finsteres Licht bei dem . . . sonnigsten . . . Tag
Grell leuchtender Schatten bei dunkelster Nacht!![46]

An English translation of Kandinsky's German translation was published by Kenneth Lindsay and Peter Vergo:

Stone-hard dreams . . . And speaking rocks . . .
Clods of earth pregnant with puzzling questions . . .
The heaven turns . . . The stones . . . melt . . .
Growing up more invisible . . . rampart . . .
Tears and laughter . . . Praying and cursing . . .
Joy of reconciliation and blackest slaughter.
Murky light on the . . . sunniest . . . day
Brilliant shadows in darkest night!![47]

It becomes evident that Kandinsky strove to be as literal as possible in the German translation while retaining the meter of the original Russian. He largely succeeded in this task, even though the dactylic tetrameter is replaced by amphibrachs in four of the eight lines. In line 4, however, the German meter falls apart, probably because Kandinsky wrongly assumed that the word "unsichtbar" (invisible) is accented on the second syllable rather than the first. Remarkably, the same word—"val," "Wall"—appears at the end of the line in both languages, taking advantage of a semantic and sonic coincidence between Russian and German. While the rhymes have disappeared in German, the number of ellipses has significantly increased, conveying to the German text a slowed-down, halting cadence. Claudia Emmert has argued that these ellipses create a semantic indeterminacy, with the word "Schmelzen" (melting) either applying to "Himmel" (sky) or "Steine" (stones), while the latter could also be syntactically connected to the "Wall."[48] The Russian text only allows for one reading (the stones are melting). The second line is also rather confusing in German. Literally it says something like "clumps with mysteries of fulfilling questions." Presumably Kandinsky meant to say "clumps filled with mysterious questions" (which the Russian text would suggest), but was pulled astray by his attempts to preserve the meter. The double exclamation mark at the end of the German version looks like an attempt to introduce an element of "intensity" into the German text by means of punctuation.

While Kandinsky made no effort to retain the rhymes in the translation of this particular hymn, he did so with the remaining lyrics inserted in his stage compositions. They include two poems in the play *Green Sound*, presenting a post-apocalyptic vision of the New Jerusalem and the rhymed monologue of a mysterious blind cripple.[49] Remarkably, in the latter case there are even more rhymes in German than in Russian—in the Russian version, only the even lines rhyme, while the German text consists of fully rhymed couplets.

The fourth, and last, example of a self-translated poem in Kandinsky's stage compositions can be found in the play *Black and White*. I will first cite the Russian original (followed by an English translation) and then the German self-translation (also followed by an English translation):

> Страх в глубине и предчувствий пороги
> Холод в вершинах. Крутые дороги.
> Ветры безумные. Смерти покровы
> Свяжи, разорвавши оковы!
> Оковы разбитые,
> Страны открытые!
> Свяжи, разорвавши оковы!
> Нарушено что — возродится
> И черное тем победится
> Свяжи, разорвавши оковы!

Fear in the depth and the sills of forebodings
Cold in the heights. Steep paths.
Insane winds. The shrouds of death
Tie together, having torn up the fetters!
Shattered fetters,
Discovered countries!
Tie together, having torn up the fetters!
What is destroyed will be reborn
And the black will thereby be vanquished
Tie together, having torn up the fetters!

Angst in der Tiefe, die Freude im Ahnen.
Kalte Berggipfeln und schwindlige Bahnen.
Schwarztote Schleier. Wildrasende Winde.
Weißes Stillschweigen. Zerreiße und binde!
Zerrissene Bänder!
Entdeckte Fernländer!
                    Zerreiße und binde!
Zerriß'nes gebunden
Das Schwarz überwunden!
                    Zerreiße und binde![50]

Anxiety in the depth, the joy in foreboding.
Cold mountain tops and vertiginous tracks.
Black-dead veils. Wild-raging winds.
White silence. Tear up and tie together!
Torn ribbons!
Discovered far-away lands!
                    Tear up and tie together!
The torn [is] tied together
The black [is] overcome!
                    Tear up and tie together!

This hymn expresses some of Kandinsky's central artistic tenets discussed in his treatise *On the Spiritual in Art*, emphasizing the need to choose an arduous upward path towards enlightenment and salvation, and the breaking of the chains of convention to reach a new synthesis. Interestingly, the concept of the "white silence," which will help to overcome the forces of darkness, appears only in the German version of the text. As in the previously quoted example, there are some oddities in German, such as the superfluous ungrammatical "n" in "Berggipfeln," or the neologism "Fernländer," which seems to have been chosen for purely metrical reasons (the correct term in German would be "ferne Länder").[51] However, another neologism in the German text, the adjective "schwarztot" ("blackdead"), is rather compelling precisely because of its strangeness. It has more poetic force than the "shrouds of death" in Russian, and it also emphasizes the dichotomy between black and white, which is worked out more explicitly in the German translation than in the Russian original. We see Kandinsky taking risks here that he eschews in his more conventionally written Russian text. We also find alliterative sound effects that are missing in Russian ("<u>Sch</u>warztote <u>Sch</u>leier. <u>W</u>ildrasende <u>W</u>inde"). The slogan "Zerreiße und binde!" ("Tear up and tie together!") sounds catchier in German than in its somewhat cumbersome Russian wording. Overall, the German translation could be considered an improvement over the Russian original. While the Russian poem looks like the work of a derivative symbolist, the German text, despite its awkwardness—or perhaps *because* of its awkwardness—shows genuine flashes of poetic inspiration.

In sum, we see that Kandinsky, in translating his stage compositions from Russian into German, tried to convey as much of the form as possible of his Russian lyrics, with somewhat mixed success. While the Russian versification is technically competent, writing German verse clearly presented a more arduous challenge. This does not mean that individual passages could not come out successfully, though. Rewriting his poems in German gave Kandinsky the opportunity to revise them and add shades of meaning that were absent in the original draft. In some cases the German version surpasses the Russian original in poetic boldness.

RUSSIAN VERSE TRANSLATIONS OF GERMAN ORIGINALS

Translating the lyric poetry in his stage compositions from Russian into German seems to have emboldened Kandinsky to try his hand at composing original poetry directly in German. By subsequently translating these texts "back" into Russian, he reversed the chronology established in the scenic compositions. The volume *Klänge* contains two poems in metric verse, entitled "Lied" ("Song") and "Hymnus" ("Hymn"). Both are German originals. The Russian version of both poems preserves the meter of the source text (iambic dimeter and trimeter in "Lied," and trochaic tetrameter in "Hymnus").[52] The second poem will be considered in more detail here. Depicting the gradual submersion of a tattered red cloth into blue waves, "Hymnus" is one of the more accomplished of Kandinsky's compositions written in formal German verse:

Hymnus

Innen wiegt die blaue Woge.
Das zerrissne rote Tuch.
Rote Fetzen. Blaue Wellen.
Das verschlossne alte Buch.
Schauen schweigend in die Ferne.
Dunkles Irren in dem Wald.
Tiefer werden blaue Wellen.
Rotes Tuch versinkt nun bald.[53]

Hymn

Inside rocks the blue wave.
The torn red cloth.
Red tatters. Blue waves.
The closed old book.
Gazing silently at the distance.
Dark erring in the wood.
Deeper grow the blue waves.
Red cloth will soon sink below.[54]

The Russian self-translation of the poem is as follows:

Гимн

В глубине вода синеет.
Краснеет в клочьях весь платок.
Красны клочья. Сини волны.
За печатью старый том.
Взгляды молча в дали; в дали.
В темном лесе черный ход.
Все синей, синее волны.
Тонет в клочьях весь платок.[55]

In the depth the water is blue.
Red in tatters is the whole cloth.
Red are the tatters. Blue the waves.
Behind a seal the old volume.
Glances silently into the distance; into the distance.
In the dark wood a black motion.
Ever more blue, more blue the waves.
In tatters will sink the whole cloth.

The "hymnic" nature of the poem becomes manifest in its stately form—trochaic tetrameters featuring alternate feminine and masculine endings, with rhymed even lines, and a musical web of sound repetitions and alliterations. This musicality is to a large extent preserved in the Russian translation, which keeps the trochaic tetrameter except for the iambic line 2. Even though there are no rhymes in Russian, the masculine endings all contain the stressed vowel "o," which creates a sense of sonic uniformity ("plat*o*k"-"t*o*m"-"kh*o*d"-"plat*o*k"). The German poem is characterized by numerous "w"-alliterations (pronounced as "v"), conveying to the text a soothing quality—"wiegt," "Woge," "Wellen," "Wald," "werden," "Wellen." While it is impossible to reproduce this exact effect in Russian, the translation nevertheless features multiple "v" sounds as well ("voda," "ves'," "volny," "volny," "ves'"). In addition, the "k" alliteration in "krasneet v kloch'iakh" and "krasnyi kloch'ia" semantically reinforces the link between the tattered cloth and the color red. The Russian version underlines the incantatory nature of the piece with repetitions ("v dali, v dali," "sinei, sinee") that are absent in the German original. The first two lines of the German poem create a contrast between bright vowels in the first half and dark vowels in the second half of each line.[56] The Russian version features a similarly conspicuous sound effect in the last three lines, with a preponderance of stressed "o" interspersed only intermittently by an occasional "e." The gradual disappearance of all vowels except for "o" at the end illustrates the drowning of the red cloth in the all-encompassing blue wave.

The Russian translation exploits a particular quality of the Russian language which has no equivalent in German (or English), namely the possibility of turning colors into verbs. "Sinet'," derived from "sinii" ([dark] blue), can mean anything from "to be blue," "to turn blue," "to appear blue" to "emitting a notion of blueness." The first two lines of the Russian version feature two such color verbs derived from the colors blue and red. Another particularity of Russian syntax is the absence of the verb "to be" in the present tense. As a result, the Russian translation features more complete sentences than the German original. Line 3, for example, contains two complete statements in Russian. By comparison, the German version appears more fragmentary and impressionistic. Technically, the second line, "Das zerrissne rote Tuch," could designate the direct object of the verb in the first line, "wiegt," but this reading is foreclosed by the period. The grammatical subject of the verb "schauen" in line 3 is equally unclear. Both in the German and Russian versions, every line of the poem ends with a period, contributing to a free-floating, meditative atmosphere that is devoid of a coherent discursive argument.

In terms of content, we can observe an interesting spatial switch in the translation of the first line, which relocates the blue wave from German "interiority" to Russian "depth." Potentially, this change makes the Russian image more metaphysical than psychological. By the same token, the apocalyptic reference to the book "behind a seal" becomes more explicit in the Russian version, while the German version merely mentions a "closed book." In addition, the outdated form "v lese" (as opposed to the modern "v lesu") conveys to the Russian text a more archaic flavor. On the other hand, the German term "dunkles Irren" is more specific than the Russian "chernyi khod." Interestingly, the image of being lost in a dark forest, possibly inspired by the opening of Dante's *Inferno*, already occurred in Kandinsky's 1903 poem to Gabriele Münter, which also featured the rhyme "Wald"-"bald."[57] Comparing the earlier poem with "Hymnus" shows the significant progress Kandinsky had made as a German poet in the intervening years. With its creative association of sounds, colors, and traditional poetic form, "Hymnus"/"Gimn" demonstrates Kandinsky's mastery of German and Russian versification and his abilities as a self-translator.

Overall, though, it seems that Kandinsky became increasingly displeased with his forays into formal poetry. In a letter to Gabriele Münter from October 27, 1910, he distanced himself from the stage compositions he had written the year before. In particular, he had grown disenchanted with the poetic passages. In his words: "For me these things are already quite outdated, *especially many of the poems in them*. I would freshen them up."[58] In Kandinsky's quest for artistic innovation, conventional rhymed and metric verse had become something that he felt he needed to leave behind. This does not mean that Kandinsky abandoned poetry, however. To the contrary: poetic writing became of increased importance to him during the years when his painting evolved from figuration to abstract art.

MOVING TOWARD ABSTRACTION: KANDINSKY'S BILINGUAL PROSE POEMS

The protean genre of the prose poem, shaped by the French poet Charles Baudelaire and introduced to Russian literature by Ivan Turgenev, became Kandinsky's preferred vehicle of poetic expression in the years after 1909.[59] Many of his prose poems are included in the volume *Klänge* (*Sounds*), the only substantial collection of Kandinsky's poetry to appear during his lifetime.[60] Published by Reinhard Piper in Munich in 1912, this luxuriously produced album, with a cover embossed in gold on fuchsia-colored material, combined 38 prose poems with 12 color and 44 black-and-white hand-printed woodcuts in an edition limited to 345 copies. The woodcuts date from 1907 to 1912, while the poems, according to Kandinsky, were written between 1909 and 1911. The relation between the images and the text is quite complex. Clearly, the woodcuts are not simply illustrations of the poems, or the poems an ekphrastic comment on the woodcuts. Rather, both media make an independent, contrapuntal contribution to a new kind of synthetic art, fulfilling an imperative voiced in Kandinsky's treatise *On the Spiritual in Art*, which appeared roughly at the same time as *Klänge*. As he wrote in that book: "And so, finally, one will arrive at a combination of the particular forces belonging to different arts. Out of this combination will arise in time a new art, an art we can foresee even today, a truly *monumental art*."[61]

How exactly the visual and verbal elements are meant to relate to each other in *Klänge* has been interpreted in various ways.[62] For our purposes, the bilingual aspect of Kandinsky's prose poems is of the most interest. Even though Kandinsky published his album in German, we know from his correspondence that his original plan was a Russian-language edition entitled *Zvuki*, which was to be published by Vladimir Izdebskii, a sculptor acquaintance in Odessa. This edition was to contain seventeen prose poems, and it displayed a different layout of texts and woodcuts than the German version. For unknown reasons, the Russian edition never materialized.[63]

Kandinsky's Russian prose poems are not simply the "originals" of the German texts that were later included in *Klänge*. Rather, he seems to have worked on the Russian and the German versions simultaneously in an act of synchronous self-translation. In some instances he first wrote a draft in Russian and then translated it into German, while in other instances he worked in the opposite direction. It is not always easy to determine which version came first. Some of the German manuscripts in the Paris archive are helpfully marked with the Russian word "perevod" (translation), indicating the primacy of the Russian text. The manuscripts themselves can also provide clues. If the German text contains additions and deletions while the Russian is a clean copy reflecting the corrected German version, this obviously suggests that the poem was first drafted in German.[64] Some of the prose poems exist only in one language and were never translated. More often than not, however, assigning the primacy to one language or the other remains a matter of conjecture. Boris Sokolov has tried to find a method for resolving this issue with a set of criteria that allegedly characterize the original version. They include "adequate" language use (as opposed to foreign calques), compactness (based on the assumption that a translation tends to expand rather than to shorten the original text), the use of euphonic effects, and neologisms.[65] Needless to say, this is far from a foolproof method, especially in view of the latitude afforded to a self-translator.[66] In any event, the fact that the first version could be either in Russian or German indicates that Kandinsky had become equally comfortable with the two languages in a sort of balanced bilingualism.

Since the form of the prose poem necessitates no attention to meter and rhyme, Kandinsky's self-translations of these texts are generally more literal than those of his formal poetry. Nevertheless, one can find subtle differences between the German and Russian versions. For example, in the poem "Hills" ("Kholmy"/"Hügel") the German color adjectives "bluish" and "yellowish" are replaced by "cold" and "warm" in Russian (in *On the Spiritual in Art*, Kandinsky describes blue as the quintessential "cold" and yellow as the quintessential "warm" color).[67] In "Bassoon" ("Fagot"/"Fagott") the "deep" sound of the instrument becomes "dark" in Russian. In addition, the branches of a tree are compared to an "etching" in Russian, but not in German. In some instances, Kandinsky added entire sentences in translation. Thus, the Russian version of the poem "Bell" ("Kolokol"/"Glocke"), after a statement pointing to the necessity of ink for writing, adds the comment "so is *today* my soul in an unbreakable fusion with ink" (Kandinsky's emphasis). Even though Kandinsky transfers the action from the German villages of Weisskirchen and Mühlhausen to the Russian Pokrovskoe and Vasil'evskoe, the bell continues to ring "in German" ("deng, deng, deng, deng, deng").[68] An interesting case of implied bilingualism can be found in the title of the prose poem "Hoboe" ("Oboe"). The text exists only in German, but the archaic term "Hoboe" (as opposed to the modern German "Oboe"), which is written in capital letters ("HOBOE"), can also be read as the Russian word "novoe" ("something new"). The title thus presents an example of Latin-Cyrillic and German-Russian double coding.

Stylistically, the prose poems collected in *Zvuki/Klänge* are quite heterogeneous. Even though Kandinsky did not date them, a chronologically early or late provenance is readily apparent from the manner in which they are written. The prose poems evolved from a fin-de-siècle symbolist style toward a radical modernism that seems to anticipate concrete poetry as well as the iconoclasm of the futurists and Dadaists.[69] Conventional narrative prose written in coherent syntax gives way to an alogical, disruptive discourse that highlights sound over semantics. In that sense, Kandinsky's literary evolution parallels the development of his visual style reflected in the woodcuts in *Klänge*, which vary between figurative ornamental Jugendstil and almost complete abstraction. The prose poems that Kandinsky continued to write both in German and Russian after the appearance of *Klänge* further developed this trajectory. As Boris Sokolov has shown, Kandinsky planned another volume of texts and woodcuts in 1914 under the title *Tsvety bez zapakha* (*Flowers without Fragrance*), but he had to abandon his plans because of the outbreak of the war. Some of these texts exist only in Russian, some only in German, and some in both languages. Overall the tone has become more pessimistic, as the messianic hope expressed in *Klänge* has given way to nightmarish and threatening forebodings.[70]

A crucial question is how the bilingual nature of Kandinsky's prose poems affected their transition toward radical modernism. It would be misguided to claim that Kandinsky was more "modern" in one language than the other. The trend towards verbal abstraction happened in both languages simultaneously. However, the authorial revision inherent in the process of self-translation allowed Kandinsky to "tune up" and sharpen his texts in accordance with the trajectory of his creative evolution. Comparing the Russian and German versions can therefore give us clues about the general development of Kandinsky's artistic technique.

An early example of how Kandinsky revised his prose poems while translating them can be found in "The Return" ("Vozvrashchenie"/"Rückkehr"). This text exists both in a Russian and German version, but it ended up neither in the planned *Zvuki* nor the published *Klänge* collection.[71] The prose poem tells the melancholy story of a young man returning to his homeland, which he finds changed into a lifeless geometrized cityscape of transparent cubic glass buildings under a black sky. In rewriting the poem in German, Kandinsky tried to tone down its decadent fin-de-siècle character. Thus, he replaced the "purple-red flowers, similar to roses" looming in the sky with "purple-red stains," and the black panthers with shining narrow green eyes who are lying in wait at each building become in German simple black stones. However, it seems that the reworked German version still did not meet with Kandinsky's approval, and he excluded this text from the published version of *Klänge*.

The prose poem "Spring" ("Vesna"/"Frühling"), included both in the *Zvuki* and *Klänge* collection, presents an example of Kandinsky's more mature style. Here is Kenneth Lindsay and Peter Vergo's English translation of the German text with a few inserted clarifications and corrections:

Be quiet, you garish fellow [literally: motley man (*bunter Mensch*)]!

Slowly, the old house slides down the hill. The old blue sky sticks hopelessly amidst branches and leaves.

Stop calling me! ["Ruf mich nicht hin" implies "Don't call me to come here"]

Hopelessly, the ringing hangs in the air, like a spoon in thick gruel.

One's feet stick in the grass. And the grass wants to prick through the invisible with its points.

Lift your axe over your head and chop! Chop!

Your words can't reach me. They're hanging on the bushes like wet tatters.

Why doesn't anything grow, only this rotting wooden cross at the fork in the road? And its arms have penetrated the air to right and to left. And its head has pierced a hole in the sky. And from its edges creep stifling [literally: strangling] red-blue clouds. And thunderbolts ["Blitze" means "lightnings"] tear and cut them in places you least expect, and their cuts and tears mend invisibly. And somebody falls like a soft eiderdown. And someone speaks, speaks—speaks—

Is it you again, you garish fellow? You again?[72]

This text, like many others in *Klänge*, expresses a necessity to become "unstuck" from an ossified material world in order to break through to a new spiritual realm, a process that may be painful and violent and entail "chopping away" at one's stultifying old habits and surroundings. The speaker seems reluctant to heed the voice calling him to engage in this transition. The religious dimension of the process is hinted at by the figure of the cross. Although seemingly in a state of decomposition, the cross will be able to pierce through the stifling confinement in which the speaker finds himself trapped. The coming apocalyptic storm, evoked in a sequence of "biblical" sentences beginning with the word "and," will be a destructive event, yet will ultimately lead to healing.[73]

Boris Sokolov lists "Spring" among the texts whose original language cannot be determined, since the Russian and German variants do not deviate from each other significantly. Nevertheless, there are some interesting differences between the two versions. The Russian text lacks the word "hopeless" ("hoffnungslos"), which appears twice in German. Did Kandinsky add or suppress this word in translation? A clue can perhaps be found in the "strangling redblue clouds" ("erwürgende rotblaue Wolken"). The corresponding Russian passage has "dushnye sizye tuchi" ("stifling blue-grey clouds"). "Erwürgend" is a rather strange German translation for the Russian adjective "dushnyi" (stifling). A more normal German equivalent would have been "stickig." "Erwürgend," the present participle of the verb "erwürgen" (to strangle), literally turns the clouds into active agents engaging in the activity of strangling. Perhaps the image was suggested to Kandinsky by the Russian verb "dushit'," which is etymologically connected to "dushnyi," but only as a faded metaphor. The actual strangulation occurs in German. By the same token, the color of the clouds changes from "sizyi," denoting a blue-grey or dove-colored hue, to a more aggressive and threatening "rotblau" (redblue). It seems reasonable to speculate that Kandinsky wrote the text first in Russian and then radicalized it when he transposed it into German, which would explain the addition of the word "hopeless."

Another interesting difference concerns the "cuts" and "gashes." The German words "Stiche" and "Schnitte" are semantically overdetermined, since they also refer to genres of visual art: "Stich" can mean "etching," while "Schnitt" is a component of the word "Holzschnitt" (woodcut), that is, the kind of picture which makes up the visual component of the album *Klänge*. Kandinsky seems to point to the role of his own art in the metaphysical "healing" process. The Russian words "prokoly" and "prorezy" do not have this double meaning, but the prefix "pro-" indicates a process of "breaking through" towards a different, more profound reality.

Kandinsky's path toward abstraction was driven by the same impetus toward a spiritual breakthrough. This impetus can be observed both in his pictorial work and in his prose poems. In his more radical texts, Kandinsky dispenses entirely with conventional syntax and semantics. Rather than narrating or describing a transition toward a new spiritual state, as happened in "Spring," the language itself reflects and embodies this transformed quality. The whimsical poem "Sonet"/"Sonett" held in Kandinsky's Paris archive presents an example of his more radical style. Both the Russian and German manuscripts are dated May 10, 1914.[74] Here is my translation of the German text:

A Sonnet

Laurentius, did you hear me?
The green circle burst. The yellow cat kept licking its tail.
Laurentius, night has not irrupted!
Cucumismatic spiral sprung up sincerely in the right direction.
The purple elephant did not stop sprinkling himself with his trunk.
Laurentius, this is not right.—Is it not right?
Labusalututic parabola did not find its head nor its tail. The red horse
    kicked, and kicked, and kicked, and kept kicking.
Laurentius, nandamdra, lumusukha, dirikeka! Diri-keka! Di-ri-ke-ka!

The nonsensical title "A Sonnet," appended to a text that is clearly not a sonnet, anticipates the absurdist writings of Daniil Kharms.[75] Like "Spring," the text is structured as a one-sided dialogue with a non-responding mysterious stranger. We also find incantatory repetitions of words and sounds, which is a frequent device in Kandinsky's prose poems. At the same time, rather than presenting a coherent discourse, the poem looks like a verbal rendition of a semi-abstract painting. The only remaining vestige of representation is provided by the animals, which are cast in expressionist colors reminiscent of the paintings of Kandinsky's friend Franz Marc.[76] They mingle with abstract geometric figures, the circle, the spiral, and the parabola. While the circle is still given a concrete color (green), the spiral and parabola are qualified with unintelligible adjectives that sound a like a parody of scientific discourse. At the end, the text turns into a sequence of neologisms that gradually disintegrate into individual syllables. Language has ceased to function in any kind of referential manner. Kandinsky's word creation parallels the verbal experiments of the Russian futurists, who tried to reach a deeper level of meaning through "transmental" (*zaumnyi*) language. It also anticipates the sound poetry of the Dadaists. The final line, which seems to evoke associations with the phonetics of an imaginary African language, resembles Hugo Ball's famous poem "Karawane" written in 1917.[77]

Kandinsky wrote the German and Russian versions of the poem on the same day. There are no major differences between the two variants, except that the Russian text is written in the present and the German in the past tense. The third line also looks different in Russian: "Lavrentii, do net eshche daleko!" ("Laurentius, it is still far to the 'no'!"). Both variants, however, can be reduced to a similar statement, the assertion that positive being, at least for now, still prevails over nothingness. The fourth line is generated in both languages by etymological play with the root denoting "right"—"*pravil'no* v *pravil'*nom na*pravl*enii" corresponds to "auf*richt*ig in der *richt*igen *Richt*ung." In the Russian version all the terms related to animals—"kot," "khvost," "slon," "khobot," "loshad'" (cat, tail, elephant, trunk, horse)— contain a stressed "o." Perhaps this sonic uniformity indicates that the poem was first conceived in Russian. In any event, the opposition between the two languages becomes neutralized in the last line, which is written in neither Russian nor German. The linguistic differences fade away as the two versions of the text converge in a sequence of more or less identical sounds.[78]

What prompted Kandinsky to write his poem simultaneously in two languages? Most likely, he was driven by the same impulse that made him create parallel and mutually interdependent sequences of texts and images. As Christopher Short has observed: "In *Sounds*, words in the poems function conventionally and, simultaneously, move toward free graphic form, becoming abstract. At the same time, the images in the album are representational and, simultaneously, move toward free graphic form, becoming abstract."[79] To name a specific example, the point and the line can function both as punctuation marks in the linear sequence of the text and as visual images in the space of the white page, where the verbal and visual texts enter into communication and competition with each other. In his theoretical writings, Kandinsky used the word "Zweiklang" (two-sound) to describe the flickering effect created by elements that allow for two conflicting readings simultaneously. His 1926 treatise *Punkt und Linie zur Fläche* (*Point and Line to Plane*) describes "Zweiklang" as "the balancing of two worlds that can never attain equilibrium."[80]

One could argue that the double incarnation of Kandinsky's prose poems in Russian and German creates an effect akin to a "Zweiklang." The two versions map on to each other while retaining their distinct characteristics. The oscillating tension between two sign systems becomes visible in instances where two contradictory readings of a graphic shape are offered simultaneously, as in the double-coded "HOBOE." The final, utopian reconciliation of the two languages can only happen when they abandon their referential function altogether, as happens at the end of "Sonett." In the final vanishing point of Kandinsky's artistic path, there is no more difference between Russian and German, as the individual idioms merge in the universal language of abstraction.

KANDINSKY'S LATE POETRY

Kandinsky continued to write occasional poetry for the rest of his life. However, compared to the burst of activity in the years before World War I, his later poetic output was much more sparse. The corpus of his published postwar oeuvre includes a total of eleven poems written in German and five written in French. During his years at the Bauhaus, Kandinsky published only one poem, "Zwielicht" ("Twilight"), which came out in 1925 in the anthology *Europa-Almanach*.[81] This "synthetic" volume contained reproductions of the works of important avant-garde artists (including Kandinsky) alongside poems by Blaise Cendrars, Else Laske-Schüler, and Vladimir Mayakovsky, among others. Most of Kandinsky's late poetry was composed after his forced departure from Germany and emigration to France in 1933. Four German poems written in 1937 appeared in the New York quarterly *Transition*, edited by Eugène Jolas, in 1938.[82] Three German poems from 1937 were published in 1939 in the fourth number of *Plastique*, a journal founded and edited by the artist Sophie Taeuber-Arp.[83] Seven additional poems in German and French appeared posthumously in the album *11 Tableaux et 7 poèmes*, which came out in 1945, and in Max Bill's book *Kandinsky* from 1951.[84] One more French poem kept in Kandinsky's Paris archive was published in 1992.[85]

Overall, Kandinsky did not radically change his poetic style in his later writings. There are fewer prose poems and more lineated "traditional" poetic texts, but without any recourse to regular meter and rhyme. The most obvious difference, compared with Kandinsky's previous poetry, is the change in languages. After his departure from the Soviet Union in 1921, Kandinsky stopped writing poetry in Russian altogether. He continued to write in German not only during his years at the Bauhaus, but also after his relocation to France in 1933. In addition, he also began writing poems in French during the final years of his life. This development obviously presents a challenge to those who posit an essential link between poetic creativity and the emotional connection offered by the mother tongue. One could speculate, perhaps, that Kandinsky felt an emotional need to cross Russian out of his psyche and distance himself from that language after his forced departure from his native land. It is not that Kandinsky completely abandoned the Russian language, however. His third wife, Nina, whom he married in 1917, was Russian, which means that his language of domestic communication remained Russian even after his final departure from Russia. Or rather, it *reverted* to Russian after the intermezzo with Gabriele Münter, when German had been for a while Kandinsky's "wife tongue." In spite of the change in domestic circumstances, however, German, rather than his native Russian, remained the primary language of Kandinsky's poetic writings for the rest of his life.

One can find pragmatic explanations for why Kandinsky ceased to write in his native language after 1921. Since he had been stripped of his Soviet citizenship and was completely cut off from the public in his country of birth, writing in Russian would have limited Kandinsky's readership to the relatively small audience of Russian émigré circles in the West. On the other hand, German was not only the language he used professionally up to 1933 in his position as a professor at the Bauhaus, it was also an idiom that he had perfected over the years as a medium of artistic expression. This may explain why he held on to it even after his forced departure from Germany. The switch to French in the late 1930s is more surprising. Of course, as an educated member of the prerevolutionary Russian intelligentsia, Kandinsky had a solid command of the French language. His interest in French literature and culture had been long-standing. Furthermore, he now lived in a French-speaking environment and was personally acquainted with some leading French poets, including André Breton.[86] Nevertheless, beginning to write poetry in a new language seems a remarkable decision, especially when we consider Kandinsky's advanced age—he was already past seventy at that time. We can surmise that it was Kandinsky's previous experience as a bilingual poet that gave him the necessary flexibility to branch out into a third language at this late stage in his life.

The two languages in which Kandinsky wrote poetry during the final decade of his life were not exactly equivalent, however. When comparing the German and French texts written in the 1930s, we notice an interesting difference. The German poems continue the linguistic experimentation of the prewar years. Many of them are written in a radical avant-garde style reminiscent of Dadaism. At the same time, Kandinsky manages to make creative use of the specific resources offered by the German language. In the poem "S," written in May 1937, he experiments with the way German builds polysyllabic words out of separate particles with their own independent meaning. The poem begins with the untranslatable lines:

Un—regel—mässig
Regel—mässig
Mässig[87]

"Irregular / Regular / Moderate," the English rendition given in the Lindsay/ Vergo edition of Kandinsky's writings, misses out on the word-building game as well as the "s"-alliteration alluded to in the title of the poem, while a literal translation of the individual components would result in the nonsensical "Un—rule—moderate / Rule—moderate / Moderate."

Some of the German poems depart even more radically from standard vocabulary. Shot through with neologisms and ungrammaticalities, they create a sort of free-floating content, as in the first stanza of "Von-Zu" ("From-To"), written on August 2, 1936:

> Kurben spritzen entblösste Striche
> Unscheinbare wollen jagen umsonst
> Au! er dreht sich tobend in Zausmal
> Unten—oben—allerseits Nichts
> Nichts.[88]

> Kurbs are splashing denuded lines
> Unprepossessing ones want to hunt in vain [or: for free]
> Ouch! he is rotating ragingly in Tusslement
> Below—above—on all sides Nothing
> Nothing

The word "Kurben," possibly a mutation of "Kurven" (curves) or "Kurbeln" (handles, cranks),[89] combines geometric shape with mechanic action, while the even more unfathomable "Zausmal" seems to contain the lexical root of the verb "zerzausen" (to ruffle up), perhaps combined with the second syllable of "Denkmal" (monument). Lacking any kind of concrete representational content, the stanza evokes a mood of frantic agitation in empty space, creating a verbal analogy to Kandinsky's paintings of the same period. The free combination of existing lexemes with neologisms resembles the juxtaposition of vaguely representational "biomorphic" shapes with abstract geometric forms in Kandinsky's late painting style of the 1930s and 1940s. The oil painting *Dominant Curve*, for example, which dates from the same year as "Von-Zu," combines overlapping monochrome circular shapes with something resembling a pink embryo and an assemblage of floating forms that look like marine microorganisms. It also features the outline of a staircase that can be read in spatially contradictory ways, offering an analogy to Kandinsky's use of polysemy in his German experimental poetry.[90]

Kandinsky's French poems are written in a quite different manner. They contain no neologisms, puns, or ungrammaticalities. Rather than experimenting with linguistic means, they follow conventional French usage and syntax, sometimes adopting a colloquial tone. Their prevalent focus is on scenes of daily life, such as a little brown chicken ruffled up by the wind in a vacant lot for sale ("Midi"), or a "nonou" (nanny) taking a stroll with a baby who, in a slight touch of surrealism, crosses paths with a large white horse moving from left to right while the nanny is moving from right to left ("Les Promenades").[91] In the poem "Le Fond," a piece of string with knots leads to a mock-philosophical debate about numerical sequences. In painterly terms, the imagery of Kandinsky's French poems rather evokes his pre-abstract period than his style of the 1930s, as can be seen in the following example, dating from March 1939:

Lyrique

C'est de la cheminée rouge
Que sort la fumée blanche.

C'est sur l'assiette jaune
Qu'est posé un concombre vert.

C'est sur la bicyclette noire
Qu'est assis un homme violet.

La route monte.
La bicyclette monte.
L'homme monte à son tour.
La fumée monte.
Elle aussi.

Le concombre ne bouge pas.
Une sinistre tranquillité. [92]

Lyric

From the red chimney
Emerges the white smoke.

On the yellow plate
Lies a green cucumber.

On the black bicycle
Sits the purple man.

The road rises.
The bicycle rises.
The man rises too.
The smoke rises.
As well.

The cucumber does not move.

A sinister calm.

Presenting a sort of cross between landscape painting and still life, the poem contains an assemblage of concrete objects that are all shown in their "natural" colors. The only exception is the purple man, who looks like a figure out of Kandinsky's earlier color dramas. Even though there is an element of movement indicated by the rising smoke and the bicycle, the overall impression is static rather than dynamic. The general upward movement is resisted by the cucumber, a symbol of material lifelessness and stasis. One wonders whether this cucumber is not conceptually borrowed and "translated" from Russian, as it were. Salted cucumbers are a typical part of humorous discourse in Russian, evoking "zakuski" and alcoholic banter.[93] There may be an element of self-deprecating sexual humor as well: if we read the cucumber as a phallic symbol, its failure to "rise" would explain the gloomy note on which the poem ends.

Kandinsky's visual art of the 1930s contains nothing resembling the content of "Lyrique." However, the poem's somewhat enigmatic title is a self-citation referring to a much earlier work, the painting *Lyrisches*. Created in 1911, this iconic image displays a jockey on a galloping horse rendered in a semi-abstract style. As a leitmotif, the horse and rider came to symbolize Kandinsky's spiritual strivings and his overcoming of figurative representation. A full-page color woodcut of *Lyrisches* was included in the *Klänge* album.[94] Is the French poem a deflating self-parody of the earlier image? The horseman has metamorphosed into a bicycle rider, the dynamism of 1911 has given way to a static mood, and the bold leap into abstraction has become a semi-comical return to representation tinged with Russian alcoholic humor. The passage from *Lyrisches* to "Lyrique" may convey Kandinsky's disillusionment with the messianic hopes expressed in the *Klänge* woodcut. By the time he wrote the poem, the anticipated dawn of a new spiritual age had been crushed by totalitarian dictatorships both in his country of birth and his adopted German homeland. Perhaps Kandinsky wrote the poem in French because he needed a new language to "defamiliarize" the image. His use of colors is also of interest. In the woodcut, the "heavenly" color blue indicates the rider's spiritual destination. But in the poem, blue has disappeared altogether. Instead, we have the green cucumber. Kandinsky's characterization of the color green in *On the Spiritual in Art* sounds almost like a comment on the cucumber in "Lyrique":

Passivity is the most characteristic quality of absolute green, a quality tainted by a suggestion of obese self-satisfaction. Thus, pure green is to the realm of color what the so-called bourgeoisie is to human society: it is an immobile, complacent element, limited in every respect. This green is like a fat, extremely healthy cow, lying motionless, fit only for chewing the cud, regarding the world with stupid, lackluster eyes.[95]

The poem "Le Sourd qui entend" ("The Deaf Who Hears"), written in the same month as "Lyrique," summarizes the poetics of simplicity that Kandinsky embraced in his French poetry, but it also functions as a more wide-ranging statement about his artistic credo:

Le Sourd qui entend

Comment dois-je raconter cette histoire?
Elle est très simple. C'est pourquoi qu'elle est compliquée.
La simplicité—voilà la difficulté.
Les choses les plus simples sont toujours les plus compliquées.
Et inversement.
Si je vous dit : au bord d'une grande route se trouve une petite pierre.
Que pensez-vous : est-ce simple ou compliqué ?
Et que pensez-vous, qu'est-ce qui augmente la simplicité ou la
    complication
Si je vous dit : une petite pierre se trouve au bord d'une grande route ?
J'ai mon opinion à moi.
Le plus simple et le plus compliqué serait de dire :
ROUTE-PIERRE (et après quelques secondes) GRANDE-PETITE.
C'est de l'impressionnisme spirituel.
Répétez encore une fois (une fois suffit)
ROUTE-PIERRE (sept secondes) GRANDE-PETITE.
La simplicité embrasse la complication.
Et inversement.
Il faudrait seulement avoir de l'oreille.
Arrêtez-vous un instant sur la grande route et regardez la petite pierre.
Regardez avec l'oreille.
Le sourd le comprend mieux encore.[96]

The Deaf Who Hears

How shall I tell this story?
It is very simple. That's why it is complicated.
The simplicity—here is the difficulty.
The simplest things are always the most complicated.
And vice versa.
If I tell you: on the side of a big road there is a small stone.
What do you think: is it simple or complicated?
And what do you think, what increases the simplicity or complication
If I tell you: a small stone is on the side of a big road?
I have my own opinion.
The simplest and most complicated would be to say:

Chapter Two

ROAD-STONE (and after a few seconds) BIG-SMALL.
This is spiritual impressionism.
Repeat one more time (once is enough)
ROAD-STONE (seven seconds) BIG-SMALL.
Simplicity embraces complication.
And vice versa.
One only would need to have an ear for it.
Stop for a moment on the big road and look at the small stone.
Look with your ear.
The deaf understands it even better.

In its combination of writing, hearing, and vision, the poem summarizes Kandinsky's program of an all-embracing synthetic and synesthetic art. Similarly to many of the texts in *Klänge*, Kandinsky directly tells the reader what to do by supplying a concrete scenario of "actions," including even a pause of prescribed length. In this sense, the poem functions as a combination of meta-discourses, including comments on the writer's own narrative technique ("How shall I tell this story"), experiments in verbal permutation and condensation reminiscent of Chinese ideograms, and a sort of theatrical script. The statement about simplicity and complexity echoes a thought that Kandinsky had expressed more than a quarter-century earlier in a letter to Gabriele Münter: "Yes, I think that ultimately and finally everything is *one*. It is a double simultaneous movement: 1. from the complex to the simple 2. vice versa. This is why subconsciously I always sought to unite these two streams in my pictures."[97]

The dialectic movement between simplicity and complexity—or between unity and difference, if we want to use the concept expressed in the letter to Münter—also provides a clue to Kandinsky's multilingual practice. The different linguistic incarnations of his parallel poems are *one* in that they express the same semantic or "spiritual" content, yet they differ in terms of their individual encoding, forming a kind of unresolvable "Zweiklang." By offering multiple wordings of the same underlying "fact," "Le Sourd qui entend" demonstrates how self-translation becomes a form of rewriting in a continuous quest for cognition and illumination.

SELF-TRANSLATION AND INTERSEMIOTIC TRANSPOSITION

In spite of his extensive practice of self-translation and his penchant for theorizing, Kandinsky never reflected explicitly on his method of translation.

However, his theoretical writings on art can provide insights into his attitude toward language as well. On a fundamental level, poetry had the same spiritual mission for Kandinsky as the visual arts, music, or any other form of artistic creation: its task was to harmonize the soul with the world. The different arts become homologous for Kandinsky and thereby translatable into each other, as suggested by the metaphorical "translation" of visual art into music that we find in the treatise *On the Spiritual in Art*, where Kandinsky writes: "Color is the keyboard. The eye is the hammer. The soul is the piano, with its many strings. The artist is the hand that purposefully sets the soul vibrating by means of this or that key."[98] Kandinsky's notion of "changing instruments," aside from denoting the switching of media or languages, can also serve more concretely as a metaphor for (self-)translation. In spite of the different sounds produced by different instruments, Kandinsky implies that the underlying spiritual message remains the same. Just as a musical piece is enriched by being played with a variety of instruments, a poetic text gains in depth by being incarnated in more than one language.

Even though Kandinsky stopped writing poetry in his native Russian after his final departure from Russia, by adding French to his poetic repertoire late in life he demonstrated to what extent bilingualism had become a crucial feature of his artistic self-definition. In writing poetry in other languages, Kandinsky did not mean to abandon his Russian roots, of course. His aspiration was to become not a German or French poet, but rather a universal artist who transcends boundaries between languages as well as artistic genres and media. This ecumenical attitude resembles Marina Tsvetaeva's embrace of a poetic universalism beyond national categorization, as we will see in the following chapter. Kandinsky's cosmopolitanism meant that he turned away from the linkage between native language and national poetry posited by German romantic philosophy. His multilingual practice rather resembles the medieval and early modern period, when poets frequently and routinely switched between different idioms. As Leonard Forster pointed out: "Language is of course the medium in which all poets work, but this was true in a different sense for poets before Romanticism, for medieval, renaissance or baroque poets, than it has been since. Just as the artist need not always paint in oils, but also in water-colour, or may draw in pencil or charcoal or silverpoint, or may have recourse to woodcut or etching, so the poet may use more than one language."[99] Similarly, as Forster has also noted, switching languages became a more common practice again in twentieth-century avant-garde and conceptualist poetry, where language is treated as simply a kind of raw material.

Kandinsky used a musical rather than a painterly metaphor to characterize his artistic border-crossing: he talked about "changing instruments." This is not surprising inasmuch as music, the abstract form of artistic expression par excellence, furnished a key conceptual framework for Kandinsky's aesthetic theories. It is not by accident that he gave his album of woodcuts and prose poems the title *Sounds*. Many of his paintings bear generic titles like "Composition," "Improvisation," or "Impression." His quest for a new synthetic art involved an attempt to appropriate the semiotic system of music in his painterly practice. Kandinsky's theoretical writings brim with references to music, where, as we have seen, colors and shapes become the equivalent of musical sounds and keys.

The Russian scholar Vladimir Feshchenko has argued that Kandinsky's interest in (self-)translation was ultimately intersemiotic rather than interlingual. In this view, the different linguistic versions of Kandinsky's poems become mere variants of a more fundamental "translation from the language of painterly perception into verbal language."[100] It is certainly true that there is an analogy between the border-crossing involved in the transition from visual to verbal expression and the act of interlingual translation. Nevertheless, one can find only a few examples of direct "translations" between specific paintings and texts in Kandinsky's oeuvre. At best, we could point to the early "White Cloud" poem and its transposition into a gouache, or the deflating parody of the painting *Lyrisches* in the poem "Lyrique." In *Klänge* there is no direct, straightforward correspondence between individual prose poems and woodcuts. The sequence of images and texts relate to each other as do the individual voices in a polyphonic composition. Rather than fulfilling an auxiliary function subordinate to the message conveyed by the visual artworks, Kandinsky's poetic texts make their own, independent contribution to his project of a synthetic "monumental" art. It is impossible to say what is primary or more important in *Klänge*, the visual or the verbal layer. Likewise, in Kandinsky's synchronous creation of parallel pairs of bilingual texts, the traditional hierarchical relation between original and translation gives way to a complementary "Zweiklang" in which both incarnations of the poem enjoy equal importance within their respective linguistic orbits.

Kandinsky's syncretic use of different media does not mean that he believed in a complete fusion of their expressive means. As he put it in *On the Spiritual in Art*: "One often hears the opinion that the possibility of substituting one art for another . . . would refute the necessity of differentiating between the arts. This, however, is not the case. As has been said, the exact repetition of the same sound by different arts is not possible."[101] The same could be said, of course, about the parallel linguistic versions of a self-translated text. While seemingly saying "the same thing," the two variants nevertheless differ completely in their outlook and expressive means. Kandinsky made it clear that his ultimate intention was to reinforce his spiritual message by conveying it in more than one medium. In his words: "Repetition, the piling-up of the same sounds, enriches the spiritual atmosphere necessary to the maturing of one's emotions (even of the finest substance), just as the richer air of the greenhouse is a necessary condition for the ripening of various fruits."[102] Translation, needless to say, is another form of *repetition*, which explains the prominent role that self-translations came to assume in Kandinsky's writings.

Kandinsky's versatility in multiple media does not mean, of course, that writing poetry had the same importance for him as creating works of visual art. There is a reason why he is more famous as a painter than as a poet. Kandinsky's metaphor of "changing instruments," if we want to take it literally, raises the underlying issue of professionalism. A gifted amateur who knows how to play more than one instrument (such as Kandinsky himself, who played the cello and the piano) is probably more inclined to change instruments than a professional musician who has spent his entire life honing and perfecting his mastery of one instrument. A celebrated cello soloist is unlikely to do double duty as a piano virtuoso, even though he might on occasion enjoy playing the piano recreationally. In this sense, one could argue that Kandinsky's poetic multilingualism was facilitated by his primary occupation as a professional artist. Since he was ultimately not as invested in poetry as he was in painting, it became easier for him to switch languages, given that he did not depend as much on a particular idiom to express his artistic design. But what about professional poets? Can they "change instruments" as easily? We will take up this question in the chapters that follow.

Marina Tsvetaeva's Self-Translation into French

MARINA IVANOVNA TSVETAEVA (1892–1941), one of the greatest of Russia's modern poets, was also the most productive Russian poetic self-translator of the twentieth century. The Russian-to-French translation of her fairy-tale poem *Mólodets* (usually referred to in English as *The Swain*), with its length of 2,146 verse lines, far surpasses the dimensions of Vladimir Nabokov's or Joseph Brodsky's later self-translated poetry.[1] Aside from the sheer volume of her translated verses, Tsvetaeva deserves attention for the boldness of her approach to writing in a non-native idiom. As Efim Etkind put it in his introduction to the French edition of *Mólodets*, "never before, in any European literature, had a poet dared to take such liberties with a foreign language."[2] In a talk at the 1992 Tsvetaeva colloquium in Paris, Etkind went even further, calling Tsvetaeva "a unique case in the history of world literature." As he explained, "it would be difficult to find another poet who wrote with so much brilliance and energy in a language other than her own, while at the same time continuing to write in her own language."[3]

Aside from the self-translation of *Mólodets*, Tsvetaeva also wrote several French prose narratives in the 1930s; she experimented with writing poetry directly in French; and, in the final years and months of her life, she translated multiple poems by Alexander Pushkin and Mikhail Lermontov from Russian into French verse. Most of Tsevateva's French writings remained unpublished during her lifetime and have only come to light relatively recently. Despite the enthusiasm expressed by Etkind and other scholars, Tsvetaeva did not succeed in publishing her French poetry, and to this day she has failed to gain recognition as a French-language poet. Unlike Nabokov and Brodsky, who have earned a distinct, if controversial, reputation within the ranks of Anglophone poetry, Tsvetaeva is perceived as a monolingual Russian poet (even though, as we will see, she herself rejected this label). For reasons that remain to be explored, her French oeuvre has been largely ignored. The fact that she ended up returning to the Soviet Union from her western European exile reinforced the narrative of a potentially cosmopolitan writer who, in spite of a trilingual upbringing and many years of residence abroad,

76

nevertheless opted to remain within the fold of Russian culture. In reality, as the example of *Mólodets* shows, Tsvetaeva was more than willing to cross the boundaries of her native language when the opportunity presented itself.

FROM *MÓLODETS* TO *LE GARS*

Tsvetaeva's status as a bilingual poet is intimately linked to the fairy-tale poem *Mólodets*. Written in 1922 and published in 1924 in Prague, it is one of several long narrative poems that Tsvetaeva based on folkloric sources. The plot derives from "Upyr'" ("The Vampire"), one of the more gruesome stories in Aleksandr Afanasiev's classic nineteenth-century collection of Russian fairy tales. Tsvetaeva's poem preserves the basic outline of its source, but it significantly expands it and gives it a radical new meaning. The heroine, a village girl named Marusia, falls in love with a handsome stranger who turns out to be a vampire. She fails to denounce him, which leads to the deaths of several family members and finally her own demise when the vampire kills her in a graphic consummation scene. Marusia is buried on a crossroad, where she becomes incarnated in a red flower. In the second half of the story, a nobleman discovers the flower and takes it to his castle. The flower metamorphoses into a beautiful woman, and the nobleman ends up marrying her. They live together for five years and have a son. One day, after the nobleman's guests at a dinner party upbraid him for having an unbaptized spouse, he forces her to go to church with him, where the vampire confronts her again. In Afanasiev's tale, the vampire kills the husband and son, but Marusia, on the advice of her grandmother, manages to destroy her tormentor by sprinkling him with holy water. She is able to resurrect her spouse and child, and they live happily ever after. Tsvetaeva's version ends very differently: when the vampire calls out to Marusia at the church service, she abandons her husband and child to reunite with him and fly off "into the blue fire."

Tsvetaeva's poem follows the plot of the fairy tale relatively closely (except for the ending), but it becomes clear that she subjects it to a fundamental reinterpretation. Her version is not the tale of an innocent victim who eventually manages to vanquish her persecutor, but a story of fatal, passionate love and all-consuming obsession. As Tsvetaeva later explained in her 1926 essay "Poet o kritike" ("A Poet on Criticism"): "Marusia loved the vampire. This is why she would not name him and kept losing, one after another, her mother, her brother, her life. Passion and crime, passion and sacrifice. Such was my task when I started working on 'Mólodets.'"[4] In more recent years, the romance between a female teenager and a vampire has become popularized in Stephenie Meyer's *Twilight* novels and their blockbuster film adaptation. But while in the *Twilight* story the relationship is facilitated by the male hero's "vegetarianism," Tsvetaeva's vampire behaves as ruthlessly and bloodthirstily as one would expect of such a creature. The scene in which he deflowers and kills Marusia combines aggressive sexuality with ritual murder. Perversely, one gains the impression that the female heroine is attracted to the vampire not *in spite of*, but rather *because* of his ferocious, bloodthirsty nature, which stands in stark contrast to the "bourgeois" conventionality of her upbringing and later married life.

The extremism of Tsvetaeva's plot is matched by what Michael Makin has called the poem's "textual violence."[5] The language of *Mólodets* is as provocative as its content. In keeping with the fairy-tale source, there is a strong folkloric influence—in fact, several passages from Afanasiev's tale are incorporated verbatim. But Tsvetaeva's language is not simply a folkloric stylization. Rather, she uses folk and archaic layers of Russian to create a modernist idiom of her own. Her use of nonstandard forms and neologisms comes close to the verbal experiments of the Russian futurists, even though she never crosses the boundary into pure "trans-sense" language. Sound and rhythm assume a major significance. In addition to the end rhymes, a multitude of internal rhymes, assonances, and alliterations lend the text an intensely musical, incantatory quality. The stirring polymetric rhythm, characterized by a folksy dance quality, creates an effect that is similar to the blend of Russian folkloric tunes with avant-garde modernism in the ballet scores of Igor Stravinsky, as Simon Karlinsky has pointed out.[6]

Mólodets received mixed reviews in the Russian émigré press. While some critics were baffled by its content and style, Vladislav Khodasevich, the greatest poet of the Russian emigration after Tsvetaeva, praised the poem's rich vocabulary and Tsvetaeva's ability to capture what he considered the genuine spirit of Russian folklore. As he put it: "A folk song is to a significant degree a joyful or plaintive wail—it contains elements of the tongue-twister and pun, of purest sound play; one always hears echoes of spells and incantations, of faith in the magic power of the word; it is always in part hysterical, turning into crying or laughter, and in part 'beyond sense' [*zaumna*]."[7] Tsvetaeva herself considered *Mólodets* a work of central importance, as we can see from the fact that she kept coming back to it in her later critical essays and letters. She mentioned it repeatedly in her correspondence with Boris Pasternak, who became the poem's dedicatee. On February 14, 1923, she wrote to Pasternak: "I just finished a long poem (one has to call it something, after all!)—not a poem, but an obsession [*navazhdenie*], and it was not I that finished it, but it finished me."[8] In subsequent letters, Tsvetaeva stressed the autobiographical significance of *Mólodets*, claiming a kinship between herself and the female protagonist Marusia.[9] She also made special efforts to have the poem translated. The British poet and novelist Alec Brown created an

English version, but no publisher was willing to take it on, and the manuscript of Brown's translation seems not to have been preserved.[10]

In 1929, Tsvetaeva made the acquaintance of the prominent Russian avant-garde painter Natalia Goncharova, who offered to do a series of illustrations for *Mólodets*. This gave Tsvetaeva the hope to publish her poem in France. Since no other translator was available, she decided to translate it herself. As she later explained in an interview published in the Paris émigré newspaper *Vozrozhdenie*: "I never thought that I would take up such a task. It happened almost accidentally: Natalia Goncharova, who knew the thing in Russian, made illustrations and regretted that there was no French text. So I began—because of the illustrations, and then I myself got carried away [*sama vovleklas'*]."[11]

Tsvetaeva's biographer Simon Karlinsky claims, somewhat misleadingly, that the self-translation of *Mólodets* obliged Tsvetaeva to learn French versification, and that, "dissatisfied with the results, she decided to write a new French poem, 'Gars,' based on 'The Swain.'"[12] It is true that in her *Vozrozhdenie* interview, Tsvetaeva states that she "attempted to translate" the poem, but ended up "writing it anew around the same core [*sterzhen'*]."[13] This does not mean, however, that Tsvetaeva considered *Le Gars* a self-standing poem only loosely based on its Russian source text. To the contrary: she regarded the French version to be a bona fide transposition of the Russian original that strove to preserve its most essential features. Moreover, Tsvetaeva was not unfamiliar with French versification, but the task that she set for herself in her translation, as we will see, was to achieve a sort of synthesis between French and Russian prosody. In a letter written in 1930, Tsvetaeva commented as follows on her progress in translating *Mólodets*: "The thing is going well. I could now write a theory of verse translation, which comes down to a transposition, a change of key while preserving the foundation. Not only with other words, but with other images. In short, a thing in another language has to be written anew. Which only the author can do."[14]

The translation turned out to be significantly more labor-intensive than the composition of the original Russian text. While it took Tsvetaeva three months to write the original *Mólodets*, she spent eight months on the French version.[15] There is no indication that she was dissatisfied with the result—to the contrary, she was proud of her achievement. The utter lack of success of *Le Gars* with the French public was therefore all the greater a disappointment to her. Tsvetaeva's reading of the poem at a Paris literary salon turned out to be a fiasco. As we know from the memoirs of E. A. Izvol'skaia, the audience reacted with "deadly silence."[16] Tentative plans to publish the poem in the journals *Commerce* and *Nouvelle Revue Française* came to nothing. As

Tsvetaeva reported in a 1931 letter: "About the French *Mólodets* there is only one refrain: '*Too* new, unusual, outside of any tradition, not even surrealism' (NB! God save me from the latter!). Nobody wants to *courir le risque*."[17] Only two brief excerpts of *Le Gars* appeared in print during Tsvetaeva's lifetime. The first chapter of the poem came out in 1930 in the journal *France et Monde*, and a short excerpt from the final chapter, under the title "La Neige" ("The Snow"), was included in a 1935 *Anthologie de la littérature soviétique* (*sic!*) edited by George Reavey and Marc Slonim.[18] The manuscript of *Le Gars* remained dormant in Tsvetaeva's Moscow archive for many decades. It was finally published in France in the early 1990s, half a century after Tsvetaeva's death.[19] A decade later *Le Gars* also appeared in Russia. A 2003 edition of *Mólodets* published in St. Petersburg includes the French text with a literal Russian translation printed *en face*, while a 2005 bilingual Moscow edition presents Tsvetaeva's Russian and French versions on facing pages. Both of these editions also include Natalia Goncharova's illustrations.[20] These publications hardly established a reputation for Tsvetaeva as a bilingual poet, however. Even among Tsvetaeva specialists, *Le Gars* has thus far received only minimal attention.[21]

"DICHTEN IST NACHDICHTEN": TSVETAEVA'S VIEWS ON POETRY AND TRANSLATION

Before engaging in a discussion of *Le Gars*, it will be useful to consider Tsvetaeva's linguistic abilities and her general attitude toward translingual poetry and translation. Tsvetaeva had an excellent command of two languages other than her native Russian. To say that her French and German were "near native" would be an understatement. In both languages she was not only a fluent speaker, but also an original stylist. As the example of *Le Gars* demonstrates, her knowledge of French also included archaic and nonstandard layers of the language. Tsvetaeva's facility with languages goes back to her early childhood. Even though she came from a less exalted class background than Vladimir Nabokov, just like him, she would have been able to claim that she grew up as a "perfectly normal trilingual child."[22] In her autobiographical sketch of 1940 she wrote: "First languages: German and Russian, by age seven — French."[23] At her Moscow childhood home there was no Russian nanny, but a series of German and French governesses. Like Wassily Kandinsky, Tsvetaeva had a Baltic German grandparent, the businessman and publisher Aleksandr Danilovich Meyn, who was her favorite relative and recited German poetry to her during visits.[24] Tsvetaeva's half-German, half-Polish mother introduced her children to German and French rather than Russian literature.[25] From age ten to thirteen, Tsvetaeva lived abroad to accompany her mother, who tried unsuccessfully to cure her tuberculosis in various European sanatoriums. Tsvetaeva attended a French-language boarding school in Lausanne, Switzerland, in 1903–04, and a German boarding school in Freiburg, Germany, in 1904–05. The latter experience turned her into a lifelong Germanophile (at least until the Nazi takeover of Czechoslovakia in 1939). At age sixteen, Tsvetaeva traveled alone to Paris to attend a summer course in medieval French literature at the Sorbonne.

In a questionnaire forwarded to her by Boris Pasternak for a planned dictionary of twentieth-century writers by the Soviet Academy of Arts and Sciences, Tsvetaeva indicated that, as a child and adolescent, she wrote poems not only in Russian, but also in German and French.[26] The same claim is repeated in the autobiographical sketch of 1940, where she writes that she composed French poems in Lausanne and German poems in Freiburg.[27] None of these texts seems to have survived, but it becomes clear that the idea and practice of writing poetry in a non-native language was certainly not alien to Tsvetaeva. She later furnished a theoretical and philosophical justification for translingual poetry in her correspondence with Rainer Maria Rilke during the summer of 1926. On July 6, 1926, she wrote to Rilke (in German):

> Goethe says somewhere that one can never achieve anything of significance in a foreign language—and that has always rung false to me. . . . Writing poetry is in itself translating, from the mother tongue into another. Whether French or German should make no difference. No language is the mother tongue. Writing poetry is rewriting it [*Dichten ist nachdichten*]. That's why I am puzzled when people talk of French or Russian, etc., poets. A poet may write in French; he cannot be a French poet. That's ludicrous.
>
> I am not a Russian poet and am always astonished to be taken for one and looked upon in this light. The reason one becomes a poet (if it were even possible to *become* one, if one *were* not one before all else!) is to avoid being French, Russian, etc., in order to be everything.[28]

"Nachdichten" is the German term for composing a poetic translation in such a way that the translated text passes muster as a valid work of poetry in the target language. As Tsvetavea herself observed in her 1929 essay "A Few of Rainer Maria Rilke's Letters": "How much better the Germans put it—*nachdichten*! Following in the poet's footsteps, to lay again the path he has already laid. Let *nach* mean follow, but *dichten* always has new meaning. *Nachdichten*—laying anew a path, all traces of which are instantaneously grown over."[29] Writing poetry, for Tsvetaeva, was akin to translation in a double sense. It means translating from the ordinary language used in daily life into a poetic idiom, but it also involves a translation from the spiritual into a material, linguistic realm. For her, contrary to popular assumptions, poetry is in principle always translatable. She explained this thought in a letter to the French poet Paul Valéry in 1937 (in French):

> One says that Pushkin cannot be translated. Why? Every poem is a translation from the spiritual into the material, from feelings and thoughts into words. If one has been able to do it once by translating the interior world into external signs (which comes close to a miracle), why should one not be able to express one system of signs via another? This is much simpler: in the translation from one language into another, the material is rendered by the material, the word by the word, which is always possible.[30]

One may object that the logic behind this statement is somewhat dubious. If we follow Tsvetaeva's argument, a successful translation of Pushkin would entail the intuition of the spiritual "interior world" behind the Russian words and its recasting into another language, which seems more complex than a horizontal transposition between equivalent external signs. How can the external form be separated from the spiritual content if they are both extensions of each other?[31] Whatever its validity, though, Tsvetaeva's belief in the fundamental translatability of poetry certainly facilitated her own self-translation of *Mólodets*.

Tsvetaeva's opinion that "no language is the mother tongue" does not mean that the choice of a particular idiom had no significance for her and that she considered all languages as essentially interchangeable when it came to writing poetry. In her letters to Rilke, Tsvetaeva also offers observations about how Russian, German, and French differ from each other as vehicles of poetic expression. She establishes a personal hierarchy, in which the top position is occupied by what she refers to as the "language of angels," the immaterial essence of the spirit of poetry. According to Tsvetaeva, German comes closest to this ideal language, followed by Russian, while French occupies the third and last position. Commenting on the poems that Rilke composed in French, she writes to him that French is an "ungrateful language for poets—that's of course why you wrote in it. Almost impossible language!"[32]

Tsvetaeva's seemingly counterintuitive decision to translate her poem into French, aside from purely pragmatic reasons, was thus determined by the particular challenge that the language presented to her as a poet. The incentive consisted precisely in overcoming a seemingly insurmountable obstacle. Like Rilke, she chose French not because it was easy, but because it was difficult. The idea of French as a problematic vehicle for writing poetry betrays Tsvetaeva's German romantic roots and prejudices. Seen from that perspective, the alleged Cartesian rationality and clarity of the French language turns into an obstacle for the expression of the spiritual and the ineffable. In her letter to Rilke, Tsvetaeva draws a contrast between German as a language of dynamic eternal becoming and French as an idiom of static finiteness, calling German an "infinite promise" ("unendliche Versprechung") and French a "gift once and for all" ("endgültige Gabe").[33] Seen from a romantic point of view, the neoclassicist straitjacket in which the French language has been dressed up since the seventeenth century may have had a deleterious effect on poetic creativity, but Tsvetaeva was surely aware of the aesthetic revolution initiated by the French symbolists. However, her own solution to overcome the perceived poetic poverty of French was not to imitate French symbolism (which had itself become a cliché by the time she wrote *Le Gars*), but to go back to more ancient, pre-classicist layers of the French language.

THE CHALLENGE OF TRANSLATING *MÓLODETS*

Even for someone who believed in the essential translatability of poetry, as Tsvetaeva did, the difficulties in translating a text like *Mólodets* are daunting. Aside from the virtuosity of its rhythm, rhymes, and wordplay, there is the issue of nonstandard language, as manifested by the presence of archaic, folk, and Church Slavonic elements alongside Tsvetaeva's own idiosyncratic style, which is characterized by neologisms, elliptic compression, and the frequent absence of verbs. The challenges that Tsvetaeva faced can be broken down into three rough categories: linguistic features of the original Russian text that can in principle be reproduced in French; formal characteristics such as meter, rhyme, and alliteration that require substantial creative rewriting; and elements of the Russian original that elude translation altogether. In what follows, I will address each category in turn.

In order to reproduce the nonstandard language of *Mólodets* with its archaic and folk connotations, Tsvetaeva resorted to the premodern vocabulary of the sixteenth and fifteenth centuries found in the works of a François Rabelais or François Villon. Thus we find archaic locutions like "onque" (75) instead of the modern French "jamais," "nenni" for "non" (37, 80), "ru" for "ruisseau" (54, 55), "choir" for "tomber" (36), "jà" for "déjà" (119), "oyez" for "écoutez" (105), and diminutive forms like "pommelettes" (26), "pauvrette" (29), "oiselet" (34), "seurettes" (46), and "enfantelet" (47) that do not exist in modern standard French. An interesting case is the word "rouble," which in modern French denotes the Russian currency, but which in ancient French meant something like a shovel.[34] The expression "Sonnez, roubles!" (117) could thus be read as an example of double coding, meaning either "Resound, shovels!" or "Resound, rubles!" In comparison with the linguistic inventiveness of the Russian text, there are fewer outright neologisms in the

French text, however. Most of the vocabulary in *Le Gars* can be found in specialized French dictionaries, with only a few exceptions that seem to be Tsvetaeva's own coinages.[35]

Tsvetaeva's archaic style pertains not only to vocabulary, but to grammar and syntax as well. For example, she uses the *passé simple* in direct speech, as in "Pourquoi cassâtes la branche / brulâtes l'arbuste?" (103; "Why did you break the branch, burn the shrub?"), which in modern usage would require the *passé composé* ("Pourquoi avez-vous cassé / brûlé," etc.). A very characteristic syntactic feature of Tsvetaeva's style, both in Russian and French, is the omission of personal pronouns with conjugated verbs. The repeated formula with which Marusia brushes off her mother's cry for help, "spliu—ne slyshu, matushka" ("[I] sleep and do not hear, mother") becomes in French "Mère, dors / et n'endends rien" (49). The phrase sounds more jarring in French because, unlike in Russian, the verbal ending does not allow for a definitive identification of the speaker ("dors" and "entends" could be either first- or second-person singular). Likewise, the frequent omission of articles creates an alien effect in French that could perhaps be interpreted as a "foreignizing" element pointing to the Russian source, but more likely is meant to evoke an archaic or folkloric style.

Tsvetaeva's French manuscript contains a few suggested corrections inserted by Robert Vivier, a professor at the University of Liège whom she had asked for advice. Mostly, Vivier proposed to amend the text by inserting missing articles and pronouns. For example, he changed "plus ne puis" ("I can't anymore") to "je n'en peux plus." As Efim Etkind correctly notes, however, the locution "plus ne puis" would have been perfectly normal in fifteenth- or sixteenth-century French.[36] Tsvetaeva ended up accepting very few of Vivier's proposed emendations, which shows that her use of nonstandard language was a deliberate strategy that she was unwilling to alter.

Another idiosyncratic feature of Tsvetaeva's Russian is a nominal style characterized by the frequent omission of verbs. In principle, this effect can be reproduced in French as well, even though it comes across as somewhat less natural, given that verbless locutions are not as common in French as they are in Russian. In his review of *Mólodets*, Dmitrii Sviatopolk-Mirskii praised the language of Tsvetaeva's poem for its "Russian 'verblessness'" ("russkaia 'bezglagol'nost'").[37] An example of this technique can be found in the stanza describing Marusia's dance in the nobleman's palace after she has metamorphosed from a flower back into human shape:

> Вплавь. Вскачь.
> Всё—в раз!
> Пляс. Плач.
> Плач. Пляс. (v. 1052–55)

Gliding in. Jumping up.
All—in one!
Dance. Cry.
Cry. Dance.

The French version preserves the nominal style of the Russian original:

Jeux d'eau.
Jeux d'air.
Pleurs. Sauts.
Sauts. Pleurs. (78)

Water games.
Air games.
Cries. Jumps.
Jumps. Cries.

As can be seen, semantic accuracy was the least concern for Tsvetaeva when she translated her poem into French. What she preserves in the present case is not the literal meaning, but the pounding staccato rhythm created by the piling up of stressed monosyllabics. Both in Russian and French, the stanza consists entirely of such words, even though the French version lacks the sonic uniformity created in Russian by the "v" and "pl"-alliterations and the preponderance of stressed "a." Clearly, sound effects were a primary concern for Tsvetaeva. If in the above example, the French version seems sonically poorer, there are many other cases where Tsvetaeva creates sound effects in French that have no equivalent in the Russian original. This includes alliterations (e.g., "Tresses traînent, bottes butent," 75), or even spoonerisms ("Le tien sonne, / et le sien—tonne," 27).

Rhymes play an extremely important role in Tsvetaeva's poetics. Both in Russian and in French, they turn up not only at the end of the verse line, but internally as well. Here, for example, is a description of the nobleman in his steam bath after having brought the red flower to his palace:

Да по притолкам — в дымá,
Да по тутолкам — в чаны . . .
И не надо мне вина!
И не надо мне жены! (v. 888–91)

Along the lintels—into the smoke!
Along the tutolki[38]—into the tubs . . .
And I do not need wine!
And I do not need a wife!

In French, the nobleman addresses the flower directly:

> M'es Dame, m'es daim,
> M'es flamme, m'es bain,
> M'es femme, m'es vin . . .
>
> —Hein? (72)

> To me you are dame, deer,
> flame, bath,
> wife, wine . . .
>
> —Huh?

With its lineup of identical rhymes in two parallel vertical rows (Dame-flamme-femme; daim-bain-vin-Hein) and the identical beginning of each verse line, the French translation is even more tightly and uniformly structured than the Russian original.

Rhyme does not only fulfill an ornamental, mnemonic, or euphonic function in *Mólodets*; it also assumes an important structural and semantic role. There are several passages where a word is left out at the end of a stanza, but has to be mentally reinserted by the reader according to the rhyme scheme. The taboo word "upyr'" (vampire), for example, is never uttered in the text, but is implied in the passage where Marusia's brother cries out to her in the middle of the night:

> Лют брачный твой пир,
> Жених твой у— (v. 369–70)

> Your wedding feast is dire,
> Your bridegroom a vam—

The interrupted utterance indicates that the brother is killed at the very moment when he is about to name and expose his murderer. The French text functions in the same way, prompting the reader to insert the word "sang" (blood):

> Sache bien qui prends,
> Un suceur de . . . (42)

> Know well whom you are marrying,
> A sucker of . . .

It goes without saying that the preservation of such effects is incompatible with a literal translation. In Tsvetaeva's approach, the rendition of structural and formal features trumps semantic accuracy.

Remarkably, this formal faithfulness pertains to meter as well. Theoreticians of verse would maintain that an equimetrical translation between Russian and French is impossible, given that the two languages use different systems of versification: syllabotonic in Russian, syllabic in French. However, Tsvetaeva simply chose to ignore this fact.[39] The polymetric twists and turns of the Russian original are replicated in the French translation. This can be seen, for example, in the description of the nobleman's palace:

> Впрочем — Богу ли соврем? —
> Столб как столб и дом как дом:
> С башнями, с банями:
> Нашего барина. (v. 872–75)

> By the way—why lie to God?—
> A column and a house like any other:
> With towers, with baths:
> Of our nobleman.

The first two lines are written in four-foot trochees (a predominant meter in *Mólodets*) before the stanza unexpectedly switches to two-foot dactyls in lines 3 and 4. In French, the text shifts from trochees to amphibrachs if we read it "à la russe," so to speak, by emphasizing the stressed syllables in accordance with the trochaic and dactylic meter and by counting the silent "e muet" as a full syllable (as is indeed the norm in French poetic scansion):

> Pic sur pic et bloc sur bloc.
> —A qui fillette ce roc
> De marbre?
>   —Pardine!
> A notre barine. (71)

> Peak above peak and block above block.
> —To whom, girl, [belongs] this rock
> Of marble?
>   —Goodness!
> To our nobleman.

Remarkably, the French translation retains *not a single word* of the original stanza aside from the closing "barin" (nobleman). Instead of the semantics, Tsvetaeva attempts to replicate the form of the Russian original as closely as possible. Aside from the metrical shift in mid-stanza, this includes the paired masculine and dactylic rhymes. Since, strictly speaking, no dactylic endings exist in French, the latter are replaced by feminine rhymes, but the sonic structure of "Pardine-barine" nevertheless suggest a trisyllabic rhyme. The rhythm of the second line in Russian with its repetition of the monosyllabic words "stolb" (column) and "dom" (house) finds an exact equivalent in the first line of the French stanza, which repeats the words "pic" and "bloc." Furthermore, the alliteration "<u>b</u>ashniami—<u>b</u>aniami—<u>b</u>arina" is echoed by the repetition of the "ar"-sound in "m<u>ar</u>bre—P<u>ar</u>dine—b<u>ar</u>ine."

As we can see, Tsvetaeva displays considerable ingenuity in replicating the formal characteristics of the Russian original in French. Of course, not everything can be preserved in translation. The different nature of the two languages makes it impossible to reproduce some key features of *Mólodets*. As already mentioned, the dactylic rhymes cannot really be replicated in French, given that all French words are accented either on the last or on the penultimate syllable (in the case of an ending on "e muet"). Some key grammatical elements of the Russian text are also impervious to translation. This includes the instrumental case, which can express, often simultaneously, the means of a performed action, a comparison, or a transformation. In her linguistic analysis of Tsvetaeva's style, the Russian scholar Liudmila Zubova calls the syncretic use of the instrumental case the "grammatical dominant" of *Mólodets*.[40] This technique is on display, for example, in the following series of free-floating nouns:

> Шаром-жаром-
> Жигом-граем . . .
> Барин, барин, барин, барин! . . . (v. 1311–13)

> Ball-fire-
> Burn-croak . . .
> Nobleman, nobleman, nobleman, nobleman! . . .

"Sharom" (simply translated as "ball" here) could mean "with a ball," "as a ball," "like a ball," or "turning into a ball." It is impossible to replicate this effect in French (or English). Tsvetaeva's French version of this passage preserves neither the form nor content of the Russian original, but creates an entirely new text, in which the narrator utters a more explicit warning to the nobleman:

> Heureux sont les bègues—ont temps
> De p-p-prendre leur temps.

> Heureux surtout les muets:
> Un mot ne revient jamais.

> Ne le sauras que trop tôt,
> Vantard! nigaud de nigaud! (89)

Happy are the stammerers—they have the time
To t-t-take their time.

Happy above all the mute ones:
A word never comes back.

You will find out only too soon,
Boaster! Dummy of dummies!

The final chapter of the poem with its inserted liturgical quotes in Church Slavonic presents another unsolvable conundrum for a French translator. Tsvetaeva uses some archaic vocabulary in her rendering of these passages, such as "agnel" instead of "agneau" (lamb) as well as her nonstandard syntax discussed above, but the difference between the (low) folkloric and (high) Church Slavonic layers in the Russian text is lost in French. A possible solution might have been to render the liturgical quotes in Latin, but this would have created its own problems, given that Latin is less intelligible to a French reader that Church Slavonic is to a Russian. By the same token, Tsvetaeva made no attempt to preserve allusions to a specifically Russian religious context, such as when Marusia is denounced as "dvuperstnaia" (two-fingered), a reference to the way in which the Old Believers make the sign of the cross. Such passages are simply omitted in the French translation.

Overall, then, the French self-translation of *Mólodets* differs significantly from the Russian original. The literal meaning of the text can alter dramatically between the two versions. At the same time, however, Tsvetaeva manages to preserve the form and nature of the poem astonishingly well. Her personal, idiosyncratic style carries over from Russian into French. Anybody familiar with Tsvetaeva's Russian poetry will find that *Le Gars* sounds very much like a poem by Tsvetaeva. In some passages, one could argue that the French version seems even more "Tsvetaevan" than the Russian original. Here, for example, is the scene describing Marusia's brother calling for help in the middle of the night:

Спит двор, спит и дом,
Спит дым над бугром,
Спит пес, спит и гусь:
—Марусь, а Марусь! (v. 353–56)

The yard sleeps, and the house sleeps,
The smoke sleeps above the hill,
The dog sleeps, and the goose sleeps:
—Marusia, hey, Marusia!

Nul bruit—tout dort.
Cour, four, coeur, corps.
Dors, dard, dors, fleur!
—Soeur! Soeur! Soeur! Soeur! (42)

No noise—everything sleeps.
Yard, oven, heart, body.
Sleep, sting, sleep, flower!
—Sister! Sister! Sister! Sister!

In the French version, the stanza becomes a sequence of phonically connected monosyllabic words, a signature feature of Tsvetaeva's poetic style. As will be shown below, "coeur," "corps," "dard," "fleur," and "soeur" create a network of semantic links with other key passages in *Le Gars*. The last line, with its fourfold repetition of the word "soeur," resembles the "Barin, barin, barin, barin!" line quoted earlier. The French text reaches a level of intensity here that surpasses the parallel passage in the Russian original, elevating Tsvetaeva's plaintive wail to an all-consuming fever pitch.

SELF-TRANSLATION AS SELF-EXEGESIS

Mólodets is not an "easy" text. Its idiosyncratic language and form create an impediment to smooth reading, and the action remains at times rather obscure. The French translation, by comparison, is somewhat more reader-friendly. Even though it is also written in a nonstandard, disruptive language, there are fewer outright neologisms and ungrammaticalities. In addition, Tsvetaeva includes some signposts that provide guidance to the reader. In the Russian text, it is often difficult to determine who the speaker is, as the text shifts abruptly between various voices, which can belong either to one of the fictional characters or to the narrator. In the French version, the speaker of an utterance is usually (though not always) indicated in the manner of a play. There are other ways in which the French text is more explicit and straightforward. For example, the first chapter features a dance scene in which various body parts (braids, breasts, cheeks) are described in the form of a riddle, but not named. In the French translation there is no guessing game, since the solution to the riddle is revealed from the start ("Oh les tresses," "Oh les seins," "Oh les joues," 26–27). This observation can be generalized. The French version sometimes makes explicit what is unspoken or only hinted at in Russian. In that sense, the self-translation can also be used as an interpretive tool to arrive at a better understanding of the Russian original.

As far as the plot is concerned, the French version often provides more details and explanations, even though the translation is overall somewhat shorter than the original (2,146 lines in French vs. 2,227 in Russian). There are entire added passages in French that help to clarify the action. The crucial scene where Marusia discovers that her beloved is a vampire is adorned with dramatic detail in the French version:

A la vitre traîtresse
Son front perlant presse.

Et du haut de son perchoir
—Vierge! Vierge! Vais-je choir?—

Que vois-je? A moi, Vierge!
Un bière, trois cierges . . .

Le voilà, mon cher,
Le voilà mon fort,
Ha-gard, l'oeil vert,
Qui croque un . . . (36)

Against the treacherous glass
She presses her forehead with beats of sweat.

And from the height of her perch
—Virgin! Virgin! Will I fall?—

What do I see? Virgin, help me!
A coffin, three candles . . .

Here he is, my beloved,
Here he is, my strong one,
Cra-zed, green-eyed,
Chomping on a . . .

The missing word suggested by the rhyme scheme is "mort" (dead person). In Russian, this entire scene is compressed into two laconic lines. The truncated word "upo-" has to be extended to "upokoinika" (the accusative case of "corpse"):

Стоит наш знакомец-то,
Грызет упо— (v. 249–50)

There stands our acquaintance,
Chomping on a co . . .

The scene where the vampire kills Marusia's brother is also adorned with details that are missing in Russian:

> Sur mon coeur—gros poids!
> Sur mon cou—dix doigts!
> Me suce! me boit!
> C'en est fait de moi! (42)

> On my heart—a heavy weight!
> On my throat—ten fingers!
> [He] sucks me! [he] drinks me!
> I am done with!

This stanza, which is entirely absent in Russian, identifies the character as a "western European" vampire who kills his victims by drinking their blood (Slavic vampires eat dead bodies, as seen in the church scene quoted above).[41]

The romance between Marusia and the vampire is fleshed out more explicitly in the French version of the poem. After the scene at the church, Marusia runs home, where she is interrogated by her mother. In French (and only in French), the mother wants to know whether she loves the young man, to which Marusia answers with "De coeur!" ("With my whole heart!" 38). Later, the vampire implores Marusia to save herself by naming him, referring to himself as an "âme damnée / mais qui t'aimait" ("A cursed soul / but who loved you," 47). In the Russian poem, the word "love" is never uttered between Marusia and the vampire.[42] In her extratextual exegesis of the poem included in the article "Poet o kritike," Tsvetaeva stressed the love between the two main protagonists, and she reinforces this point in her French self-translation. To make matters even clearer, the preface to the French translation begins with the words: "This is the story of a young human who preferred losing her family, herself, and her soul to losing her love" (129).

Efim Etkind has argued that Marusia's sacrifice becomes more radical in the French translation: in French, she is ready not only to give up her life, but even her immortal soul for the sake of her lover.[43] Such a reading is not incompatible with the Russian text either, though. When the vampire implores Marusia to save her soul, she replies "Na koi mne dusha?" (v. 589–90; "What do I need a soul for?"). A bit later she adds that "hell" is "paradise" as long she remains in the company of her beloved (v. 601–3). All of these passages are translated more or less literally into French. In addition, the French version contains a sentence describing Marusia as "une âme qui se damne" ("a soul condemning herself," 54), and the vampire utters the warning "Ame perds et rien ne gagnes!" ("[You] are losing [your] soul and gaining nothing!" 55). What we are seeing in the French translation is not so much an alteration and radicalization of the plot, as Etkind argues, as a clarification. Tsvetaeva sharpens the message of the poem with added details that can only be found in the French version.

The courtship between Marusia and the vampire[44] develops around four key scenes: their first dance, the marriage proposal, the consummation of the relationship, which leads to Marusia's physical death, and their final reunion. In each case, the French translation adds some significant components. In Russian, the first dance is rendered in a striking series of alliterating verbs and nouns:

> Прядает, прыщет,
> Притопот, присвист.
> Пышечка! — Пищи!
> Пришепот, прищелк. (v. 102–5)

> [He] jumps, gushes,
> Stamping down, whistling.
> Cutie!—Squeak!
> Whisper, click.

In French, this becomes:

> Feu qui saute, feu qui souffle,
> Feu qui fauche, feu qui siffle.
>
> LE GARS: Feu—suis,
>   Faim—ai,
>   Feu—suis,
>   Cendres—serai! (29)

> Fire that jumps, fire that blows,
> Fire that mows, fire that whistles.
>
> THE SWAIN: Fire—am,
>   Hungry—am,
>   Fire—am,
>   Ashes—will be!

The hissing sound, a sonic leitmotif of the vampire throughout the poem, is realized both in the Russian and French text. The Russian "pr"-alliteration is replaced by alternating "f" and "s" sounds in French, which underline the impression of hissing and whistling. At the same time, the French version draws an explicit connection between the vampire and the element of fire, and it adds an explanatory monologue, which highlights both the fiery, predatory nature of the character and hints at his longing for self-annihilation.

At the end of the first chapter, the vampire proposes to Marusia with the following quatrain:

> Сердь моя руса,
> Спелая рожь —
> Сердце, Маруся,
> Замуж пойдешь? (v. 167–70)

> My blond mid-heart,[45]
> Ripe rye —
> Heart, Marusia,
> Will you get married?

In the French version this becomes:

> Maroussia, ma fleur,
> Maroussia, mon fruit,
> Maroussia, ma soeur,
> Me veux-tu pour mari? (31)

> Marusia, my flower,
> Marusia, my fruit,
> Marusia, my sister,
> Do you want me as your husband?

The prevalent "s"-"m"-"r" sound pattern of the Russian text, a permutation of the consonants contained in Marusia's name, becomes in French a flow of "m"-alliterations, with the final word, "mari" (husband), echoing the beginning of the word "Marusia." In both the Russian and French texts, the vampire refers to his beloved with plant and agricultural imagery, but the French rhyming words carry a more significant semantic charge. "Fleur" anticipates Marusia's later symbolic and literal transformation into a flower. "Fruit" repeats an earlier statement made by the vampire, who told Marusia "c'est toi le fruit" ("you are the fruit," 30), creating an allusion to the forbidden fruit in Genesis 1:3 (in the Russian text, Marusia refers to herself as a "red fruit" ["alyi plod"] at the beginning of chapter 2, v. 176). "Soeur" (sister) hints at a "family resemblance" between Marusia and the vampire. The female heroine is herself endowed with qualities that make her an equal and willing partner of her male suitor. The word "soeur" is all the more surprising here since the expected rhyme with "fleur" could easily have been "coeur" (heart), which would have been an obvious solution for rendering the "serd'" and "serdtse" of the Russian original. The identical rhymes "coeur"-"fleur"-"soeur" (together with "peur" [fear]) form the structural backbone in the French version of the consummation scene, to which we turn next.

In the physical union with her lover, Marusia becomes the metaphorical "flower" announced by the "fleur"-rhyme in the French proposal scene. The image of a flower and an insect conveys the conflation of lovemaking with vampiric bloodsucking. The symbol of the sting combines the action of the insect (a bumblebee in Russian, a hornet in French) with phallic connotations, while at the same time evoking the proverbial "sting of death" evoked in 1 Corinthians 15:55:

> —Час да наш,
> Ад мой ал!
> К самой чашечке
> Припал.
>
> —Конец твоим рудам!
> Гудом, гудом, гудом!
>
> —Конец твоим алым!
> Жалом, жалом, жалом!
>
> —Ай — жаль?
> —Злей — жаль!
> С дном пей!
> Ай, шмель!
>
> Во — весь
> Свой — хмель
> Пей, шмель!
>
> Ай, шмель! (v. 685–700)

> The hour is ours,
> My hell is red!
> To the very cup
> He pressed himself.
>
> —An end to your blood!
> Buzzing, buzzing, buzzing!
>
> —An end to your red!
> With the sting, the sting, the sting!

—Ai!—does it hurt?
—Fiercer—sting!
Drink from the ground!
Ai, bumblebee!

In—all
Your—drunkenness
Drink, bumblebee!

Ai, bumblebee!

Droit au coeur
Dard très long.
Fille—fleur.
Gars—frelon.

Frère et soeur?
Non—et oui.
Dard et fleur,
Elle et lui.

—Hôtesse! Nourisse!
Suce, suce, suce!
—Ma fraîche! Ma grasse!
Glace, glace, glace.

—Te
fais-
je
mal?

—Dieu
te
fit tel.

—Te
fais-
je peur?

—Dieu
me
fit
fleur (57–58)

Straight into the heart
Very long sting.
Girl – flower.
Guy – hornet.

Brother and sister?
No – and yes.
Sting and flower,
She and he.

—Hostess! Nurse![46]
Suck, suck, suck.
—My fresh one! My fat one!
Ice, ice, ice.

—Do
I
hurt
you?

—God
made
you so.

—Do
I scare
you?

—God
made
me
a flower

    The Russian and the French texts emphasize different semantic connotations. While the Russian version foregrounds the metaphor of the cup and of drinking, the French version focuses on the sting image. The rhymes and monosyllabic words in French create a clear link with the proposal scene, as well as with Marusia's brother's earlier cry for help ("Dors, dard, dors, fleur! / —Soeur! Soeur! Soeur! Soeur!"). At the same time, the French version contains information that is unavailable in the Russian original. We are again reminded that Marusia and the vampire are potentially related to each other, as the question of whether they are brother and sister is first denied and then affirmed. Nothing of the sort ever happens in the Russian text. Moreover, in a passage arranged in the manner of a Russian modernist *stolbik*, which breaks up the verse line into a vertical column of monosyllabic words,[47] Marusia affirms that the vampire's actions and her relationship with him are God's will. A similar statement of metaphysical justification is lacking in the Russian text.

    The poem ends with the final reunion of the two protagonists at the church service and their flight up into the sky. This scene is also rendered differently in Russian and French:

Та — ввысь,
Тот — вблизь:
Свились,
Взвились:

Зной — в зной,
Хлынь — хлынь!
До — мой
В огнь синь.(v. 2220–27)

She — up,
He — close:
Winding together,
Soaring up:

Heat—in heat,
Surge — surge!
Ho-me
Into the blue fire.

Un coeur
Un corps
Accord
Essor

Unis
Étreints
Au ciel
Sans fin. (125)

A heart
A body
Accord
Rise

United
In hugs
To the sky [or heaven]
Without end.

The French translation reproduces the rhythmic structure of the Russian original with two syllables per line, but it is written in a more transparent
language than the Russian text, which contains neologisms ("khlyn'," derived
from the verb "khlynut'" [to surge]) and archaisms (the monosyllabic "ogn'"

instead of the common "ogon'" [fire], and "sin'" instead of "sinii" [blue]). The penultimate line in Russian features another typical device of Tsvetaeva's poetics. The word "domoi" (home) is broken down with a dash into individual syllables, which each assume a semantic significance of their own. Rewritten as "do-moi," the word becomes a combination of the preposition "do" (toward) with the possessive pronoun "moi" (mine). Tsvetaeva uses the same technique a few lines earlier in the French text, where the vampire addresses Marusia as "Ma-rie!" combining the possessive pronoun "ma" with the imperative "rie!" (laugh!).

Overall, the French ending makes a different impression than the original Russian conclusion. Rather than with a dramatic movement into the fire, the poem ends with an almost placid statement of harmony and unity. Significantly, the word "ciel" has a double meaning, denoting both "sky" and "heaven." The pairing of "coeur" and "corps" harkens back to an earlier utterance made by Marusia at the beginning of chapter 2. When her mother asks her: "Le sais-tu d'où il sort?" ("Do you know where he comes from?"), she responds with "Un seul coeur, un seul corps! ("A single heart, a single body!" 33). The corresponding Russian dialogue is "A skazal tebe iz ch'ikh?"—"Odno serdtse—na dvoikh!" (v. 180–81; "And did he tell you from whose [family]?"—"One heart—for two!"). Tsvetaeva takes advantage of the similar sound of the words "coeur" and "corps," which form a phonemic minimal pair in French, to emphasize the unity between her two principal characters and to create linkages between individual passages in the poem that do not exist in Russian. The harmonious "happy ending," which seems more evident in the French than in the Russian version, is also supported by extratextual comments that Tsvetaeva made about her poem. In the same letter to Boris Pasternak where she identified Marusia as her alter ego, Tsvetaeva wrote: "I breathed a sigh of relief when the poem was done, happy for Marusya—for myself. What are they going to do in fire-blue? Fly around in it forever? Nothing satanic."[48]

Tsvetaeva took care to preserve in her translation a crucial formal feature of her poem: both in Russian and in French, the text begins and ends with the same word. In Russian, the first line of the poem is "Sin' da sgin'—krai sela" ("Blue, and be gone—edge of the village"). In French, the poem opens with the lines "Fin de terre, / Fin de ciel, / Fin de village" ("Edge [or 'end'] of the earth / edge of the sky / edge of the village"). "Sin'" and "fin" reoccur as the final words in the Russian and French version, respectively. Not only do the two words play the same structural role in the text, they even have a similar phonic shape. The French self-translation helps to elucidate the meaning of "sin'" in the original text. It becomes evident that the color blue denotes the infinity from which the story emerges and into which it flows back, ending in the romantic eternal flight that Tsvetaeva described in her letter to Pasternak.

The French version not only helps to clarify the plot of the poem, it also reinforces the implicit symbolic links built into the Russian text. In her analysis of *Mólodets*, the German scholar Christiane Hauschild has noted the prominent role of religious imagery, in particular the blasphemous connection between the consummation scene and the ritual of Holy Communion. As she points out, Marusia's sexual encounter with the vampire, who ends up killing her by drinking her blood, draws an implicit parallel with the Eucharist. In Tsvetaeva's poem the scene turns into a literal, cannibalistic consumption of blood, in which Marusia offers herself to the vampire as the sacramental "cup."[49] Earlier in the text, while he is interrogating Marusia, the vampire refers to his activity of eating corpses in the church as a "tainoe delo" ("secret act," v. 637), echoing the Orthodox terminology for the Eucharist, "tainodeistvie."[50] In the French translation of this passage, this connection is made much more explicit by mentioning bread and wine:

LE GARS:

— Fille, pèse bien:
Le sais-tu quel pain
(Fais-le bien, ton choix)
Mange, quel vin bois? (56)

THE SWAIN:

Girl, ponder it well:
Do you know what bread
(Make your choice well)
[I] eat, what wine [I] drink?

The French version is also more explicit with regard to color symbolism. As the Russian scholar N. M. Gerasimova has shown, the dichotomy between red and white forms the dominant color contrast in the poem.[51] In many instances this effect is merely implied in the Russian text, whereas in the French translation it becomes affirmatively marked with the adjectives "rouge" (red) and "blanc" (white). Thus, the lines "Vkrug berezynki—koster" ("Around the birch tree—a bonfire," v. 98) and "Vkrug chasovenki—pozhar!" ("Around the chapel—a conflagration!" v. 101) become "Brasier rouge, bouleau blanc" ("red blaze, white birch") and "Brasier rouge, clocher blanc" ("red blaze, white steeple," 28). The word "rouge" dominates in the French version from the very beginning. Marusia is introduced with the line "Ses joues sont rouges, sa bouche est rouge" ("Her cheeks are red, her mouth is red," 25). The corresponding Russian line "Doch' Marusia rumianista" ("The daughter Marusia is ruddy," v. 8) displays a more subdued and less sensual redness, while at the same time creating a paronomastic pun with the name Marusia. The double mentioning of the adjective "rouge" in the French version creates a strong link between Marusia and the vampire, who is introduced as a "Gars en chemise rouge," "Chemise rouge comme feu" ("A young man in a red shirt," "A red shirt like fire," 26).

The color red appears in various guises in the Russian text. This includes the adjectives "rumianyi" (ruddy) and "alyi" (crimson) aside from the standard "krasnyi" (red). The latter word can also mean "beautiful" in Russian folk language. Tsvetaeva consciously plays with this double meaning. In calling Marusia a "krasnaia devitsa" she is not simply using a folkloric cliché for "beautiful girl," but is also pointing to the inherent "redness" that links her to her male partner. In French this same effect is impossible to achieve, of course. More often than not, when facing the choice of translating "krasnyi" with either "beautiful" or "red," Tsvetaeva chose the latter option. For example, the vampire's boast that he trades in "krasnym tovarom" ("precious merchandise," v. 161) becomes in French "C'est du rouge que je vends" (31), suggesting that he is trading in red wine. In this sense, the French version creates an anticipation of the later Eucharistic symbolism. The word "sang" (blood) also occurs more frequently in the French version than in the original Russian. At the dance, the vampire addresses Marusia with the words "Tvoi malinovyi naliv— / Ssudi, devka, podelis'!" ("Your raspberry sap— / lend, girl, share!" v. 124–25). In French this becomes a much more literal "En est-tu riche de sang rouge! / Cède-m'en à ton amoureux!") ("You are rich in red blood! Give [some of] it to me, your beloved!"). Overall, "rouge" is the most frequently used adjective in the French text. This coloration is reflected in Tsvetaeva's statement at the end of her preface to the French translation: "Et voici, enfin, la Russie, rouge d'un autre rouge que celui de ses drapeaux d'aujourdhui" ("And here, finally, is Russia, red from a different red than the one of her present-day banners," 130).

LE GARS AS METATEXT

Until now, we have focused mainly on the ways in which the French translation of *Mólodets* replicates or reinforces certain key aspects of the Russian original despite dramatic deviations in wording and imagery. Nevertheless, it goes without saying that *Le Gars* is not identical with its source text (no translation is). In writing her poem anew seven years after its original composition, Tsvetaeva could not help becoming aware of how she herself, and therefore also her relation to the original text, had changed over time. Christiane Hauschild has argued that *Mólodets* contains a metatextual dimension, inasmuch as the title word refers both to the (nameless) male protagonist of the story and to the fairy-tale poem itself.[52] If the figure of Marusia is a

self-portrait of Tsvetaeva, her obsessive relationship with the male protagonist mirrors the author's attitude to her own poetic work. This metatextual
awareness increased in the process of self-translation, given that the author-
translator was now facing a text that was both intimately familiar and yet
"other." If *Le Gars* differs in a significant way from the original *Mólodets*, it is
perhaps precisely in this added self-awareness and self-reflection.

A major shift between the Russian and French incarnations of the
poem concerns the way in which the story is framed. Both versions are
divided into two parts with five chapters each, but the individual chapter
headings vary substantially. While the two principal parts of the poem have
no title in Russian, they are called "La Danseuse" ("The Dancer") and "La
Dormeuse" ("The Sleeper") in French. We might consider this as yet another
example of the more explicit and "reader-friendly" nature of the French version, which provides signposts that are absent in the Russian original. However, it is also worth emphasizing that these added titles, using the feminine
form, foreground Marusia as the central character of the story. In doing so,
the two titles create a contrast to what seems to be implied by the poem's
principal title, *Mólodets*, which emphasizes the male hero.

An analysis of the chapter headings reveals a similar shift away from
"male dominance."[53] In the Russian original, the female protagonist is banished from all the titles. As Christiane Hauschild has noted, this creates an
inherent contradiction between the chapter headings, which foreground the
male character as the main hero, and the fact that the story is presented from
the point of view of the female protagonist.[54] The title of the opening chapter,
"Mólodets," reinforces this effect by simply repeating the title of the poem.
In the French version, the contradiction disappears, or is at least significantly
attenuated. While the main title, *Le Gars*, still highlights the male protagonist, the chapter titles correct this impression. In Russian, they refer mainly
to the three male characters (the vampire, the nobleman, and the son) and
to spatial parameters denoting a liminal experience (ladder, gate, and thresh-
old). In French, the female protagonist is named in three of the titles ("Soeur
et frère," "Mère et fille," "L'Épousée"). In the latter case, she replaces the
son, who provided the chapter heading in the Russian version. The male
protagonist also drops from the title of the first chapter. In short, while the
chapter titles of the Russian version omit any mention of the female heroine,
the French titles turn her into a central focus of attention, emphasizing her
two main hypostases as "dancer" and "sleeper" and embedding her into a
network of familial relations as "sister," "daughter," and "spouse."

It appears that Tsvetaeva, while reworking her poem in French, became
more attentive to issues of gender. The figure of Marusia not only serves as a
self-portrait, but gains additional weight as a specifically female character. A
telling detail in the French version reinforces this impression. The nobleman,

after discovering that the red flower that he brought to his palace has turned into a woman, engages in a protracted physical struggle with her to prevent her from assuming her previous shape as a flower. In the French text, we find the following passage (which has no equivalent in Russian):

> Combattante
> Surhumaine!
> En démente
> Se démène.
>
> Amazone?
> Ballerine?
> En démone
> Le domine. (80)
>
> Superhuman
> Fighter!
> Madly
> Struggles.
>
> Amazon?
> Ballerina?
> As a demon
> She dominates him.

Tsvetaeva had always been fascinated by female fighters. As Simon Karlinsky points out in his biography, commenting on Tsvetaeva's poetry written at age seventeen and eighteen, "the most attractive role of all for Tsvetaeva, then and later, was that of an Amazon, a role she had in her grasp and voluntarily relinquished."[55] The word "Amazone," introduced with a question mark as a possible hypostasis of the female protagonist, was to resurface in Tsvetaeva's 1933 essay on lesbian love written in French, "Lettre à l'Amazone." Tsvetaeva argues there that lesbian love, as beautiful and rewarding as it may be, is ultimately doomed because of the more powerful maternal instinct (which was also the reason, according to Karlinsky, why Tsvetaeva relinquished her own role as an Amazon). In that sense, the plot of *Mólodets* offers a scenario of compensatory wish fulfillment. Marusia abandons her son and husband in pursuit of her passion, something that Tsvetaeva herself, despite numerous affairs, never was able or willing to do. The word "Amazone," inserted into the French text, but missing in Russian, provides a hint of what might have been. Other signposts in the French translation mark the struggle between Marusia and the nobleman as a manifestation of a more generalized gender conflict:

Homme veut.
Femme hait:
Gagne – perd. (81)

Man wants.
Woman hates:
Gains – loses.

This stark, almost schematic statement, which presents the conflicting as-pirations of the two genders as a sort of zero-sum game, has no equivalent anywhere in the Russian text.

Aside from the author's becoming more self-conscious as a woman, the reworking of the poem in French also seems to have made Tsvetaeva more aware of her Russian identity. Interestingly, the French version contains nu-merous allusions to Russia that are absent in the Russian original. The vam-pire refers to "saintly Russia" (47), he tells Marusia that she should be buried "a hundred versts from the temple . . . in the vast land, the Russian land" (60), snow is called "Russia's manna" (68), Marusia has "Russian braids" (76), the nobleman's valet asks him reproachfully "Are you Russian?" (92), the noble-man's guests abuse him with "Russian curses" (96), and the nobleman boasts about his spouse that "[she is] mine—Russian" (105). In addition, there are other clichéd "Russian" elements that exist only in the French text: Marusia's mother orders "a liter of eau de vie" (i.e., vodka) for the brother's funeral (43), the wind is blowing "in the steppe" (46), Marusia's grave is haunted by wolves (60), and midnight is personified as a "tsarina" (73 and 74).

A possible explanation for these additions may be that Tsvetaeva, in transplanting the poem from a Russian to a French linguistic medium, was trying to compensate for the loss in "Russianness" by asserting it discursively. As Etkind has noted, the language of the Russian version is intimately rooted in Russian folklore, whereas the French version displays more of a "neutral" folkloric style that cannot be located in a specific national tradition.[56] If Tsve-taeva wanted to signal to her French readers the "Russian" nature of her poem, she had to do it by other means. Interestingly, as Anna Lushenkova Foscolo has observed, the Ukrainian word "khata" (hut), a non-Russian ele-ment in the original Russian text, becomes a Russian "izba" in the French translation, thus preserving the foreignness of the word but recasting it in a Russian key.[57] In addition, it is important to note that the heroine herself is intimately connected to a personification of Russia. The very name "Marusia" contains the root "Rus'." That this phonic similarity is no accident becomes clear in the nobleman's exclamation "Moia Rus'-to!" ("Russia is mine!" v. 1983) when he is on his way to church. In uttering these words, the nobleman unwittingly comes close to pronouncing Marusia's name, which is unknown to him.[58] The name "Marusia" also contains the hair color "rusyi" (dark blond). This connection becomes evident when the vampire addresses her in the proposal scene as "Serd' moi rusa" (rhyming with "Serdtse, Marusia").

These connotations work somewhat differently in French. The name "Maroussia" can be linked with the color "rousse" (red-haired) as well as with "russe" (Russian), a similarity exploited in the tongue-twisting juxtaposition "rousses russes tresses" ("red Russian braids," 76). To be sure, in spite of the phonic similarity, "roux/rousse" is not the same color as "rusyi" (dark blond). One could argue that the French "roux" works even better than the Russian "rusyi" in the color symbolism of the poem, since it associates the female character more explicitly with the theme of "redness." If Tsvetaeva persisted in seeing the female heroine of her poem as a self-portrait, the "Maroussia" of the French version gains additional poignancy as a rebellious "redhead" and as a "Russian" living in an alien environment, as Tsvetaeva herself did in her French exile.

Finally, coming back to the metatextual dimension, the French version contains some clues that underline a deeper layer of meaning in the poem: Marusia's (and Tsvetaeva's) "obsession" is ultimately about poetic creation, with the vampire assuming the gender-bending role of a male muse to a female poet.[59] As Sibelan Forrester has pointed out, "the plot lets [Tsvetaeva] work out her own concern with the poet's devotion to a cause above and beyond a stereotypical female fate."[60] As frequently happens in the process of self-translation, the rewriting of the text takes on features of a self-commentary. The most extensive part of the Russian original omitted from the French version is an episode in the final chapter, where the nobleman engages in inquiries about the owner of the land and buildings that they pass on the way to church. In the French text, the sixty-six lines of this passage are replaced by just three:

> Choses tardent,
> Art abrège:
> Neige – barbe – barbe – neige . . . (117)

> Things are getting late,
> Art abridges:
> Snow – beard – beard – snow . . .

Read as a metacommentary on Tsvetaeva's own activity as self-translator, these words indicate that the retardation of the plot brought about by the original Russian episode now seems superfluous to her. She therefore takes the liberty to "abridge" the text in her capacity as the "artist" behind it, compressing the whole omitted episode into a minimalist, repetitious line.

An even more obvious intrusion of the author-translator into the text occurs in the description of the nobleman's palace at the beginning of chapter 2 of part 2:

> Qu'est-ce que ce monument
> Porté par douze géants?
> Barbaresque, surhumain,
> Déluge marmoréen?
>
> Rien qu'à le dire si haut
> Chevilles me font défaut.
> Malaise des cîmes
> (Connu à qui rime). (71)
>
> What is this monument
> Carried by twelve giants?
> Barbarian, superhuman,
> Deluge of marble?
>
> Just by naming it so high
> My ankles give in.
> Dizzy spell of the mountaintops
> (Known to those who rhyme).

Through her French translation, Tsvetaeva speaks here as a poet to fellow poets. Those "who rhyme" will be able to connect to the feeling of vertigo induced by her poetic creation. Significantly, no comparable wording exists in the Russian original. The feeling described here is entirely an effect of self-translation: it expresses the dizziness caused by the reencounter with one's own "monument" and the daunting task of having to write it again, anew, in a different language.

TSVETAEVA—A FRENCH POET MANQUÉ?

There is evidence that French became an increasingly dominant language for Tsvetaeva in the final decade of her life. Her notebooks from 1932–33 are almost entirely written in French.[61] Aside from the self-translation of *Mólodets*, she also experimented with writing poetry directly in French. Her notebooks contain the drafts of three French poems, which were composed around 1927, that is, two years before she translated *Mólodets*.[62] Written in a very different, much "smoother" style than *Le Gars*, these poems betray the influence of French symbolism in their attempt to create an atmosphere of refined musicality. They also show, incidentally, that Tsvetaeva was well acquainted with the technique of French syllabic versification.[63] The abundance of variants and the drawing up of columns with possible rhyme words testify to a serious effort, but Tsvetaeva did not produce a final version or make any effort to have these poems published.

If writing poetry directly in French remained a marginal activity, translating poetry into French took on a much greater significance during the final years of Tsvetaeva's life. In June 1936 she began to translate the poems of Pushkin, hoping that the upcoming centennial of his death in 1937 would provide her with opportunities for publishing her translations.[64] Aside from the pleasure of re-creating some of her favorite Russian poems in French, Tsvetaeva was also motivated by the desire to finally give the French public the "right" kind of translation of the Russian national poet. Pushkin had been translated into French before, but mainly into prose and free verse. By contrast, as Tsvetaeva asserted in a letter to Iurii Ivask, her version was written "in verses, of course, and *correct* verses" ("stikhami, konechno, i *pravil'nymi* stikhami"). [65] As with *Le Gars*, however, her efforts to publish her translations of Pushkin met with little success. Only three of them appeared during her lifetime.[66] The rest were published decades after her death. Thus far, a total of eleven poems by Pushkin in Tsvetaeva's translation have appeared in print.[67]

Tsvetaeva's translations of Lermontov all date from the final period of her life after her return to the Soviet Union in 1939. As with Pushkin, they were originally prompted by upcoming anniversaries. In August 1939, the Soviet French-language journal *Revue de Moscou* commissioned three translations on the occasion of Lermontov's 125th birthday in October. Two of them did appear in the October issue of that year, but without any credit given to Tsvetaeva as the translator. In April 1941, the year of the centennial of Lermontov's death (and the year of Tsvetaeva's own death), the journal *Internatsional'naia literatura* approached Tsvetaeva with a request for additional French translations of Lermontov. She did send them ten poems, of which the editors selected three, but publication was halted because of the German invasion of the Soviet Union. Like her other French-language poems, Tsvetaeva's Lermontov translations languished for decades in the Russian State Literature Archive. An incomplete version of ten poems by Lermontov in Tsvetaeva's translation appeared in France in 1986.[68] A complete bilingual edition, containing twelve poems as well as a facsimile reproduction of Tsvetaeva's drafts, came out in Moscow in 2014.[69]

Tsvetaeva's translations of Pushkin and Lermontov are more "faithful" than her self-translation of *Mólodets*. There are no large-scale deviations from the original such as added or left-out stanzas. At the same time, Tsvetaeva does take semantic liberties in an effort to preserve formal and structural features. This includes not only the rhyme scheme, but also, as in *Mólodets*, an attempt to reproduce the Russian meter within the system of syllabic French verse.[70] As far as the selection of poems is concerned, Tsvetaeva clearly gravitated toward texts that she identified with on a personal level. The result is a remarkable fusion of Pushkin's and Lermontov's poetics with her own. These are not "imitations" in the manner of Robert Lowell's free English renditions of Mandelstam or Pasternak. While Lowell was unscrupulous in transforming and appropriating the poets that he translated, Tsvetaeva respected the integrity of Pushkin and Lermontov, but she made them resonate with her own poetic voice.[71]

Many of the poems by Pushkin that Tsvetaeva selected for translation concern the theme of the poet, his art, and his fate. With Lermontov, whom she translated after her return to the Soviet Union, the predominant focus of the selection is a premonition of death. Clearly, Tsvetaeva understood this somber theme as a comment on her own situation. This can be seen in her rendition of Lermontov's famous 1841 poem "Vykhozhu odin ia na dorogu" ("Lonely I walk out unto the road"). Here is the third stanza in Lermontov's original and in Tsvetaeva's translation:

> Уж не жду от жизни ничего я,
> И не жаль мне прошлого ничуть;
> Я ищу свободы и покоя!
> Я б хотел забыться и заснуть!

> I am not expecting anything anymore from life,
> And I don't regret the past in any way;
> I seek freedom and rest!
> I would like to forget myself and fall asleep!

> Dans ce rude sein plus rien ne vibre,
> Rien — ni avenir, ni souvenir.
> Je voudrais finir tranquille et libre, —
> Ah! m'évanouir — mourir —dormir![72]

> In this rough breast nothing vibrates anymore,
> Nothing —neither future, nor memory.
> I would like to finish quiet and free—
> Ah! to faint —to die — to sleep!

As is frequently the case with Tsvetaeva, the translation takes the content of the original to a more extreme level while trying to preserve or amplify its aesthetic qualities. In the present example, we can point to the sonorous richness of the assonances "rude sein plus rien" and the profuse internal rhymes (avenir, souvenir, m'évanouir, mourir, dormir). At the same time, the idea of impending death emerges more clearly and categorically in French. The verb "to die" ("mourir") is directly named in the fourth line, and is anticipated with "finish" ("finir") in line 3. "To faint" ("m'évanouir") seems more ominous than the peaceful falling asleep evoked in Lermontov's poem. Rather than having no more expectations and no regrets, the speaker in Tsvetaeva's version is already internally dead, with no thoughts of the future and no memory of the past. This "nihilist" quality is expressed in the prominently repeated word "nothing" ("rien").

In the notebook where she copied Lermontov's poem together with the draft of the French translation, Tsvetaeva underlined the words "svobody" and "pokoia" ("freedom" and "rest") and wrote in the margins "NB! Ia!" ("Nota bene: I!").[73] Aside from this gloss, the autobiographical significance of the poem also becomes visible in Tsvetaeva's lexical choices. The word "sein" (breast), while theoretically applicable to both genders, usually refers to the female anatomy. "Ce rude sein," then, could point to Tsvetaeva's own aging body (the word "sein" is also repeated in the following stanza). Furthermore, the adjectives "tranquille" and "libre" are not marked for gender, which makes the speaker of the stanza potentially feminine. Lermontov's poem was written not long before the poet's death in 1841. In translating this text a hundred years later, shortly before her own suicide on August 31, 1941, Tsvetaeva not only engaged in a dialogue with a beloved poetic predecessor, she also made a poignant statement about herself.

Given her evident abilities in writing French verse, why did Tsvetaeva not compose more poems in French (or in German, for that matter, which she considered a language more suitable for poetry than even her native Russian)?[74] In her study of bilingual Russian writers of the First Emigration, Elizabeth Beaujour calls Tsvetaeva a "particularly interesting case: a poet who could have become a real bilingual—perhaps even a *trilingual*—writer, but who ultimately rejected bilingual practice although she did not believe that poetry was 'national.'" Beaujour adds that "Tsvetaeva's resistance to writing in French was ferocious and emotional."[75] This is certainly an overstatement. Tsvetaeva's decision to self-translate *Mólodets* into French may initially have been prompted by purely external and accidental circumstances rather than a desire to write in French, but she did get "carried away" while working on the project. Her French version of *Mólodets*, as well as her subsequent translations of Pushkin and Lermontov, show not only an unquestionable ability to write French poetry, but also an emotional engagement. Beaujour argues that the typical trajectory of bilingual writers usually goes through several stages, beginning with self-translation, and leading via a "major translation project" from the first into the second language (Nabokov's English version of *Eugene Onegin* being a prominent example) and then to balanced bilingual writing.[76] If we apply this scheme to Tsvetaeva's career, her translations of Pushkin's and Lermontov's poetry could be seen as fulfilling the function of the "major translation project" following the initial self-translation. What is missing, evidently, is the subsequent unfolding of a mature bilingual oeuvre.

According to Beaujour, what ultimately made Tsvetaeva cling to her Russian *Muttersprache* was her maternal instinct. While she may not have regarded Russian as her "mother tongue" in the spiritual sense of the word, "it was the language *in which she was a mother*; and, of all Tsvetaeva's passions, none was stronger than the maternal one."[77] In order to prevent her son from growing up as a Frenchman, she agreed to return with him to the motherland—with fatal consequences for all involved. Of course, with Tsvetaeva's life tragically cut short, we do not know what might have been. It is certainly remarkable that, even after her return to a Russian-speaking environment, Tsvetaeva still expended considerable efforts to translate Russian poetry into French. Michael Makin has even speculated that Tsvetaeva "was becoming increasingly unhappy with Russian as a poetic medium" and that her French oeuvre "expresses her alienation from her native tongue"[78]—an alienation that may hardly have been remedied by moving from her French exile to Stalin's Russia.

To characterize Tsvetaeva's French writings as a "failure," because she was allegedly unable to realize her creative designs outside her native tongue, strikes me as misguided.[79] Still, how can we explain Tsvetaeva's utter lack of success with the French reading public? Part of the problem was certainly her inability or unwillingness to fit into any recognizable pattern or tradition. To an audience accustomed to free verse and prose poetry, rhymed and metrical translations appeared freakish and artificial. Furthermore, a reader attuned to syllabic verse cannot be expected to appreciate the subtleties of syllabotonic prosody, which may come across as monotonous to a French ear.[80] The eminent émigré critic Vladimir Weidlé, who had a solid understanding of both Russian and French versification, described his reaction to Tsvetaeva's translations of Pushkin as follows: "Tsvetaeva unwittingly exchanged French with Russian metrics. For a Russian ear these translations are superb, but as soon as I mentally switched to the French system, I noticed myself that for the French they will not sound good."[81] Significantly, the few positive appreciations of Tsvetaeva's French translations all have come from Russian native speakers (or, in the case of Jean-Claude Lanne, from a French Slavist with a good command of Russian). The British-born scholar Robin Kemball, who undertook a detailed metrical analysis of Tsvetaeva's translations of Pushkin, demurred on the question of their quality, which he felt could be judged adequately only by a French native speaker (even though Kemball was a professor at the University of Lausanne and had an impeccable oral and written command of French).

Perhaps the secret for appreciating Tsvetaeva's French translations of Pushkin and Lermontov and her self-translation of *Mólodets* is that one has to read them together with the Russian originals. In other words, contrary to Kemball's opinion, the ideal reader and judge of Tsvetaeva's translations may not necessarily be a French native speaker, but someone familiar with both versions of the text. Whether such a person is a native speaker of French or Russian (or yet a third language) is less important than the ability to read and understand both linguistic incarnations of the poem. Only a bilingual receptor can fully appreciate Tsvetaeva's achievement. Perhaps it was this "stereoscopic" effect created by parallel texts in two different languages that made Tsvetaeva a fertile translator and self-translator, but impeded her writing of self-standing poetry in French. As we have seen, Tsvetaeva defined the essence of poetry as translation. It is not surprising, then, that she realized her ideal of transnational and translingual poetry first and foremost as a self-translator.

It is evident that Tsvetaeva had no intention of becoming a "French poet" (she explicitly rejected such mononational labels, as we have seen). Rather, her double self-portrait as Marusia/Maroussia in Russian and French illustrates a translingual metamorphosis evoked symbolically in the fairy-tale heroine's shape-shifting between woman and flower. By stepping out of her native idiom, Tsvetaeva came closer to her proclaimed ideal of being a universal poet outside the confines of a nationally or monolingually defined literature. At the same time, by retaining some key elements of Russian prosody such as syllabotonic verse and a discursively stated "Russianness," her French self-translation paradoxically reasserted her Russian roots. *Le Gars* thus exists in a hybrid transnational domain that cannot be associated unequivocally with either Russian or French poetry.

Whether an audience for such writing exists *in the real world* is a different question, of course. There is certainly something utopian about Tsvetaeva's maximalist bio-aesthetic agenda propelling her to crash through the boundaries of national belonging in the same way that she broke through all sexual, political, linguistic, and even grammatical barriers. Tsvetaeva's lack of recognition as a French-language poet may to a significant degree be explainable by the fact that she created for herself an ideal readership so attenuated as to be "not of this world."

Vladimir Nabokov's Dilemma of Self-Translation

VLADIMIR VLADIMIROVICH NABOKOV (1899–1977) is known as a master of Russian and English prose. The fact that he began his literary career as a poet and continued to write poetry throughout his life has received comparatively little attention.[1] Nabokov's poetic oeuvre, much of it unpublished, is in fact of gigantic dimensions. In the preface to his 1970 bilingual volume *Poems and Problems,* Nabokov claimed that the thirty-nine Russian poems collected in this book "represent only a small fraction—hardly more than one per cent—of the steady mass which I began to exude in my early youth."[2] Overall, somewhat more than 500 of his Russian poems have appeared in print. Nabokov's poetic oeuvre in English is much smaller in scope. Some of it was written during his student years at Cambridge, but the bulk of it belongs to Nabokov's American period, when he continued to write occasional poetry both in Russian and English.[3]

In addition to 23 published poems written directly in English, Nabokov self-translated 39 of his Russian poems. While the translations he made of his novels and memoirs have attracted a fair amount of critical attention, almost nothing, aside from a few cursory remarks, has been written about his self-translated poetry.[4] This neglect is all the more puzzling since these translations postdate his controversial edition of Alexander Pushkin's novel-in-verse *Eugene Onegin.* Nabokov made it quite clear that the literalist method of translation he championed in the preface to *Eugene Onegin* and other related publications did not only apply to his English rendition of Pushkin's verse, but was meant as a prescription for the translation of poetry *tout court.* One might wonder, then, to what extent Nabokov adhered to his literalist credo when it came to translating his own work.

A closer look at Nabokov's self-translated poetry reveals a rather inconsistent picture. Many of these translations deviate from his publicly proclaimed literalist doctrine by retaining vestiges of rhyme and meter. Clearly, translating his own poetry was different for Nabokov than translating Pushkin. "Killing" the original text and replacing it with a hypertrophied commentary, as he did with *Eugene Onegin*, was not a viable solution when his own work was at stake. Instead, he resorted to a somewhat haphazard approach, with the decision to reproduce or ignore the formal features of the original poem determined on a case-by-case basis. With their mixture of rhymed and unrhymed lines and with the presence or absence of meter, Nabokov's self-translated poems differ markedly from his originally composed poetry in Russian and English. They also differ from the translations he did of the work of other poets—not surprisingly, perhaps, if we maintain that the fidelity of the translator is primordial only when the translator is translating someone other than himself. By reaching a sort of compromise between his literalist theory and the method used in his earlier translations, where he closely adhered to form, Nabokov was tacitly stepping back from the extreme position that he had embraced in his *Onegin* writings when, relatively late in life, he began to self-translate his own poetry from Russian into English.

FROM "RIGID FIDELITY" TO "RUGGED FIDELITY"

The majority of Nabokov's poems in English (39 out of 62, to be exact) are self-translations of texts that he had originally written in Russian between 1917 and 1967. The English versions of these poems first appeared in the 1970 volume *Poems and Problems*. This rather strange book is a collection of 39 Russian poems with English self-translations *en face*, 14 poems that Nabokov wrote directly in English, and 18 chess problems (hence the title, *Poems and Problems*). The word "Problems" could also hint at the difficulties Nabokov faced in transposing his poetry from Russian into English. In his preface, Nabokov drew an explicit connection between his method of self-translation and the literalist theory he developed while preparing his English edition of *Eugene Onegin*, which had appeared six years earlier. As he put it:

> For the last ten years, I have been promoting, on every possible occasion, literality, i.e., rigid fidelity, in the translation of Russian verse. Treating a text in that way is an honest and delightful procedure, when the text is a recognized masterpiece, whose every detail must be faithfully rendered in English. But what about faithfully englishing one's own verse, written half a century or a quarter of a century ago? One has to fight a vague embarrassment; one cannot help squirming and wincing; one feels rather like a potentate swearing allegiance to his own self or a conscientious priest blessing his own bathwater. On the other hand, if one contemplates, for one wild moment, the possibility of paraphrasing and improving one's old verse, a horrid sense of falsification makes one scamper back and cling like a baby ape to rugged fidelity. (14)

Nabokov's remarks reveal the ambivalence and uneasiness that frequently accompany the process of self-translation. When translating his own novels and memoirs, Nabokov alternated between relative fidelity and creative rewriting. However, taking liberties in the rendition of verse is a risky procedure in Nabokov's theory of translation. It exposes the translator to charges of "paraphrase," a method defined and dismissed in the preface to *Eugene Onegin* as "offering a free version of the original, with omissions and additions prompted by the exigencies of form, the conventions attributed to the consumer, and the translator's ignorance."[5] According to Nabokov, when it comes to the translation of poetry, only the "literal method," which strives to preserve the "exact contextual meaning of the original," deserves to be called a "true translation."[6] Nabokov is nothing less than absolute in his condemnation of alternative approaches. As David Bethea put it, "the mere thought that anyone would consider the prosodic structure of the work as worthy of transposition drives him into a smoldering rage."[7]

One wonders, however, whether the "rigid fidelity" demanded for the translation of *Eugene Onegin* is really identical with the "rugged fidelity" that Nabokov applied in his self-translated poetry.[8] The shift from "rigid" to "rugged" seems to open the door to a certain flexibility. Nabokov's approach to rhyme offers a case in point. In discussing previous translations of *Eugene Onegin*, Nabokov categorically condemned "poetical versions," which he castigated for being "begrimed and beslimed by rhyme."[9] However, in the preface to *Poems and Problems*, he states that "whenever possible, I have welcomed rhyme, or its shadow." He goes on to qualify this statement by assuring the reader that he "never twisted the tail of a line for the sake of consonance; and the original measure has not been kept if readjustments of sense had to be made for its sake."[10] To be sure, the absolute primacy of sense over form had not always been Nabokov's credo—it constitutes a kind of conversion that he underwent in late middle age. Earlier in life he had no qualms about producing the kind of "poetical" translations that he later so vehemently attacked in others. By the time he published *Poems and Problems*, however, having proclaimed his literal approach to be the only legitimate way to translate poetic texts, Nabokov had no choice but to declare his allegiance to this method, since any other public stance probably would have opened him up to charges of inconsistency, if not hypocrisy.

Contemporary reviewers were aware of Nabokov's literalist theory of translation and blamed it in part for the shortcomings of his self-translated poems, which contributed to the lukewarm critical reception of *Poems and Problems*. Richmond Lattimore, the celebrated translator of Homer, noted in his review that Nabokov's insistence on "strict fidelity" led to various "oddities" such as inverted phrases or, in the poem "To Russia," a bumpy meter that feels like "driving on a flat."[11] It should be pointed out that the bumpiness criticized by Lattimore (who did not know Russian) is not the result of semantic, but of metrical fidelity, namely the decision to retain the original anapests in English. Konstantin Bazarov, a reviewer who did know Russian, opined that Nabokov's "translations often turn moving Russian poems into banal and embarrassing English ones" whose "obscurity can often only be clarified by reference to the original lucid Russian," thus implying that Nabokov's literal method not only did a disservice to Pushkin's poetry but to his own as well.[12] Echoing similar criticism voiced about the *Onegin* translation, reviewers complained about Nabokov's predilection for rare and obscure English vocabulary to render commonplace Russian expressions. For example, both Bazarov and John Skow, who reviewed *Poems and Problems* in *Time* magazine,[13] took Nabokov to task for translating the ordinary Russian noun "zhimolost'" (honeysuckle) in the opening poem of the volume with the incomprehensible word "caprifole."

Nabokov's framing of his self-translated poems steered the critical reception in a specific direction. Publishing the poems together with a collection of chess problems was an unusual decision and looked like an attempt to dazzle the public with a display of technical virtuosity in an arcane discipline accessible only to specialists. The inclusion of the Russian original poems must have had a similar effect—as something of an unfathomable riddle encoded in an illegible script—given that most readers of the book had no knowledge of this language. The spatial arrangement of the Russian and English versions *en face* presents the Russian poems as "problems," so to speak, to which the English translations offer the "solution." In his preface, Nabokov draws an explicit analogy between the creation of chess problems and poetry:

> Chess problems demand from the composer the same virtues that characterize all worthwhile art: originality, invention, conciseness, harmony, complexity, and splendid insincerity. The composing of those ivory-and-ebony riddles is a comparatively rare gift and an extravagantly sterile occupation; but then all art is inutile, and divinely so, if compared to a number of more popular human endeavors. (15)

Statements such as these could only reinforce the notion of Nabokov as an aloof formalist given to self-referential games, or, to quote Bazarov's review once more, a "player whose approach to writing is that of an intellectual puzzle-maker producing artifacts which are all clever construction and stylistic acrobatics, an aesthete trapping glittering bejewelled butterflies in his lepidopterist's net."[14] Surely, though, the referential function of language makes writing and translating poetry a more complex phenomenon than composing chess problems devoid of semantic content.

Let us come back to the question, then, of how faithful Nabokov remained to his self-proclaimed theory of translation when translating his own poetry. Rather than relying on Nabokov's comments about his own practices (which always have to be taken with a grain of salt), this question is best approached with a systematic survey of the thirty-nine self-translated poems in *Poems and Problems*. First of all, it has to be noted that there is no consistent, generally applicable method in Nabokov's self-translations. He uses a variety of approaches between individual poems and even within a single poem. Contrary to the principles outlined in Nabokov's *Onegin* writings, this can include the reproduction of the original meter and rhyme scheme. Overall, fourteen translations (36 percent of the total) show evidence of systematic rhyming, even though the rhyme scheme is not always completely realized— sometimes only the "b" rhyme is preserved in an "abab" stanza, and occasionally Nabokov resorts to slant rhymes and assonances instead of exact rhymes. Individual rhymed lines also occur in otherwise unrhymed translations.

The rendition of meter presents a similarly inconsistent picture. Twenty-five translations (64 percent of the total) show regular metric patterns. Sometimes the translation preserves the meter, but not the exact line length of the original, for example by replacing iambic hexameters with pentameters (a sensible solution, given the shorter average word length in English), or by using iambic lines of varying length. An effort to preserve the original meter is particularly visible in the poems "Vecher na pustyre"/ "Evening on a Vacant Lot" (68–69) and "Slava"/"Fame" (102–13), which are the only two known polymetric works in Nabokov's canon.[15] The English translation replicates the trajectory from trochees to iambs to anapests back to iambs in the first poem, and the switch from mixed ternaries to alternating anapestic tetrameter and trimeter in the second. A total of nine translations (23 percent) are metered *and* rhymed. It becomes evident, then, that Nabokov's translational practice in *Poems and Problems* deviates from the principles promulgated in his *Onegin* writings, which proscribe preserving formal features in translation aside from a vague adherence to Pushkin's iambic meter.

A more interesting question is whether the decision to reproduce or ignore the prosodic features of the original poem was a matter of randomness or whether there was a method to Nabokov's inconsistency. In his preface to *Poems and Problems*, Nabokov states that he welcomes rhyme (and presumably meter) in those instances when they can be realized without "readjustments of sense." This would suggest that the preservation of rhyme or meter is only permissible if it occurs more or less "naturally" as the by-product of a literal translation. In reality, though, the relative frequency of rhyme and meter in Nabokov's self-translations is far too high to be explained as a random effect. Clearly, it is evidence of a conscious effort. At the same time, there is no attempt, in most cases, to achieve a complete reproduction of the original's formal features. The result is a sort of halfway solution, a compromise, perhaps, between the conflicting goals of preserving semantics and form in translation. To be sure, such a compromise violates the absolute primacy of sense over form proclaimed in Nabokov's *Onegin* writings.

The footnotes appended to individual poems in *Poems and Problems* almost never address the issue of translation. The only exception is "K Rossii"/ "To Russia" (96–97), where Nabokov provides the following comment:

> The original, a streamlined, rapid mechanism, consists of regular three-foot anapests of the "panting" type, with alternating feminine-masculine rhymes. It was impossible to combine lilt and literality, except in some passages (only the third stanza gives a close imitation of the poem's form); and since the impetus of the original redeems its verbal vagueness, my faithful but bumpy version is not the success that a prosy cab might have been. (99)

As can be seen, Richmond Lattimore's disparagement of the "bumpy" anapests in this translation was lifted from Nabokov's own self-critical footnote. Nabokov does make an exception for the third stanza, however, which he singles out for successfully combining "lilt and literality." This stanza reads as follows in Russian and English:

> Навсегда я готов затаиться
> и без имени жить. Я готов,
> чтоб с тобой и во снах не сходиться,
> отказаться от всяческих снов;

> I'm prepared to lie hidden forever
> and to live without name. I'm prepared,
> lest we only in dreams come together,
> all conceivable dreams to foreswear;

The English translation is indeed quite close to the original both in semantics and form, reproducing not only the original anapestic trimeter, but also the syntax of the Russian source text. The "AbAb" rhyme scheme with its alternation of feminine and masculine endings is preserved as well, albeit with slight imperfections. However, as Nabokov correctly points out, this quatrain has no real equivalent elsewhere in the poem. The other six stanzas are also written in a three-beat ternary meter in English, but in at least one line of each stanza one or more syllables are missing from the anapestic scheme, making the meter more akin to a Russian *dolnik* than to an anapestic trimeter. Similarly, some rhymes are replaced by assonances or are

117

missing altogether, even though the alternation of feminine and masculine endings is carried through.

Presumably it was this lack of formal perfection that prompted Nabokov's musings that a "prosy cab" à la *Eugene Onegin* might have been a more successful English rendition of this poem. Are Nabokov's poetic self-translations a tacit admission and illustration of the theoretical impossibility of translating poetry, which, aside from an occasional "lucky break," can in practice only result in a half-baked muddling through? Why, then, one might wonder, did he not render his own poetry as a "prosy cab" in English?

"LOSS" AS "GAIN": NABOKOV'S USE OF STRATEGIC IMPERFECTIONS

While an element of sheer randomness or compromise cannot be ruled out, a closer study of Nabokov's self-translated poems reveals a more complex and interesting picture. In some cases, Nabokov uses the inevitable differences between the Russian original and the English translation and the formal irregularities of the English verse as a means to illustrate and reinforce the semantics of the original. Seen from this angle, the translation is not necessarily always an inferior, deficient copy of the source text, but a creative rewriting that can even be, in some respects, "richer" than the original Russian poem.

"Neokonchennyi chernovik"/"An Unfinished Draft" (66–67) offers a simple example of a poem where the English translation embodies the idea of the original more closely than the Russian source text. Written in Berlin in 1931, the poem launches an attack against opportunist "litterateurs" who are motivated by lust for gain and glory. By contrast, the speaker presents himself as someone who has weighed his "life and honor on Pushkin's scales, and dared to prefer honor." While the Russian poem ends with a rhymed couplet, the English version breaks off after the first word of the final line, thus creating a concrete, if rather obvious, visualization of the "unfinishedness" announced in the title of the poem. Significantly, the last word of the English text is "honor." By breaking off the poem at this exact moment, Nabokov highlights this concept more prominently in English than he does in Russian with the terminal rhyme "chest'"—"predpochest'" ("honor"—"to prefer").

A similar, more subtle self-referentiality occurs in the poem "Nepravil'nye iamby"/"Irregular Iambics" (144–45), a nature scene written 1953 in Ithaca, New York, which equates the leaves shaken by an impending thunderstorm with the "foliage of art." As Nabokov explains in a footnote, the irregularity alluded to in the title concerns the use of the word "esli" (if) in a "scudded" position. "Scud" (more commonly called a pyrrhic) is Nabokov's term for an unfulfilled stress at a place in the verse line where the metric scheme would call for a stressed syllable.[16] Three lines in the final quatrain of the Russian poem begin with the words "esli b ne." Since the word "esli" is accented on the first syllable, the iambic foot at the beginning of the line is inverted. Such an inversion is quite common both in Russian and English, but in Russian it is only permissible if the stressed position falls on a mono-syllabic word.[17] By using the disyllabic "esli" in such a position, Nabokov intentionally violates the conventions of Russian prosody. The English trans-lation of the poem opens with the line "For the last time, with leaves that flow." Since the stress in this sentence falls most naturally on the word "last," the iambic rhythm is disrupted with an inversion in the second foot. Iambic verse in English generally exhibits a wider range of rhythmic variation than that found in Russian, which makes it debatable whether such a line really qualifies as "irregular."[18] Nevertheless, it seems reasonable to speculate that Nabokov intended the opening verse of his English translation to illustrate the title "Irregular Iambics." Before criticizing Nabokov for his bumpy ver-sifying, then, one would do well to consider whether the seemingly clumsy English prosody is not at times an intentional strategy.

"Nepravil'nye iamby" contains other irregularities aside from the un-orthodox metrical use of the word "esli." In two instances, Nabokov rhymes masculine with dactylic endings, a modernist technique that was virtually unknown before the twentieth century. Even though the English version is not rhymed, Nabokov creates a vaguely analogous effect by placing the last stress sometimes on the final and sometimes on the penultimate syllable of the line. Finally, both the Russian and English versions contain abundant enjambments. In the Russian text, which is divided into three quatrains, they create a striking lack of syntactic breaks at the borders of the stanzas. The English version is printed as one continuous twelve-line stanza, which makes the enjambments run more organically, perhaps in order to illustrate the "flow" mentioned at the beginning of the poem. The English layout of the text thus creates an analogy between the thunderstorm evoked in the poem and the stream of words on the page.

The examples provided so far may reinforce the impression of Nabokov as a master of clever, but ultimately sterile formal games. We should not for-get, though, that Nabokov's self-proclaimed goal in translating poetry was the preservation of "sense." The manipulation of form merely serves an auxiliary function in this endeavor. Nabokov's self-translated poems present multiple examples where the seeming technical irregularities or flaws of the English translation follow the semantic or narrative content of the Russian original.

The English version can not only become more self-referential than the Russian original with regard to formal criteria, it can also serve as a meta-commentary on Nabokov's own situation as a self-translator. The poem "My s toboiu tak verili"/"We So Firmly Believed" (88–89), written in Paris in 1938, expresses the alienation of Nabokov's current self from his younger persona, who now seems an entirely different person. This alienation, one assumes, became even more pronounced when Nabokov translated the poem into English thirty years later. The English version, unlike the Russian original, illustrates the idea of non-continuity in its very form. In the opening line of the poem, the translation faithfully replicates the anapestic tetrameter of the Russian original ("We so firmly believed in the linkage of life" corresponds to "My s toboiu tak verili v sviaz' bytiia"), but already in the second line ("but now I've looked back—and it is astonishing"), the meter of the English text falls apart in mid-line. It is never recovered in the rest of the poem, except, in a somewhat weaker form, in line 9 ("You've long ceased to be I. You're an outline—the hero"). The disappearing anapest illustrates on a formal level the illusionary nature of the presumed "linkage of life," that is, the idea that a person's identity survives intact through the flux of time. The Russian version keeps the anapestic meter throughout the poem and thus displays a constancy that is belied by the poem's content. Moreover, in keeping with the absence of "linkage," the English translation, unlike the Russian original, remains unrhymed. It is true that "linkage of life" has an alliteration absent in the Russian, but, significantly, this phonic "linkage" occurs in the opening line of the poem, which is written in flawless anapests. In the context of self-translation, this poem thus acquires an additional poignancy as a commentary on the situation of the aging Nabokov translating the work of his younger self and discovering in the process that he has become a different person than the author of the original poem, which makes the attempted "linkage" with the past a tenuous undertaking.

The strategic use of the presence or absence of rhymes, as well as a metafictional awareness of Nabokov's situation as self-translator, can also be found in the long "Parizhskaia poema"/"The Paris Poem" (114–25). The lines "and I'm flying at last—and 'dissolving' / has no rhyme in my new paradise" become self-referential in the English translation. The word "dissolving" is paired with "straying" in a weak assonance, while in the Russian original "taiushchikh" forms a perfect dactylic rhyme with "plutaiushchikh." At best, one could argue that the words "dissolving" and "paradise" create a sort of "eye-rhyme" in the English text.[19] Later in the same poem, when talking about "this life, rich in patterns," Nabokov inserts a passage that, especially when read in English, sounds like another metafictional gloss on his attempt to recapture the meaning and form of his previously written Russian text:

> no better joy would I choose than to fold
> its magnificent carpet in such a fashion
> as to make the design of today coincide
> with the past, with a former pattern (123)

By replacing the full rhymes of the original with assonances in which only the final consonant carries over, the English translation illustrates the difficulty of achieving the desired coincidence between the "former pattern" and the "design of today." In the Russian text, the word "pattern" ("uzor") rhymes perfectly with the word for "carpet" ("kover"). While recapturing the pattern of the former life seems still possible in the Russian poem, recapturing this recapturing in English proves to be highly problematic. The poverty of rhymes in this particular place is all the more conspicuous because the rhyme scheme is to a large extent preserved in the rest of this 136-line poem. Nabokov draws additional attention to this fact by segmenting the English version into quatrains, which are absent in the print layout of the Russian original.

An even more intriguing game with rhymes is played in the rather risqué poem "Lilith" (50–55), which anticipates the *Lolita* plot by several decades.[20] The poem describes in explicit detail the sexual encounter of the speaker with an alluring underage woman. In the original Russian, all 62 lines are rhymed. In English, rhyme is only used sparingly, with a total of 14 rhyming lines, or a few more if we include half-rhymes such as "wind"— "in," or "eye"—"trice." The English rhymes are not distributed randomly, however—they predominate in the middle of the poem, which is devoted to the consummation of the relationship. This event is conveyed in three consecutive "abcb" rhyming sequences. Before the speaker can come to a climax, the girl withdraws, leaving him, frustratingly, "at half the distance / to rapture." It is at this exact moment of coitus interruptus that the rhymes disappear from the English version. Only one more full rhyming pair appears later in the poem, tellingly linking "lust" with "dust." In English, the penetration scene also stands out metrically because it is written in consistent iambic tetrameters, as opposed to a mixture of tetrameter and pentameter elsewhere in the poem, thus underlining the rhythmic intensity and regularity of the speaker's thrusting movements. The Russian version, using rhymed tetrameters throughout the poem, provides no such differentiating effect.

Two poems in the collection *Poems and Problems*, "K muze"/"To the Muse" (56–57) and "Tikhii shum"/"Soft Sound" (58–61), deserve particular attention because of the self-reflective light they shed on Nabokov's own poetic evolution and on his status as a Russian-language poet writing in English. "K muze" was written in Berlin in 1929. Nabokov identified it in the preface to the collection *Stikhotvoreniia: 1929–1951* as a pivotal work in his poetic development, marking the end of his youthful art.[21] The six stanzas of the poem draw up a sharp contrast between the past and the present. The first three stanzas describe the speaker's youthful infatuation with the Muse, an enchanting female who appears to him on a moonlit balcony. This encounter results in lyrics that are said to be smiling with "red-lipped rhymes."

The self-parodying nature of these clichéd images is reinforced with a subtle literary allusion: "Ia schastliv byl" ("I was happy") in line 9 echoes Antonio Salieri's monologue in Pushkin's *Mozart and Salieri*. The second half of the poem presents the aging speaker at the present time. He has now become "experienced, frugal, and intolerant," worries about ambition, produces "polished verse" that is "cleaner than copper," and talks with the Muse only on rare occasions "across the fence, like old neighbors." One suspects that the transition discussed here concerns not only the evolution of Nabokov's poetry from youthful effusion to the "robust" style of his mature years, but also the larger shift from poetry to narrative prose.

The English translation of the poem follows the Russian original relatively closely, as the example of the two opening stanzas will demonstrate:

> Я помню твой приход: растущий звон,
> волнение, неведомое миру.
> Луна сквозь ветки тронула балкон,
> и пала тень, похожая на лиру.
>
> Мне, юному, для неги плеч твоих
> казался ямб одеждой слишком грубой.
> Но был певуч неправильный мой стих
> и улыбался рифмой красногубой.

> Your coming I recall: a growing vibrance,
> an agitation to the world unknown.
> The moon through branches touched the balcony
> and there a shadow, lyriform, was thrown.
>
> To me, a youth, the iamb seemed a garb
> too rude for the soft languor of your shoulders;
> but my imperfect line had tunefulness
> and with the red lips of its rhyme it smiled.

The inverted syntax, which does not always reflect the actual word order of the Russian original, and the use of the passive voice in the first stanza convey to the English version a certain stiffness. In terms of form, the translation preserves the iambic pentameter of the original and, at least in the first stanza, reproduces the "b" rhyme of the Russian quatrain. This, however, turns out to be a deceptive maneuver calculated to create false expectations similar to the beginning of "We So Firmly Believed." Even though the English version, just like the Russian original, is segmented into quatrains, at the end of the second stanza the reader's anticipation of another rhyme is frustrated: "Smiled" does not rhyme with "shoulders." At best, it hints at the missing rhyme with the repeated letters "s," "l," and "d." This effect is all the more surprising, or ironic, since the absence of an expected rhyme occurs at the precise moment where the poem brings up the phenomenon of rhyme.[22] It is as if the poet, rather than living up to the promise of a rhymed ending created by the previous stanza, and teasingly alluded to in the assonance of "rhyme" and "smiled," instead decided to provide a retroactive illustration of an "imperfect line."[23] Clearly, the English translation engages in a formal self-parody that has no equivalent in the Russian original. In this connection, one wonders whether the word "lyriform," seemingly another example of Nabokov's eccentric predilection for obscure or nonexistent English vocabulary, was not prompted by the same strategy of exposing the implied author of the poem as a pretentious blunderer.

In the remaining four stanzas of the English translation, rhyme disappears. The verse remains a consistent iambic pentameter—with one notable exception. The crucial lines 17 and 18 ("Ia opyten, ia skup i neterpim. / Natertyi stikh blistaet chishche medi") are translated as "I am expert, frugal, intolerant. / My polished verse cleaner than copper shines." The first of these lines is devoid of any discernible metrical structure in English. Had it been Nabokov's intention to reproduce the iambics of the Russian original, the line could easily have been "fixed" with an elision and word-for-word translation ("I'm expert, frugal and intolerant"). Surely, the lack of a metrical structure here cannot be caused by Nabokov's difficulty in writing iambic verse in English, but must be the result of a deliberate decision. His design seems to illustrate the prosaic qualities evoked in the passage by switching to actual prose. Even by the more flexible standards of English prosody, "I am expert, frugal, intolerant" cannot possibly be read as an iambic line.[24] The second line also makes a clumsy impression in English, with its unnatural syntax and the word "cleaner" awkwardly protruding from the iambic scheme. As in the first stanza, the syntax cannot be explained as an effect of literalism. The unnatural word order of placing the verb in final position is not dictated by the structure of the original, but seems to be chosen for its own sake. As a result, the "polished verse" alluded to in the poem turns out to be not all that polished. One could add that while the phrase "polished verse" has a positive connotation in English, the Russian "natertyi stikh" seems more unusual. The word "natertyi" is more likely to appear in connection with a floor than with verse, and to a Russian speaker it sounds similar to "zatertyi" (trite, shopworn).[25] The Russian expression has thus perhaps a slightly negative or ironic tone, which Nabokov manages to convey in English by making the line (and its predecessor) purposefully "unpolished."

This discrepancy between content and form, that is, the evocation of formal perfection through an imperfect line that undercuts its own stated meaning, could be read as another subtle metacommentary. The enumeration of simple objects in the final quatrain of the poem—"leaf of grape-vine, pear, watermelon halved"—indicating, in Paul Morris's interpretation, Nabokov's "heightened interest in the phenomenal specificity of the world and experience,"[26] amounts to a programmatic statement about his goals as an artist. His novelistic work comes closer to his mature artistic credo than his poetry ever did. The inadequacy of the English translation per-haps reflects the inadequacy of poetry to capture Nabokov's ultimate artistic ideal. This insight may have become clearer to him when he self-translated "K muze" many years after the poem's original composition, and when narra-tive prose, rather than poetry, had become his preferred genre.

The experience of loss associated with the impossibility of creating a perfect self-translation can serve as an emblem of Nabokov's own exilic condition. The unfathomable quality of the sound of his native language be-comes the topic of the poem "Tikhii shum"/"Soft Sound," written in 1926, which follows immediately after "To the Muse" in *Poems and Problems*. The speaker, presumably vacationing in a French coastal town, listens to the nightly roar of the sea. As in "To the Muse," this poem is divided into two symmetrical halves. While the first four quatrains evoke the romantic com-munion of man and sea in rather traditional terms, the sound of the sea turns in the second half of the poem into a mysterious evocation of his native land. When the noise of the day recedes in the silence of the night, the speaker begins to hear a "soft sound" containing shades of dear voices, the singing of Pushkin's verse, and the murmur of familiar pine woods. Pushkin's poem "K moriu" ("To the Sea," 1824) is of particular relevance here with its link-ing of the sound of the sea with the theme of exile. The "softness" of the sound also creates a thematic connection with Nabokov's own 1941 poem "Softest of Tongues," which is not included in *Poems and Problems*. In this poem, Nabokov laments the necessity of giving up his native idiom and being forced to "start anew with clumsy tools of stone."[27] The absence of this poem from *Poems and Problems* is interesting in itself—was it a moment of self-protection?

As Paul Morris has pointed out, Nabokov's original Russian poem, "Tikhii shum," which is replete with conspicuous alliteration and assonance, creates an "arrangement of whispering sibilants" calculated to "mimic the sound of the sea and to communicate the quiet though relentless intensity of the poet's experience."[28] It goes without saying that the English translation can only provide a faint echo of this sonorous quality. "Shum moria, dyshash-chii na sushu" becomes "the sound of seawaves breathing upon land," with the English "s"-alliteration a poor substitute for the rich sound texture of the Russian original. One can imagine that the feeling of loss and alienation expressed in the poem became even more poignant when Nabokov was con-fronted with the task of translating it into an idiom that had little in common with the beloved "soft sound" of his native language.

The English version is also sonorously poorer because of the absence of rhymes. The original is written in aBaB quatrains, as was "K muze." The translation retains only one pair of rhymes in the fifth stanza. The Russian iambic tetrameter is replaced in English with iambic lines of varying length. As in "To the Muse," some of them are of questionable regularity. Once again, however, the distribution of "smooth" and "bumpy" lines is not random, but follows the semantic logic of the poem. Following a romantic cliché,[29] Nabokov sets up a strong dichotomy between "day," characterized by the distracting noises of hustle and bustle, and "night," when the stillness allows for the perception of the roaring sea and the unfathomable sound of waves emanating from the Russian past. The passages pertaining to the diurnal world tend to be metrically "unruly," as demonstrated by the third stanza:

> Daylong the murmur of the sea is muted,
> but the unbidden day now passes
> (tinkling as does an empty
> tumbler on a glass shelf);

The jarring enjambment separating adjective and noun ("empty / tumbler") also occurs in Russian ("pustoi / stakan"), but the onomatopoetic effect created by the alliteration of "tinkling" and "tumbler," disrupting the iambic scheme with a stressed syllable at the beginning of the line, is unique to the English text. By contrast, the nocturnal world is rendered in evenly flowing iambic lines, as shown by the stanza where the lost Russian past makes its mysterious appearance. The sequence of feminine rhymes, which appear at the end of the even lines and also internally in line 4 ("reverberation"—"respiration"—"pulsation"), conveys a sense of melodious "Russianness" to the stanza (even though they may not strike a native speaker of English as particularly felicitous):

> Not the sea's sound . . . In the still night
> I hear a different reverberation:
> the soft sound of my native land,
> her respiration and pulsation.

Yet the apparition of the native land remains fleeting. In the subsequent stanzas, the diurnal world with its noise returns. As a result, the rhythm begins to lose its regularity and turns "unruly" again:

> Repose and happiness are there,
> a blessing upon exile;
> yet the soft sound cannot be heard by day
> drowned by the scurrying and rattling.

The stresses at the beginning of the last two lines, announcing the return of the diurnal noise, replicate the rhythm of the earlier "tinkling" and "tumbler," which now leads to a similar cacophony of "scurrying and rattling."

In the final stanza, the poem returns once more to the nocturnal apparition of the homeland:

> But in the compensating night,
> in sleepless silence, one keeps listening
> to one's own country, to her murmuring,
> her deathless deep.

In the Russian original, the stanza has a changed rhyme scheme (aBBa instead of aBaB). The English translation gestures towards the BB rhymes with "listening" and "murmuring." It also introduces alliterations that are absent in the Russian original ("sleepless silence," "deathless deep"). The s-alliteration of "sleepless silence" echoes the earlier "sound of seawaves" as well as the "Soft Sound" of the poem's English title. The word "compensating" in the first line seems a rather strange choice (the Russian simply says "v polnochnoi tishine" ["in the silence of midnight"]). Perhaps it provides another metacommentary on the status of the English text: a translation can compensate for the inevitable loss of some of the original's features by adding features that are unique to the target text, such as the alliterations present in English and absent in Russian.

It should be emphasized once more that the effects discussed here occur *only in the English translation*. The originals in *Poems and Problems*, like most of Nabokov's Russian poetry, are written for the most part in a formally conservative style. Nabokov was not much given to modernist experimentation, possibly because he associated such an approach with left-wing politics. At most, he engaged in unconventional verse forms in an intentional parody, as he did, for example, in the poem "O praviteliakh"/"On Rulers" (128–33), which is written in the form of a Mayakovsky pastiche. Most of Nabokov's poetic oeuvre in Russian, following the example of his beloved nineteenth-century classics, resorts to conventional meters, rhymes, and stanza forms, with a strong predilection for iambic tetrameter, exact rhymes, and AbAb quatrains. The poems that he originally wrote in English also gravitate toward conventional forms, with some occasional, but moderate use of slant rhymes and unusual stanzas.[30] Formal experimentation is very rare in Nabokov's original poetry. One of the few exceptions, discussed by Barry Scherr, occurs in the poem "Vecher na pustyre"/"Evening on a Vacant Lot" (68–73), where Nabokov resorts to approximate and heterosyllabic rhymes to highlight his agitated state while looking back on his youth and the death of his father. Scherr notes that "such occasional departures from nineteenth-century norms in poetry are all the more striking for standing out against the background of [Nabokov's] generally traditional versification."[31]

Gerald Smith has come to a similar conclusion in his comprehensive formal analysis of Nabokov's Russian poetry, where he notes that "Nabokov viewed departure from exactitude as a specific device, to be used to mark certain particular texts, rather than as a generally available formal resource which it became in Russian poetry during his time."[32] In Nabokov's original poetry this strategic "departure from exactitude" remains very infrequent, and it mostly pertains to rhyme. The more radical stratagem of using a deliberately clumsy, broken, or disappearing meter is nowhere to be found in his original Russian or English work—it can only be observed in his self-translated poetry.[33]

THE QUANDARY OF SELF-TRANSLATION

How can we explain the discrepancies between Nabokov's originally composed poems and his self-translated ones? Possibly, he felt that he had "nothing to lose" when he translated his own work, given the impossibility of reproducing the same poem in a different language. The perceived hopelessness of the task may have given him a particular kind of experimental freedom. Julia Trubikhina, in her monograph on Nabokov and translation, argues that "pessimistic would be a mild way" to describe Nabokov's attitude toward translatability.[34] His literalist version of *Eugene Onegin* is not just a utilitarian crib—it is ultimately meant to illustrate the impossibility of translating Pushkin, or any other poet. The translator assumes here—to quote Douglas Robinson—the role of an "angry, disgusted parent, using the T[arget] L[anguage] text to castigate the receptor for not having read the text in the original."[35] In a strange displacement, rather than the deliberately "ugly" translation, it is the hypertrophied commentary, with "footnotes reaching up like skyscrapers to the top of this or that page,"[36] that attempts to replicate the digressive charm, wit, and metafictional self-irony of Pushkin's original.[37]

This is not the solution that Nabokov adopted in *Poems and Problems*. Theoretically, following the model of the novel *Pale Fire*, he could have become his own Kinbote by making his poetry the object of a monumental (pseudo-)scholarly apparatus. Although Nabokov does resort to footnotes in *Poems and Problems*, some of them flippant, ironic, and digressive, they are infinitely more modest in scope than the gargantuan commentaries in *Eugene Onegin* and *Pale Fire*. It was not a viable option for Nabokov to treat his own oeuvre in the same manner as he did Pushkin's. Although he never suffered from false modesty, framing his own poetry as a sacrosanct classic of world literature would have smacked of narcissism or megalomania, to say the least.[38] The strategy of what Trubikhina calls an "allegorical" approach to translation, in which "the violence done to the original by the process of translation is sublated by acknowledging the limitation of language and producing an allegorical model, the Other, the Commentary,"[39] was not available to Nabokov when it came to the translation of his own poetry. Given his pessimism regarding the possibility of translating poetic texts, he was thus left in a dire predicament.

Nabokov tends to comment on translation with metaphors of violence and desecration. His programmatic 1955 poem "On Translating *Eugene Onegin*," which he included in *Poems and Problems*, opens with the memorable image of the "poet's pale and glaring head" offered by the translator on a platter (175). If translating is tantamount to murdering the author of the original text, does this mean that self-translation becomes for Nabokov a form of self-mutilation, or self-beheading? The remarks he made about the translation of his own prose fiction indeed display a sense of physical violence and self-inflicted pain. In the 1930s Nabokov complained that translating his own work was like "sorting through one's own innards and then trying them on for size like a pair of gloves."[40] Nevertheless, it would be problematic to conclude that Nabokov treated self-translation as symbolic suicide. Precisely because he dealt with his own work, "killing" the original text in translation, as he did with Pushkin's *Eugene Onegin*, was not desirable when it came to the translation of his own poetry. This may explain why Nabokov refrained from eradicating "the last vestiges of bourgeois poesy and concession to rhythm" from his own self-translated poetry as radically as he claims he did with *Eugene Onegin*.[41] Some of the English versions in *Poems and Problems* even look like a throwback to the old days when Nabokov still produced "poetical" translations. A perfect example can be found in the poem "Provans"/"Provence" (26–27), where the English translation faithfully replicates the meter and rhyme scheme of the Russian original. Not coincidentally, this poem describes a moment of unmitigated harmony and happiness, a sentiment otherwise rarely encountered in *Poems and Problems*. The speaker expresses his "bliss to be a Russian poet" in a Mediterranean landscape brimming with picturesque life and singing. Perhaps Nabokov felt that a traditionally rhymed equimetrical translation was the most adequate way to express the somewhat conventional and stereotypical character of the original Russian poem.

The prevalent emotional experience related in *Poems and Problems* is not one of happiness and bliss, but rather of anxiety, tedium, loss, and exilic alienation. One could argue, then, that the lack of conventional "poeticity" in the translation illustrates the original's "sense" more aptly than the deliberate ugliness of Nabokov's *Onegin*. The few conventionally rendered "beautiful" moments in *Poems and Problems* stand out all the more starkly against a background of prosaic drabness.[42] The ruined landscape of the English translation serves as a memento of the lost paradise of the original Russian poems with their rich euphony and elegant formal polish. The best that the English translation can do, in Nabokov's pessimistic view, is to hint at the loss a reader inevitably experiences when an adulterated, coarse simulacrum takes the place of the unrecoverable splendid original.

POEMS WRITTEN BY FICTIONAL CHARACTERS

A consideration of Nabokov's poetic self-translations would not be complete without taking into account, if only briefly, the poems written by his fictional characters. Nabokov took it upon himself to personally translate the poetry contained in his novels and stories even if the translation of the book was entrusted to an extraneous translator. His practice in rendering these fictional poems deviates even more strongly from his literalist principles than do the self-translated texts in *Poems and Problems*. For the most part, the poems in his narrative fiction keep the original meter and rhyme scheme in translation even at the cost of significant semantic reshuffling and alterations.

The only major exception occurs in the first chapter of the novel *Dar (The Gift)*, where the poems of the protagonist Fyodor Godunov-Cherdyntsev are given in an English prose rendition (although printed with line breaks). Joseph Schlegel, in an article devoted to Andrei Bely's impact on Nabokov's poetics, has analyzed the form of Godunov-Cherdyntsev's poems cited in *Dar*. Using Bely's method of plotting the graphic patterns resulting from skipped stresses, which had a huge impact on Nabokov's own understanding of prosody, Schlegel shows that these poems display an unusually high level of rhythmical richness.[43] Perhaps Nabokov felt that trying to reproduce the same effect in English would have been futile or too cumbersome. This is not to say that it was impossible: when Godunov-Cherdyntsev creates a poem that is deliberately designed to produce a particular diagrammed shape, Nabokov's English translation retains not only the meter and rhyme scheme, but also the distribution of stresses in each line. Starting with the final poem in chapter 1, the poetic texts quoted in the novel, whether by Godunov-Cherdyntsev or other poets, are rendered in an equimetrical rhymed translation. The same is true for all the other occasional poetry encountered in Nabokov's fiction.

This principle of formal fidelity also applies to Nabokov's English-to-Russian translation of *Lolita*. The most extensive inserted poem in that novel is Humbert Humbert's thirteen-stanza paean to the female heroine. Here are stanzas 3 and 4 in the English original and the Russian self-translation:

Where are you riding, Dolores Haze?
What make is the magic carpet?
Is a Cream Cougar the present craze?
And where are you parked, my car pet?

Who is your hero, Dolores Haze?
Still one of those blue-caped star-men?
Oh the balmy days and the palmy bays,
And the cars, and the bars, my Carmen!

Где разъезжаешь, Долорес Гейз?
Твой волшебный ковер какой марки?
Кагуар ли кремовый в моде здесь?
Ты в каком запаркована парке?

Кто твой герой, Долорес Гейз?
Супермен в голубой пелерине?
О, дальний мираж, о, пальмовый пляж!
О, Кармен в роскошной машине![44]

A literal English translation of the Russian translation would look as follows:

Where are you traveling, Dolores Haze?
What make is your magic carpet?
Is a cream-colored Cougar fashionable here?
In which park are you parked?

Who is your hero, Dolores Haze?
Superman in a blue cape?
O, distant mirage, o, palmy beach!
O, Carmen in a luxury car!

The Russian translation replicates the ternary rhythm and the aBaB rhyme scheme of the original. The only exception is the line ending on "pliazh," where the internal rhyme with "mirazh" takes precedence over the rhyme with "Geiz" (Cyrillic for "Haze"). Nabokov spends great efforts in re-creating the rather outré sound effects of Humbert Humbert's poem. The almost comically melodious "balmy days—palmy bays" becomes an equally sonorous "dal'nyi mirazh—pal'movyi pliazh" in the Russian translation. While Nabokov's Russian version of the poem can certainly be enjoyed in its own right, it nevertheless falls short of the American original both with regard to sound instrumentation and the use of punning rhymes. Dissecting "carpet" into "car pet" and extracting the words "car" and "men" from the name "Carmen" reveals a foreigner's defamiliarizing glance at the English language.

As we can see, there is a vast discrepancy between Nabokov's approach to translating the poems in *Poems and Problems* and those contained in his narrative prose. What explains this difference? There are cases where Nabokov had little choice but to reproduce the meter and rhyme of his fictional poems, of course. This is true for the typographically unmarked pieces of poetry "smuggled" into the prose fabric of *Dar*, such as Godunov-Cherdyntsev's love poem to Zina in chapter 3 or the Onegin stanza hidden in the novel's final paragraph. A translation without meter and rhyme would have made these poems indistinguishable from their prosaic surroundings.[45] One wonders, though, why the work of a mediocre poet like Humbert Humbert receives the courtesy of a full-fledged "poetical" translation that is refused to Pushkin, or, for that matter, to Sirin (aka Vladimir Nabokov). The answer, probably, lies precisely in Humbert's mediocrity. When it comes to the rendering of middling poets, fictional or real (we might also include here the poetic oeuvre of Nikolai Chernyshevsky quoted in *Dar*), a "paraphrase" exhibiting the otherwise derided qualities of "bourgeois poesy" might be what is called for in Nabokov's theory. In other words, the effectiveness of a "poetical translation" seems to stand in inverse proportion to the poetic quality of the original text. The divergent approach in translation shows that Nabokov saw an essential difference between the poems that he published under his own name (or the pen name Sirin) and those that he attributed to his fictional characters. Unsurprisingly, he located himself closer to Pushkin than to Humbert Humbert on the scale of poetic greatness.

"OTSEBYATINA" AND THE DISCONTENTS OF BILINGUAL WRITING

Clearly, translating his own poems presented a different challenge to Nabokov than translating the work of other poets, whether they be real or fictional. Notwithstanding his claim that writing poetry is similar to composing chess problems, many of Nabokov's poems are of an intensely personal nature, which made self-translation inevitably a dialogue with his own former self. As a result, the principles of fidelity proclaimed in his *Onegin* writings became problematic. How can one be "faithful" to one's former self, if, as Nabokov himself points out in the poem "We So Firmly Believed," the immovable nature of the self across time is an illusion? It is very possible that looking at his old verse made him uncomfortable because he felt it needed improvement. However, because, according to his own theory, any improvement or paraphrase would amount to falsification, he had to fall back on "fidelity" if he wanted to remain consistent with his self-proclaimed ideal.

In reality, Nabokov had largely abandoned the principles embraced in his *Onegin* writings when he translated his own poetry in the late 1960s. Nevertheless, he remained insistent that he had not wavered in his allegiance to literalism, and he never retracted his polemical attacks against formal poetic translation. As a shorthand for his disdain for such practices, he resorted to the term "otsebyatina," a pejorative used by Russian translation critics to denounce gratuitous insertions and alterations inflicted on a text by the translator. In his 1964 article "Pounding the Clavichord," Nabokov translated the word "otsebyatina" into English as "come-from-oneselfer" or "from-oneselfity" and defined it as "the personal contributions of self-sufficient or desperate translators (or actors who have forgotten their speeches)."[46] While meant as a club to hit Nabokov's rivals in the "englishing" of *Eugene Onegin*, the notion of "otsebyatina" takes on rather peculiar overtones in the context of self-translation. One could argue that a "self-sufficient or desperate translator" is in fact a pretty apt characterization of Nabokov's own role in *Poems and Problems*, given that self-translation inevitably involves a form of "otsebyatina."

In considering Nabokov's career as a bilingual poet and self-translator, we are left with a paradox, which can be put into sharper focus if we compare his theory and practice of translation with that of Marina Tsvetaeva discussed in the previous chapter. Nabokov's English rendition of his own poems differs fundamentally from Tsvetaeva's French self-translation of *Mólodets*, even though there are some obvious biographical parallels between the two poets. They were roughly the same age (Nabokov was born seven years after Tsvetaeva), and both grew up trilingually in Russia before being forced into exile after the Bolshevik Revolution. However, while Tsvetaeva is considered to be a monolingual Russian poet, Nabokov is celebrated for having successfully crossed the linguistic boundary. In their theoretical pronouncements, as we have seen, the two poets took diametrically opposed positions. Tsvetaeva embraced poetic creation outside the mother tongue and asserted a belief in the fundamental translatability of poetry, while Nabokov, even though he is considered a paragon of bilingual virtuosity, expressed skepticism on both of these accounts. His apprehension about writing outside the native tongue is captured in his well-known lament, in the afterword to the American edition of *Lolita*, of having to abandon his "untrammeled, rich, and infinitely docile Russian language for a second-rate brand of English."[47] Moreover, Nabokov exhibited a radical skepticism about the translatability of poetry. His literalist version of *Eugene Onegin* is ultimately meant to demonstrate the impossibility of translating Pushkin. Not surprisingly, then, poetic self-translation becomes for Nabokov a form of self-torture.

The differences between Nabokov's conflicted self-translations in *Poems and Problems* and Tsvetaeva's virtuoso performance in *Le Gars* stem not only from a discrepancy in poetic talent. The two had very different styles, of course. As a Russian poet, Nabokov was a post-symbolist attached to classic forms. He was also in his bones a "pictorial" and visual image-oriented poet who cared about finding the "mot juste" or exact phrasing in the poetic line, rather than creating a sense of sweeping musicality. Unlike Tsvetaeva, he did not feel the "choric" movement of the poetic line or stanza. Nabokov's translational efforts were also hemmed in by his theoretical rigidity and his pessimism about bridging the linguistic gap in poetic creation. His belief in the impossibility of translating poetry, which hardened with his long labor over *Eugene Onegin*, seems to have turned in *Poems and Problems* into a self-fulfilling prophecy, even though he couldn't resist the temptation to deviate from his own literalist credo by smuggling vestiges of poetic form into the English text.[48]

Nabokov's skepticism about bilingual creation does not mean that he was unable to write compelling poetry in English, of course. Nabokov's biographer Brian Boyd even argues that "English poetry has few things better to offer than 'Pale Fire.'"[49] Perhaps the most remarkable English poem in *Poems and Problems* is not a self-translation, but a text written directly in English. "An Evening of Russian Poetry," composed in 1945 in a semi-comical style that seems to mimic a lecture by Nabokov's own Professor Pnin, offers a reflection on Russian poetry and the difficulty or impossibility of capturing its form and spirit in English. Nabokov's English-language evocation of the shapes and sounds of his native language and his lost Russian past acquire here an elegiac and wistful tone:

> Beyond the seas where I have lost a scepter,
> I hear the neighing of my dappled nouns,
> soft participles coming down the steps,
> treading on leaves, trailing their rustling gowns,
> and liquid verbs in *ahla* and in *ili*,
> Aeonian grottoes, nights in the Altai,
> black pools of sound with "l's" for water lilies.
> The empty glass I touched is tinkling still,
> but now 'tis covered by a hand and dies. (159–60)

In a sort of "meta-self-translation," Nabokov addresses the unbridgeable gap between Russian and English while at the same partially overcoming it by imbuing the English lines with the lilting sounds of Russian past-tense endings. For a tantalizing moment, in a sort of spiritist performance, the two languages seems to fuse into one, rendering the "problem" of translation redundant, before the speaker himself brings the seance to an abrupt and willful halt.

Joseph Brodsky in English

IOSIF ALEKSANDROVICH BRODSKII (1940–1996), better known in English as Joseph Brodsky, was the most visible and successful Russian literary immigrant to the United States after Vladimir Nabokov. As the winner of the 1987 Nobel Prize for Literature and the American poet laureate in 1991, Brodsky gained more official recognition than any other Russian-American writer before or since (even though, unlike Nabokov, his writings did not make him a wealthy man). Nabokov and Brodsky have a superficial outward similarity. Both were Russian-born bilingual authors who were given to strong opinions. Both insisted that literary creation was a cerebral rather than an emotional activity, and both rejected "smooth," domesticating translations. Forced into exile from their country of birth, they created a poetic oeuvre in Russian and English of comparable proportions, with the native tongue predominating by an approximately ten-fold margin over the poetry written in the second language.[1] Last but not least, both Nabokov and Brodsky engaged in poetic self-translation. Brodsky translated fifty-three of his Russian poems into English on his own, in addition to collaborating with extraneous translators on many more texts.[2]

In spite of these parallels, there are more differences than similarities between Nabokov's and Brodsky's bilingual trajectories and reputations. Nabokov's status as a major English-language novelist is firmly established, while his poetry, Russian or English, has received little attention and is generally considered of secondary importance. Most critics agree that Nabokov's talent as a prose writer surpassed his poetic gift.[3] Matters stand differently for Brodsky, who was a poet first and foremost. He did receive high praise for his English-language essays (the collection *Less Than One* won the National Book Critics Award in 1986), but the reception of his English-language poetry has been mixed at best. Given that for most American readers, Brodsky's Russian poems are only accessible in translation, and in view of the active role that Brodsky took in shaping the English renditions of his Russian poetic oeuvre, the quality of his self-translations has become a source of considerable controversy and acrimony. Brodsky's decision as a non-native speaker of

English to take the translation of his poems into his own hands, or—perhaps even worse—to edit and "correct" the work of prominent Anglophone poets who had agreed to translate his work—was bound to raise eyebrows. How could an immigrant who spoke English with a thick foreign accent dare to lecture experienced American-born and British-born poets about the finer points of English verse? To many critics, such behavior seemed, at best, presumptuous, and at worst, self-destructive in terms of Brodsky's reputation. Some of the premises on which this criticism is based, in particular Brodsky's alleged insecure grasp of the English language, are open to challenge. In reality, Brodsky's command of English was more solid than what his accent suggested, or what his critics were willing to give him credit for. A consideration of Brodsky's self-translations has to begin with an assessment of his relationship with the English language.

BRODSKY AND THE ENGLISH LANGUAGE

Not everyone holding forth on Brodsky's English skills, or lack thereof, is aware of the unusual circumstances under which he acquired this language. The genesis of Brodsky's bilingualism differed markedly from that of Nabokov, or any other of the poets discussed thus far. Brodsky was essentially a self-made bilingual. Unlike Nabokov, he did not benefit from an aristocratic multilingual upbringing. He grew up in Leningrad as a "normal" monolingual Soviet child. Even though he was ethnically Jewish, there was no exposure to Yiddish or Hebrew, given the Stalinist erasure of Jewish cultural memory after World War II. Brodsky's Baltic-born mother knew German, but did not pass the language on to her son. The English-language instruction that he received in school was of subpar quality and thoroughly uninspiring. According to Brodsky's own account, the reading material consisted of "the standard propaganda garbage translated into English . . . A biography of Stalin, a memoir of some party faithful meeting, Lenin in his Finnish hideout."[4] Brodsky's aversion to English class was so strong that he came close to being kept back in fourth grade because of his poor grades in that subject. He quit school voluntarily at age fifteen. From then on, his education was entirely autodidactic. The first foreign language that he taught himself was Polish, which allowed him to read Western literature in Polish translation that was otherwise unavailable in the Soviet Union. Polish was followed by English— possibly under the influence of Anna Akhmatova, who had become Brodsky's mentor.[5]

A key moment in Brodsky's appropriation of English was his discovery of John Donne and other poets of the English metaphysical school during his exile in Norenskaia, the small village near the Arctic Circle where he had been banished on charges of "social parasitism." Equipped with only a bilingual dictionary, Brodsky proceeded to translate Donne's poetry into Russian. Donne exerted a considerable influence on the development of Brodsky's own Russian-language poetry, not only in terms of themes, imagery, and poetic technique, but even rhythm and prosody.[6] In addition to Donne, Brodsky studied and translated a number of twentieth-century English and American poets, in particular W. H. Auden, who became an important inspiration (and, after Brodsky's emigration in 1972, a personal friend).

There was inevitably a huge gap between Brodsky's passive and active knowledge of English, at least as long as he remained in the Soviet Union, where the opportunities for speaking the language were extremely limited. Clarence Brown reports that when he heard Brodsky recite an English poem by George Herbert during a visit to Leningrad in 1966, he thought that Brodsky was speaking Lithuanian.[7] Even later, when he had achieved fluency in English, Brodsky still retained a very noticeable foreign accent. The peculiarities of his pronunciation and intonation could easily obscure the fact that Brodsky, while clearly not a native speaker of the language, had an intimate familiarity with English poetry that surpassed by far the knowledge of an educated British or American native speaker. He was able to recite hundreds of lines of English poetry by heart. We should not forget Brodsky's Anglophile leanings that preceded his actual residence in an English-speaking environment. Motivated by literary and poetic considerations rather than biographical happenstance, Brodsky's appropriation of the English language was essentially a labor of love.

Brodsky contrasted his attitude to the English language with that of Nabokov in several interviews. In conversation with David Bethea, he claimed that for Nabokov the change from Russian to English was "easy," since, "like any civilized person, he felt at home in several languages, two or three." Brodsky saw himself as a different kind of bilingual: "For me, the English language means nostalgia for world order. And for him English was simply one of his languages. . . . When looked at more closely, I have a pretty sentimental attitude toward the English language. That's the whole difference."[8] He elaborated on this thought in an interview with an Estonian newspaper in 1995 a few months before his death:

> For Nabokov, English was practically a native language, he spoke it since his childhood. But for me English is my personal position. It gives me pleasure to write in English. An additional pleasure comes from a feeling of incongruity: inasmuch as I was not born to know this language, but the exact opposite, not to know it.
>
> Moreover, I think that I began to write in English for a different reason than Nabokov—simply out of delight with this language. If I were confronted

with a choice—to use only one language, Russian or English—I would simply lose my mind.[9]

Clearly, Brodsky came to see his existence in two linguistic spheres as a gain rather than a curse. Writing in English was more than a pragmatic decision prompted by the exigencies of living in an Anglophone environment—it fulfilled a genuine creative need. Having two languages at his disposal became an existential and psychological necessity that he was unwilling to part with. In conversation with Solomon Volkov, Brodsky described his bilingualism as "a remarkable situation psychically, because you're sitting on top of a mountain and looking down both slopes. . . . You see both slopes, and this is an absolutely special sensation. Were a miracle to occur and I were to return to Russia permanently, I would be extremely nervous at not having the option of using more than one language."[10]

There is evidence that Brodsky had already experimented with writing English verse at a time when his active command of the language was still extremely limited. A letter from his Arctic exile written in 1965 contains a semi-serious rhymed English quatrain:

> My window is
> immoral kiss
> of white
> twilighte[11]

Aside from the shaky spelling (perhaps influenced by seventeenth-century usage?), the rhyme "is"/"kiss" betrays a Russian accent, which occasionally persists also in Brodsky's later and more confident English verse. Four years later, that is, still long before his emigration, Brodsky translated a poem by his friend Vladimir Ufliand into English. It shows that even then he envisioned his translational activity between English and Russian as potentially a two-way street.[12]

Brodsky's first serious attempts at writing poetry in English were prompted by the death of two Anglophone poets who had become personal friends. His elegy in commemoration of W. H. Auden, written in October 1973, that is, only a year and a half after his emigration, appeared in the *New York Review of Books* in December 1974 and was later included in a 1975 volume of tributes to Auden edited by Stephen Spender. If we are to believe Brodsky, Auden was the reason why he began to write in English in the first place. In his 1983 essay "To Please a Shadow," he writes:

When a writer resorts to a language other than his mother tongue, he does so either out of necessity, like Conrad, or because of burning ambition, like

Nabokov, or for the sake of greater estrangement, like Beckett. Belonging to a different league, in the summer of 1977, in New York, after living in this country for five years, I purchased in a small typewriter shop on Sixth Avenue a portable "Lettera 22" and set out to write (essays, translations, occasionally a poem) in English for a reason that had very little to do with the above. My sole purpose then, as it is now, was to find myself in closer proximity to the man whom I considered the greatest mind of the 20th Century: Wystan Hugh Auden.[13]

Brodsky's statement, while no doubt heartfelt, probably needs to be taken with a grain of salt. In any event, his elegy for Auden is a rather weak poem that has not been reprinted in the later editions of his poetry. Brodsky himself later expressed regret for allowing its publication in the first place.[14] Four years later, however, Brodsky composed another elegy for an Anglophone poet, Robert Lowell, which first appeared in *The New Yorker* in October 1977. This poem, the first one in English to be collected in a book, shows a greatly improved command of English verse writing, evoking Lowell's Boston and New England "with remarkable economy and vividness," as David Bethea has noted.[15] For the sake of illustration, here is the first stanza:

> In the autumnal blue
> of your church-hooded New
> England, the porcupine
> sharpens its golden needles
> against Bostonian bricks
> to a point of needless
> blinding shine.[16]

The stanza displays some of the trademark features of Brodsky's poetic style, such as the daring enjambment "New / England," as well as ingenious rhyming. One wonders whether the unusual rhyme "needles"—"needless," which depends as much on graphic as on sound, would have occurred to an English native speaker. Possibly it betrays the fresh perspective of someone who is looking at the language from the outside.

The elegy for Robert Lowell clearly shows Brodsky to be a capable English-language poet. Nevertheless, when questioned by interviewers in the late 1970s, he denied that he had any ambition to write serious poetry in English. Here is how he answered a question (in Russian) by John Glad, who wanted to know whether Brodsky wanted to become a bilingual poet:

You know, no. This ambition I do not have at all, although I am perfectly capable of writing entirely decent poems in English. But for me, when I write verses in English, this is rather a game, chess, if you want, putting bricks together. But I frequently realize that the psychological, emotional-acoustic processes are identical. The same mechanisms are mobilized that are active when I compose verses in Russian. But to become a Nabokov or a Joseph Conrad, such ambitions I do not have at all. Even though I imagine that this would be completely possible for me, I simply don't have the time, energy, or narcissism for this. However, I fully admit that someone in my place could be one and the other, i.e., write poems in English and in Russian.[17]

Brodsky's answer is strangely coy and self-contradictory. Almost every sentence begins with a hedging word—"no" (but), "khotia" (even though), "odnako" (however). Essentially, Brodsky seems to be saying that, even though he has no plans to become a bilingual poet, there would be no real impediment for him to be a great poet in more than one language. The only thing that stops him is his alleged lack of ambition, or his unwillingness to become another Nabokov (which, as far as Brodsky is concerned, is not a flattering comparison). Writing poetry in English looks at first sight like a mere "game" devoid of serious artistic value. However, at second sight it turns out to be not all that different from writing poetry in the native language after all. It is not surprising, then, that Brodsky began to write poems in English on a more and more regular basis. As Eugenia Kelbert has pointed out, "while Brodsky only published one original English poem in the 1970s, fifteen were published in the 80s and this number almost doubled (28) in the short half-decade before the poet's death in 1996. These numbers speak for themselves: clearly, Brodsky's English career, cut short at the age of fifty-five, was only just unfolding."[18]

BRODSKY'S EVOLUTION AS A SELF-TRANSLATOR

It is important to keep in mind that Brodsky's "English career" did not only consist of poems originally composed in English. A large number of his English poems are self-translations of texts originally written in Russian. This raises a number of questions: Are these translations part of Brodsky's larger corpus of English-language poetry, or do they belong to a category of their own?[19] Is there a difference, stylistic or otherwise, between the self-translations and the poems written directly in English? Should the translations be viewed as inferior simulacra of the Russian source texts, or as English poems in their own right, which ought to be appreciated independently of their original Russian incarnations?

The history of Brodsky's poetry in English translation evolves along the lines of a steadily increasing intrusion of the author into the translational process. While Brodsky originally had no role at all in shaping the English versions of his Russian poetry, at the end he took complete control and responsibility. The first edition of Brodsky's poetry in English came out in 1967 without any involvement by Brodsky.[20] He did have a more active role in George Kline's translation of his *Selected Poems* published in 1973, even though he still resided in the Soviet Union. Essentially, Brodsky answered various queries by the translator, which were delivered to him via hand-carried messages. Given his still limited knowledge of English, he did not presume to interfere in the poetic shape of the translated text. In particular, Kline's imperfect preservation of rhymes did not seem to bother Brodsky at that time. In a note to Kline he declared himself to be "highly delighted" by the translation, adding "To hell with the rhymes, if it works out this way."[21]

This "hands off" attitude changed considerably after Brodsky moved to the United States. The next collection of his poetry in English, *A Part of Speech*, was published by Farrar, Straus and Giroux in 1980. The roster of translators, in addition to Kline, included such illustrious names as Richard Wilbur, Anthony Hecht, and Derek Walcott, among others. Brodsky appended the following note to the book:

> I would like to thank each of my translators for his long hours of work in rendering my poems into English. I have taken the liberty of reworking some of the translations to bring them closer to the original, though perhaps at the expense of their smoothness. I am doubly grateful to the translators for their indulgence.[22]

In reality, the translators were not as indulgent as Brodsky's comment suggests. His intervention in the translational process resulted in a number of bruised egos. The translators, some of them prominent English-language poets, resented Brodsky's interference in a domain in which they felt they possessed more competence than he did. Brodsky's insistence on the exact preservation of meter and rhyme in translation seemed to them exaggerated and misguided. They also objected to Brodsky's cavalier attitude of treating what they considered polished poetic translations as mere drafts that could be altered, rewritten, or discarded at will by the original author.[23]

Brodsky, for his part, did not hide his apprehensions about the quality of the translational work done by his Anglophone peers. In an interview with Grace Cavalieri in 1991, he described his reaction to reading the English translations of his poetry as a mixture of pleasure and horror: "On one hand you're terribly pleased that something you've done will interest the English. The initial sentiment is the pleasure. As you start to read it turns very quickly into horror and it's a tremendously interesting mixture of those two sentiments."[24] Interestingly, Brodsky claimed that his displeasure with the English translations of his poetry stemmed not so much from the fact that they were inadequate renditions of his poems, but from a general concern with the quality of their English language. As he stated to Sven Birkerts in 1979:

> The thing that bothers me about many of those translations is that they are not very good English. It may have to do with the fact that my affair with the English language is fairly fresh, fairly new, and therefore perhaps I'm subject to some extra sensitivity. So what bothers me is not so much that the line of mine is bad—what bothers me is the bad line in English.[25]

Coming from an immigrant who was faulted by native speakers of English for his imperfect or unidiomatic command of their language, such a statement was cheeky, to say the least. But Brodsky clearly did not mind being provocative and ruffling feathers. His displeasure with the translations done by extraneous translators, and probably also the fatigue induced by the need for constant haggling with them, eventually prompted Brodsky to take matters into his own hands. He suggested, semi-facetiously, that he became his own translator so that he could himself take the blame for the deficiencies of the translation:

> One thing I can say is that the reason I translate myself is simply . . . it's not because of vanity or enthusiasm for my own work. Quite the contrary. It's simply because very often it quickly develops into a great deal of bad rub, especially if the man is older than yourself. Whereas, you can correct the translator, you change the poem once, twice, three times, a fourth time. People would say, it's lousy English, but in the original it's great. In order to avoid that association, I decided to do it myself, so I could be blamed. I would take the responsibility. I would rather reproach myself than what some other gentleman would say.[26]

This semi-jocular statement raises two points that are crucial for Brodsky's understanding of translation: the necessity of constant, multiple revision, and the need to look at the translation as a poem in its own right rather than as the imperfect copy of an elusive original.

Brodsky did end up assuming total responsibility and control over the English versions of his poetry. In his collections *To Urania* (1988) and *So Forth* (1996), the majority of translations—20 in the first and 31 in the second book—are executed by himself without any external collaborator. Even when he was not the sole translator, he remained firmly in charge of the translational process. A note informs the reader that all extraneous translations in *To Urania* were "commissioned and revised by the author." The note to *So Forth* suggests an even stronger involvement on Brodsky's part:

"Translations, where not made by the author, were commissioned by him and executed under his direction."[27] It looks as if Brodsky, when he retained an extraneous translator at all, preferred not to rely on the "big name" poets of his earlier collection, but on people who were more pliable to his own wishes.

While Brodsky could be quite ruthless and dictatorial in his dealings with translators of his work, he was not completely unreasonable. In some instances he was willing to listen to the advice of English native speakers. George Kline reports that in "infrequent cases . . . Brodsky made unacceptable suggestions for revision because he misunderstood an English word" or because he mistakenly "assumed that certain kinds of Russian word-order, in particular inversions, will work in English."[28] In those instances Brodsky usually backed down and deferred to Kline's judgment. The same holds true for questions of prosody—Brodsky accepted, for example, Kline's contention that "here" and "near" cannot be treated as two-syllable words.[29] Overall, Kline remained diplomatic in describing his collaborative relation with Brodsky, which he summarizes as follows:

> Working closely with a Russian poet who has a deep and subtle, even if fallible, command of one's own language—the language into which one is struggling, with that poet's help, to transpose his work—is a unique experience, always stimulating, sometimes illuminating, occasionally humbling or frustrating.[30]

Other translators who collaborated with Brodsky were less reticent than Kline in expressing their frustration with the poet's interference in their work. Daniel Weissbort writes that "the main problem . . . was that Brodsky found it hard, or impossible, to accept his translator's notion of what was tolerable in English. He was constantly, it seemed to me, trying as it were to transform English into Russian, to colonize English and oblige it to do things I did not believe it could do."[31]

Did Brodsky's interference in his translators' work enhance or damage the quality of their translations? In order to arrive at a conclusive judgment about this issue, one would need to compare their initial versions with Brodsky's revisions. Making use of the Brodsky papers at Yale's Beinecke Library, Zakhar Ishov has done just that by painstakingly collating the multiple drafts of George Kline's translation of the poem "A Second Christmas by the Shore" with Brodsky's suggested emendations. The textual evidence supports Ishov's claim that Brodsky's intervention resulted in an improved translation. Ishov shows that Brodsky's version, as opposed to Kline's original drafts, matches the original more closely in both content and form while also resulting in a more compelling English poetic text.[32] Daniel Weissbort arrived at a similar conclusion with regard to Brodsky's substantial reworking of his translation of the sequence "A Part of Speech." This is worth noting, given that originally Weissbort had been so piqued by Brodsky's dismissive treatment of what he considered a polished translation that he asked to have his name withdrawn from the published version, for which he wanted to assume no responsibility as co-translator. Yet, when revisiting the text after Brodsky's death, Weissbort conceded that "with all its imperfections" Brodsky's version was still "patently superior" to his own. He now admitted that Brodsky, after all, may have been "right about translation."[33] What precisely, then, was Brodsky "right" about?

BRODSKY'S THEORY OF TRANSLATION

Brodsky's insistence on preserving meter and rhyme, while a common feature of English-to-Russian verse translation, went very much against the grain of prevalent contemporary practices in the United States. This attitude put him on a collision course with established American translators of Russian poetry. As early as 1973, long before he engaged in his own self-translational project, Brodsky had begun to attack the American translation industry. In reviewing the work of English-language translators of Russian poetry, he did not hold back in castigating what he perceived as a fundamental abdication of the aesthetic, and even ethical, task of the translator. Here is how he commented on Stanley Kunitz's translation of Anna Akhmatova's poems:

> . . . in order to translate, one must . . . have some conception of not only the author's complex of ideas, his education, and the details of his personal biography, but also his etiquette, or better the etiquette of the poetry in which the poet worked . . .
>
> . . . Then there will be no temptation to omit some things, emphasize others, use free verse where the original is in sestets, etc. That is, the translator must have not only the technical but also the spiritual experience of the original. . . . In translation, some loss is inevitable. But a great deal can be preserved too. One can preserve the meter, one can preserve the rhymes (no matter how difficult this may seem each time), one can and must preserve the meaning. Not one of these things, but all together. Images exist, and one must follow them—and not propound fashionable theories in the introductions.[34]

Brodsky took an even sharper tone in his review of the translations of Osip Mandelstam's poetry by W. S. Merwin, Burton Raffel, and David McDuff, which he characterized as "the product of profound moral and cultural ignorance" resulting in translations that "bear the imprint of self-assured, insufferable stylistic provincialism." As he elaborated:

Translation is a search for an equivalent, not for a substitute. Mandelstam is a formal poet in the highest sense of the word. For him a poem began with a sound, with a "sonorous molded shape of form," as he himself called it. Logically, a translator should begin his work with a search for at least a metrical equivalent to the original form . . . A poem is a result of a certain necessity: it is inevitable, so is its form. . . . Form too is noble . . . It is the vessel in which meaning is cast; they sanctify each other reciprocally—it is an association of soul and body. Break the vessel, and the liquid will leak out.[35]

It is interesting to contrast Brodsky's approach to that of Nabokov, who could be equally uncompromising in his attack against American translators of Russian poetry. Both Nabokov and Brodsky were absolutists, and both shared a common contempt for what they called "smooth" translations. At the same time, Brodsky's formal absolutism is the polar opposite of the semantic absolutism that Nabokov propagated in his later years. In his preface to *Eugene Onegin*, Nabokov writes:

In transposing *Eugene Onegin* from Pushkin's Russian into my English I have sacrificed to completeness of meaning every formal element including the iambic rhythm, whenever its retention hindered fidelity. To my ideal of literalism I sacrificed everything (elegance, euphony, clarity, good taste, modern usage, and even grammar) that the dainty mimic prizes higher than truth.[36]

This stubborn "in-your-face" attitude, presenting the translation as a challenge to the philistine tastes and prejudices of the presumptive audience, also characterized Brodsky's approach to translation. Like Nabokov, he was not willing to make any concessions to public preferences and established practice in his pursuit of what he considered the only legitimate and "true" translation method. Valentina Polukhina's description of Brodsky's (self-) translational approach as a series of stunning "sacrifices" in the service of a stubbornly pursued ideal sounds rather similar to Nabokov's declaration, as long as we substitute form for semantics. As Polukhina put it: "He was willing to sacrifice rhetorical figures to rhyme, syntax to prosody—everything, including meaning, to form. And he did."[37]

Of all the poets discussed thus far, Brodsky's method of self-translation comes closest to that of Marina Tsvetaeva. This is probably no accident: Brodsky considered Tsvetaeva the greatest poet of the twentieth century, not only in Russian, but in any language.[38] Neither Tsvetaeva nor Brodsky had any patience for free verse in the translation of formal poetry. As Tsvetaeva did in her French version of *Mólodets*, Brodsky was willing to introduce significant semantic alterations in his self-translated poems for the sake of preserving the formal energy of the original text. Moreover, both Tsvetaeva and

Brodsky were ready to violate the norms of the target language when it suited their purpose, creating a "Russified" version of French and English that left some of their readers baffled or indignant.

Many of Brodsky's self-translations are a tour de force seemingly designed to prove the presupposition that formal equivalence between Russian and English is an achievable goal. Rather than picking "easy" texts, he gravitated toward poems that presented a particular formal challenge. Thus, the first poem that he translated on his own in 1980, "December in Florence," is written in triple-rhymed tercets, a feature preserved in the English version.[39] The poem "Portrait of Tragedy," first published in 1996, presents an even greater tour de force, featuring twelve stanzas with AAAABBB rhymes.[40] The English text maintains not only the rhyme scheme of the Russian original, it even preserves the feminine nature of all the rhymes, a feat not easily achieved in English. A listing of the rhyming words in the English translation of the poem demonstrates Brodsky's verbal creativity (words in italics designate the lexemes that also rhyme in the Russian text):

Stanza 1: "*creases*-rhesus-rises-wheezes," "lately-lazy-lady"
Stanza 2: "senseless-lenses-else's-pretenses," "heroes-eras-chorus"
Stanza 3: "gnashes-flashes-ashes-blushes," "*surprise us*-devices-crisis"
Stanza 4: "*Gorgon*-golden-burden-broaden," "fashion-ashen-crush on"
Stanza 5: "ardor-under-fodder-founder," "cartridge-courage-garbage"
Stanza 6: "feces-faces-save this-laces," "cheer up, *cherub*, stirrup"
Stanza 7: "hidden-heathen-mitten-smitten," "decent-distant-*instant*"
Stanza 8: "statues-much as-catch is-matchless," "martyrs-starters-tatters"
Stanza 9: "evening-beginning-being-grieving," "vowels-bowels-ovals"
Stanza 10: "gargle-ogle-ogre-goggle," "of us-sofas-surface"
Stanza 11: "stir it-Spirit-serried-buried," "badly-buggy-ugly"
Stanza 12: "torrent-warrant-weren't-worried," "oven-cloven-open"

Aside from occasional slant rhymes, the consistent "femininity" of the rhyming is produced more than once by means of compounds. Such rhymes have a tendency to sound comical in English, although several compound rhymes also occur in the Russian original, with similar implications. The scansion of "weren't" as a two-syllable word possibly betrays the peculiarities of Brodsky's oral performance in English. The potentially comic implication of the compound rhymes is not necessarily a distraction here—they serve to underline Brodsky's tragicomic representation of tragedy as a grotesque female character. In terms of phonetics, some of the English rhymes manage to reproduce the hissing sound characteristic of the Russian original ("creases-rhesus-rises-wheezes" corresponds to "morshchiny-muzhchiny-chertovshchiny-prichiny"). The reproduction of form in translation, especially such a challenging one as a stanza consisting of quadruple and triple feminine rhymes, necessitates inevitable semantic shifts. Natalia Rulyova, in her detailed comparison of the Russian and English versions of the poem, has observed that the autobiographical references to Brodsky's Soviet past are toned down in English, where tragedy is represented in more abstract than historically concrete terms and the irremediability of tragedy is less pronounced than in the Russian original.[41]

FROM "OCTOBER SONG" TO "OCTOBER TUNE"

How did Brodsky's emigration to the United States affect his attitude towards his earlier poetry? In order to explore this question, I propose to analyze Brodsky's self-translation of the brief poem "Oktiabr'skaia pesnia" ("October Song"). Written in 1971, the year before Brodsky left the Soviet Union, "October Song" evokes an evening spent with a female companion in a house by the seaside. The atmosphere moves from an initial mood of lifeless stasis— evoked by the "objective correlative" of a stuffed quail on a mantelpiece, the chirring of an old clock, and the depiction of a morose nature scene in late fall—toward a sort of domestic idyll. The speaker's request to the female addressee to put aside her book does not, as one might expect, lead to an erotic scene (Dante's line "that day we read no further" comes to mind) but to housewifely needlework, with the female character mending the speaker's linen. The poem ends on a note of romantic sublimity with the evocation of the female character's radiant golden hair illuminating the dark room. While the seascape setting, gloomy weather, and references to time and inanimate objects are trademark features of Brodsky, the poem is uncharacteristically simple and straightforward—there are no daring enjambments, virtuoso rhymes, or other rhetorical fireworks.

Октябрьская песня

Чучело перепелки
стоит на каминной полке.
Старые часы, правильно стрекоча,
радуют ввечеру смятые перепонки.
Дерево за окном — пасмурная свеча.

Море четвертый день глухо гудит у дамбы.
Отложи свою книгу, возьми иглу;
штопай мое белье, не зажигая лампы:
от золота волос
светло в углу.[42]

A literal English translation of the poem would look as follows:

> October Song
>
> A stuffed quail
> Stands on the mantelpiece.
> The old clock, regularly chirring,
> Pleases in the evening the crumpled membranes.
> The tree behind the window is a dull candle.
>
> The sea for the fourth day roars hollowly at the dike.
> Put your book aside, take the needle,
> Mend my linen without lighting the lamps:
> from the gold of the hair
> it is bright in the corner.

Brodsky's English translation of the poem was first published in *The New Yorker* on October 5, 1987, under the title "October Tune:"

> October Tune
>
> A stuffed quail
> on the mantelpiece minds its tail.
> The regular chirr of the old clock's healing
> in the twilight the rumpled helix.
> Through the window, birch candles fail.
>
> For the fourth day the sea hits the dike with its hard horizon.
> Put aside the book, take your sewing kit;
> patch my clothes without turning the light on;
> golden hair
> keeps the corner lit.[43]

As in all of his self-translations, Brodsky tries to preserve as much as possible of the original form. In the case of "Oktiabr'skaia pesnia" this is more easily achieved with the meter than with the rhymes. The two five-line stanzas are written in a relatively loose *dolnik* with generally increasing lines in the first stanza and progressively decreasing ones in the second stanza. This feature is highlighted by the graphic arrangement of the English text, which presents the lines centered rather than flush left. Given that English words have fewer syllables on average than Russian words, the English lines tend to be generally shorter.[44] There is one significant exception, however: line 6 stands out by being longer in English than in Russian. "More chetvertyi den' glukho gudit u damby" ("The sea for the fourth day roars hollowly at the dike") becomes "For the fourth day the sea hits the dike with its hard horizon." We can clearly see that the increased line length in English is the result of semantic expansion.

The re-creation of rhymes was a major priority for Brodsky when he translated his poems. In the case of "Oktiabr'kaia pesnia," the Russian AAbAb CdCEd scheme is slightly altered in the English version, and Brodsky also replaces feminine with masculine endings and vice versa, producing the scheme aaBBa CdCed. One peculiar feature that carries over from Russian to English is the fact that line 9, evoking the adressee's golden hair, does not rhyme with anything. Making the line stand out in this way underlines a semantic point: just as the golden hair of the female companion is able to illuminate the room on its own without any other source of light, the word "hair" does not need a rhyming partner in order to "shine" in the text. In consequence, both the Russian and the English versions feature the same lexeme in this (non-)rhyming position.

Aside from the identical word at the end of line 9, only one other lexeme in rhyming position is the same in Russian and English: "perepelki"/"quail" in line 1. In addition, the rhyme words "iglu" (needle) and "sewing kit" (line 7), "lampy" (lamps) and "light on" (line 8), and "v uglu" (in the corner) and "keeps the corner lit" (line 10) have a similar effect. Overall, though, Brodsky engages in considerable semantic adjustments in his pursuit of English rhymes. How much do they alter the poem? The first two lines look like a rather forced attempt to introduce a rhyme at any price. "Chuchelo perepelki / stoit na kaminnoi polke" ("A stuffed quail / stands on the mantelpiece") becomes "A stuffed quail / on the mantelpiece minds its tail." Purely for the sake of rhyme, it seems, the English version ascribes agency to what is presented as a lifeless object in the Russian original. Other English rhyming solutions are more ingenious. In lines 3 and 4, "healing" rhymes with "helix." These words more or less convey the semantic information given in the Russian text, where the chirring of the old clock is said to be pleasing to the speaker's "crumpled membranes." To be sure, "helix" focuses on a different part of the human ear than the Russian "membrane," but both images refer to the auditory sense. While "healing" is more explicit than the Russian "pleasing," given the apparently damaged state of the speaker's ear, it is plausible that the sound of the old clock would have a soothing effect.

Somewhat paradoxically, the English version of the poem is more explicit and yet at the same time more difficult to understand. The line "Derevo za oknom—pasmurnaia svecha" ("The tree behind the window is a dull candle") becomes "Through the window, birch candles fail." The Russian original features a nonstandard use of the adjective "pasmurnyi." Meaning something like "dull," "gloomy," or "overcast," this word usually qualifies the weather. Using it to describe a candle is clearly unidiomatic. In the present case, the gloomy weather semantically "infects" the tree in front of the window and spreads from there to its metaphorical representation as a candle, resulting in a quasi-oxymoronic "dull candle." In other words, what should be a source of light becomes instead a focus of darkness in the poem.[45] This dark candle fulfills a specific purpose in the poem's economy: it stands in contrast to the woman's hair in the second stanza, which is able to illuminate the room better than a lamp. In the English version, the tree in front of the window is explicitly identified as a birch tree. The common essence of whiteness or brightness helps to motivate the metaphorical presentation of the tree as a candle. However, the English text does not really make clear that "candle" is used as a metaphorical stand-in for the tree ("birch candles" rather suggests something like candles made of birch wood, or candles placed on a birch tree). The fact that these candles "fail," prompted by the rhymes with "quail" and "tail," lacks the oxymoronic energy of the original image and creates a rather enigmatic impression for a reader who is unacquainted with the Russian original.

The most significant deviation between the original and the translation occurs in the already mentioned line 6, where "The sea for the fourth day roars hollowly at the dike" becomes "For the fourth day the sea hits the dike with its hard horizon." The "hard horizon" in the English version is nowhere to be found in the Russian original. Did Brodsky simply add these words because he needed a rhyme with "light on" (similarly to the "tail" added to the "quail")? In general, he was not averse to introducing semantic material into his self-translations for the sake of rhyme—something that, if done by a translator other than the author, would almost certainly be condemned as illegitimate "padding." However, the need for a rhyme is not a sufficient explanation for what is happening here. Alexandra Berlina has made the interesting observation that "the horizon as a source of pain, a hard or sharp thing, is one of Brodsky's favorite images."[46] This image is realized with greater intensity in English than in Russian. Depictions of a hard horizon appear in nine of Brodsky's published English translations, but only in three of the corresponding Russian originals (three more source poems contain the word "horizon," but without further qualification). "October Tune" is one of the three poems where the word "horizon" is absent in the Russian version, but has been added in the English one. Interestingly, all three of these self-translations date from 1987, the year when Brodsky received the Nobel Prize. Berlina argues that the image of the "sharp horizon" represents the ocean separating the United States from Russia and at the same time indicates the irretrievable temporal abyss between Brodsky's American present and Russian past. It is not by accident that the self-translation of "Oktiabr'kaia pesnia" seemingly bridges the gap between Brodsky's pre-emigration Russian and post-emigration English oeuvre. In 1987, thanks to the political changes affecting the Soviet Union, Brodsky could have returned for a visit to his homeland. By inserting the crucial image of the "hard horizon" into the English version of his poems that he self-translated in that year, Berlina argues, "it is as if he was reminding himself that he could not return: even if he went back in space, he still could not go back in time."[47]

As we can see, "October Tune" is more than a simple reconstruction of the Russian original in English. It also functions to some extent as a self-commentary, expressing Brodsky's changed attitude toward a poem that he composed while still living in the Soviet Union and was now revisiting in America sixteen years later. In that sense, the English self-translation becomes an "American" poem. The slightly altered title, substituting a "tune" for the Russian "song," puts the translation in dialogue with other poems from Brodsky's American period, all of them written directly in English, such as "The Berlin Wall Tune" (1980), "Belfast Tune" (1986), and "Bosnia Tune" (1992).[48] All of these poems exist in a tension between the soothing musicality suggested by the title and the violent world of war and ethnic conflict evoked in the text. By the same token, the seemingly idyllic world of "October Tune" hints at an underlying darker reality. Overall, Brodsky's rather uncharacteristically simple Russian poem gains an increased complexity through its transposition into English. Paradoxically, as Berlina has argued, this transformation may make "the self-translation more characteristic of the poet than the original."[49]

BRODSKY'S ENGLISH OEUVRE AND THE CRITICS

While Brodsky is undoubtedly the most canonical Russian poet of the second half of the twentieth century, the validity of his English oeuvre remains an issue of ongoing controversy. In a 2015 review published on her blog *The Book Haven*, Cynthia Haven, a former student of Brodsky's and the editor of his collected interviews in English, opined that Brodsky's reputation in the English-speaking world is "marred by the ambitious, ill-advised self-translations that would have torpedoed a lesser genius."[50] Haven's remark prompted a reply from Ann Kjellberg, Brodsky's literary executor and the editor of his collected English poetry, who argued that "Brodsky's effort to enliven and expand the formal repertoire in English, which met with considerable resistance at the time, can surely now be judged a success."[51] The disagreement between Haven and Kjellberg replicates a dispute that has persisted for decades at this point. The most vociferous attacks against Brodsky's English-language writings came from two well-established British poets and critics, Christopher Reid and Craig Raine, in the 1980s and 1990s. The titles of their reviews—"Great American Disaster" and "A Reputation Subject to Inflation"—speak for themselves.[52] Reid's complaints about the "generally 'un-English' quality of Brodsky's performance" were amplified by Raine's claim that Brodsky, a "world-class mediocrity" in his opinion, was "unable to achieve more than a basic competence in his adopted language." While Raine's dismissive characterization of Brodsky's English skills is demonstrably wrong, Reid was on somewhat more solid ground when he pointed to the "un-English" quality of Brodsky's performance. However, in an age that values "foreignization," one has to wonder whether the non-idiomatic handling of the target language is a sufficient argument to disqualify a translation. Moreover, the perception of traditional meter and rhyme as an expression of conservatism, which had led some American critics on the Left to attack Brodsky on political grounds,[53] has given way to a more tolerant and pluralist attitude in recent years. It now seems permissible again to use forms other than free verse in English-language poetry without being labeled a reactionary.

Nevertheless, even among critics sympathetic to Brodsky who acknowledge his ability to write compelling poetry in English, one can find a certain apprehension about his self-translations. David Bethea, in his monograph *Joseph Brodsky and the Creation of Exile*, leaves no doubt that, in his opinion, Brodsky was able to write great poetry in English.[54] Yet, when discussing the poem "May 24, 1980," one of Brodsky's most famous texts, Bethea adds the following qualifier: "It is an exceptionally powerful poem in Russian, especially if one has heard Brodsky read it aloud. Sadly, much of that power is lost in translation (the author's own)."[55] Bethea does not elaborate in what ways he considers the translation deficient. Others have done this job for him: in their anti-Brodsky sallies, Reid and Raine (neither of whom knew Russian) honed in on that particular text as an especially egregious example of Brodsky's mishandling of the English language. Skeptical assessments of Brodsky's self-translation have also come from more balanced critics who were able to compare the English version with the Russian original, such as Charles Simic or Valentina Polukhina.[56]

The most extensive comparisons of "May 24, 1980" with its Russian source text have been undertaken by Daniel Weissbort and Alexandra Berlina.[57] Berlina sidesteps an ultimate judgment about the quality of Brodsky's self-translation. Her main point, which corresponds to the overall argument offered in her monograph *Brodsky Translating Brodsky*, is that the English version makes the poem more "Brodskian." As she observes, the translation adds trademark features of Brodsky's personal style that are missing in the Russian source text such as enjambments, switches in register, punning references to idioms, and compound rhymes. Weissbord's discussion of "May 24, 1980" is yet more extensive, taking up a total of thirty-eight pages of his book

From Russian with Love. Weissbord keeps coming back to this text again and again in an almost obsessive manner. The poem develops into a cornerstone of his attempt to come to terms with Brodsky's method of translation, which at one point had led to a serious rift between himself and the poet. Written in the form of a diary, Weissbord's account traces the evolution of his own shifting attitude, which vacillates between disapproval and cautious respect for Brodsky's translational enterprise. He never arrives at a conclusive judgment, but does allow for the possibility that Brodsky may have been more right than wrong after all.

The question of whether the idiolect of Brodsky's self-translations is a viable or attractive form of English poetic discourse ultimately remains a matter of personal taste. It is interesting to note that the most positive assessments of Brodsky's English-language poetry and self-translations have all come from Russian-born scholars (Zakhar Ishov, Alexandra Berlina, Eugenia Kelbert) rather than from native speakers of English.[58] This creates another parallel with Tsvetaeva's French version of *Mólodets*, which has drawn more praise from Russian than from native French readers. In her Ph.D. thesis devoted to Brodsky's self-translations, Natalia Rulyova—another Russian native speaker—concludes that Brodsky's English texts should be read not as if they originated in English, but "with an awareness of the value of their foreignness."[59] This may be good advice, but it is worth pointing out that it is not necessarily what Brodsky intended, or hoped to achieve. Rather, he wanted his translations to be appreciated as self-standing English poems. In consequence, he published his self-translations in monolingual English-language editions rather than in a bilingual version that would facilitate a comparison between source and target text. Whether he was right or wrong about this is a question we will need to come back to.[60]

The ambiguity surrounding Brodsky's achievement as a self-translator is perhaps best conveyed in the comment of his fellow Nobel Prize winner and friend Seamus Heaney, who shall for now have the last word here:

> So, in spite of his manifest love for English verse, which amounts almost to possessiveness, the dynamo of Russian supplies the energy, the metrics of the original will not be gainsaid and the English ear comes up against a phonetic element that is both animated and skewed. Sometimes it instinctively rebels at having its expectations denied in terms of both syntax and the velleities of stress. Or it panics and wonders if it is being taken for a ride when it had expected a rhythm. At other times, however, it yields with that unbounded assent that only the most triumphant art can conjure and allow.[61]

Self-Translation among Contemporary Russian-American Poets

ALTHOUGH NABOKOV AND BRODSKY were the most prominent Russian-to-English self-translators of the past century, they are by no means the only ones. In recent decades, there has been a substantial influx of Russian-speaking immigrants to the United States, creating a new wave of so-called Russian-American literature. These authors are part of a larger global cohort of translingual Russian diaspora writers, many of them of Jewish descent.[1] While some of them continue to write poetry in their native Russian, even though they have a fluent command of English, and others write exclusively in English, while still highlighting their Russian origin, some write poetry in both Russian and English, or even in multiple languages.[2] Not all of these authors are self-translators, of course. In fact, very few of the Anglophone Russian immigrant novelists who have emerged in the United States since the turn of the millennium have engaged in self-translation. To borrow the terminology proposed by Steven Kellman, most of these authors belong to the category of "monolingual translinguals" rather than "ambilinguals."[3] The only major exception is the novelist, journalist, and screenwriter Michael Idov, who self-translated his debut novel *Ground Up* and published it in Russia under the title *Kofemolka*.[4]

While rare among contemporary Russian-American prose writers, self-translation occurs somewhat more frequently among poets. In this chapter, I will analyze the work of Andrey Gritsman and Katia Kapovich, two contemporary bilingual Russian-American poets who have both engaged in self-translation.[5] They represent two different approaches to the question of how, or why, a poet should translate his or her own work. While Gritsman invites a comparison between source and target text and the gaps between them in a bilingual *en face* edition, Kapovich camouflages her self-translated poems as English originals. For both authors, the geographic and cultural displacement caused by the move to a new continent and language becomes a productive principle affecting their translational practice. By stressing difference rather than similarity, their self-translated texts illustrate and explore their own bifurcated identities.

ANDREY GRITSMAN'S *VIEW FROM THE BRIDGE*

Andrey Gritsman has been the most prolific self-translator among the current generation of Russian-American poets. A medical doctor by training and profession, Gritsman was born in Moscow in 1947 and has lived in the United States since 1981. In 1998 he received an M.F.A. in creative writing from Vermont College of Norwich University. Aside from his daytime job as a physician, he runs a Russian-American bilingual poetry reading series in New York, as well as the journal *Interpoezia*. Gritsman was also the coeditor of an anthology of American poetry written in English by non-Anglophone immigrants, entitled *Stranger at Home: American Poetry with an Accent*.[6] Since 1995 he has published multiple volumes of poetry, about half in Russian and half in English. Many of them have titles that signal a sense of in-betweenness and movement between cultures: *Nicheinaia zemlia* (*No Man's Land*), *Vid s mosta / View from the Bridge*, *Dvoinik* (*The Double*), *Peresadka* (*Transfer*), and *In Transit*.

The volume *Vid s mosta / View from the Bridge* is of particular interest for a consideration of self-translation. It is a bilingual edition, with the Russian and English versions of the same poem printed on facing pages. Most of the English translations are by Gritsman himself, while a few are by two extraneous translators, Alex Cigale (himself a Russian immigrant) and Jim Kates. The volume also contains an extensive introduction, in which Gritsman comments on his own status as a bicultural poet and his method of translation. Interestingly, two versions of this introduction are offered, one in Russian and the other in English. Strictly speaking, these two texts are not equivalent, as the Russian version contains entire sentences and paragraphs that are left out in the English one. Furthermore, the English text is written "with an accent," so to speak—there are omitted articles and other telltale signs that identify the author as a native speaker of Russian.

Gritsman's bifurcated introduction becomes an illustration of its own content by stressing difference rather than similarity in translation. As he puts it, the Russian and English versions of his poems should not be considered "direct translations," but "parallel poems" written in two languages on the same subject and in the same "emotional waves." Gritsman stresses sound and rhythm as the primary criterion, and he attacks what he calls the "American translation industry" for generating products that are "predominantly intellectual and related to vocabulary," rather than to the sound or emotion of the original.[7] He also draws a contrast between Joseph Brodsky and himself. While Brodsky, in Gritsman's opinion, was "a major original English language poet," he was not really an American poet, given that his interest resided elsewhere than in the local American landscape.[8] By contrast, Gritsman claims that he has adjusted "to the power field of the new language," with English becoming a "second self (alter ego) amazingly different from the still existing first self of a native language."[9] He elaborates: "a distant powerful surf of the Russian poetry has been humming in my head since childhood," but "my poems in English derive from the American landscape: from the hot dog man, bar, office, highway, a New York City street, an old saxophone player on the corner of Lexington Avenue, the fuel refineries of Houston."[10]

What does this mean for Gritsman's practice of self-translation? I will examine a concrete example, the poem "Sheremet'evo" / "Moscow International Airport." This poem is in itself emblematic of Gritsman's transcultural themes inasmuch as it deals with international travel, border-crossing, and leaving his native Russia behind en route to America.

ШЕРЕМЕТЬЕВО

Так широка страна моя родная,
что залегла тревога в сердце мглистом,
транзитна, многолика и легка.
Тверская вспыхивает и погасает,
такая разная: военная, морская, —
и истекает в мерзлые поля.
Там, где скелет немецкого мотоциклиста
лежит, как экспонат ВДНХ.

За ним молчит ничейная земля,
в аэродромной гари светят бары,
печальных сел огни, Камазов фары,
плывущие по грани февраля,
туда, где нас уж нет.
И слава Богу. Пройдя рентген,
я выпью на дорогу
с британским бизнесменом молодым.
В последний раз взгляну на вечный дым
нагого пограничного пейзажа,
где к черно-белой утренней гуаши
рассвет уже подмешивает синь.[11]

A literal English translation of this poem would look approximately as follows:

SHEREMETYEVO

So wide is my motherland
that alarm took root in the hazy heart,
transit-like, many-faced, and light.
Tverskaya [street] flares up and dies down,
so diverse: martial, maritime —
and flows out into the frozen fields.
There, where the skeleton of a German motorcyclist
lies, like an exhibit item at the VDNKh.[12]

Behind him the no man's land is silent,
in the airport fumes, the bars shine,
the fires of sad villages, the headlights of Kamaz trucks,
floating along the border of February,
to where we are no more.
And thank God. Having passed the X-ray,
I will have a drink for the road
with a young British businessman.
For the last time, I will look at the eternal smoke
of the bare border landscape,
where, in the black and white morning gouache,
dawn already stirs in blue color.

Gritsman's English version of the poem deviates considerably from its Russian source text:

MOSCOW INTERNATIONAL AIRPORT

This country of mine is beautiful indeed.
So be it, my heart is untroubled.
My sadness is so light
so transient, fluid.

And as we drive along
Tverskaya street is flickering with lights,
all changing, variable, flowing,
streaming as if a military parade
was winding down to the frozen fields
on the outskirts of Moscow.

There lies the carcass of the Nazi motorcycle ranger
like an exhibit from
the All-Union Fair of the Socialist Labor.
And further is a no-man's-land

where the lights of the airport bars
float over the airfield's trembling haze.
The lights of the sad villages
and the headlights of heavy trucks
flow along February's frozen border

to the life that goes on without us.
Well, then, thank God!
I pass the X-ray control
and have a drink for the road
at the Irish Bar
with an Englishman from Kent —
O, such a Russian custom!

For the last time
I look at the eternal bitter smoke
over the bare landscape
of the invisible state border zone,
gently drawn in a black-and-white gouache
as the late dawn
adds some light,
a touch of wind
and a tint of blue.[13]

A few immediate observations can be made about the differences in form between the Russian and the English version. The Russian text consists of twenty iambic, mostly rhymed lines of varying length, which are broken down into two stanzas. The English self-translation is considerably longer. It contains thirty-five lines, arranged in five stanzas, of unrhymed free verse (although some lines have an iambic feel). One thing that becomes clear at once is that Gritsman is no Brodsky: in spite of his criticism of the American "translation industry," he jettisons meter and rhyme in favor of free verse. This is a common approach of American translators, but it is something that Brodsky severely criticized and did not tolerate in the translation of his own poems. Gritsman replaces the constraints of meter and rhyme, which are still prevalent in contemporary Russian poetry, with a looser, more "American" form.

Aside from meter and rhyme, another feature of the Russian poem that presents difficulties to a translator is what one could call its citationality. The Russian text reads like a patchwork of quotes. The first line reproduces the opening of a famous Stalinist patriotic song, Isaak Dunaevskii's and Vasilii Lebedev-Kumach's "Shiroka strana moia rodnaia" ("Wide Is My Motherland"), which was first featured in the Soviet film *Circus* of 1936. The poem contains many more allusions to the classic canon of Russian poetry. The second line, "zalegla trevoga v serdtse mglistom" ("alarm took root in the hazy heart"), is a verbatim quote from a 1922 poem by Sergei Esenin, "Ia obmanyvat' sebia ne stanu" ("I will not deceive myself"), except that "trevoga" (alarm, anxiety) has replaced Esenin's word "zabota" (care, concern). It looks as if Gritsman is offering an emotionally intensified version of Esenin's line. The phrase "pechal'nykh sel ogni" ("the fires of sad villages") in line 11 is borrowed from Mikhail Lermontov's poem "Rodina" ("Motherland," 1841), where we find the same expression with a slightly changed syntax and a different synonym for "village" ("ogni pechal'nykh dereven'"). Line 13, "gde nas uzh net" ("where we are no more"), echoes a famous line from Aleksandr Griboedov's play *Gore ot uma* (*Woe from Wit*, 1823): "Gde zh luchshe? Gde nas net" ("Where is it better? Where we are not"), as well as another famous passage from the final stanza of Pushkin's novel-in-verse *Eugene Onegin*, written in 1832, "Inykh uzh net, a te daleche" ("Some are already gone, and others are far away"). The "smoke" ("dym") in line 17 can be connected to another quote from Griboedov's *Gore ot uma* that has become proverbial in Russian culture: "I dym otechestva nam sladok i priiaten" ("Even the smoke of the fatherland is sweet and pleasant to us"). Interestingly, in the English self-translation, Gritsman "corrects" Griboedov, as it were, by making the smoke bitter rather than sweet, thereby undermining the patriotism expressed in the Russian source text.

What is the effect of saturating the Russian poem with quotations? It is as if, in taking leave of his native country at Moscow Airport, the speaker catches not only a final glance of the Russian landscape, but revels for one more time in the verbal landscape of Russian poetry with its tight-knit network of intertexts. This feature of the Russian poem cannot be preserved as such in the English translation, of course. A possible experimental solution, perhaps, would have been to substitute a patchwork of quotes from American poetry and patriotic songs. This is not what Gritsman does, however. The opening line, "This country of mine is beautiful indeed," sounds more like a reflection of Gritsman's American persona commenting on the text of the Russian song quoted in the original poem. The melancholy of the Esenin line, reinforced by the substitution of "zabota" with "trevoga," has turned into its opposite in the English version: the heart is now "untroubled." Is this a sign that American optimism has replaced Russian gloom?

Interestingly, the next line in the English version, "my sadness is so light," is another quote from a classic text of Russian poetry, Pushkin's 1829 poem "Na kholmakh Gruzii" ("On the Hills of Georgia"): "pechal' moia svetla" ("my sadness is light"). This allusion is not present in the Russian version, however: it can only be found in the English translation. One could speculate that Gritsman is carrying over the citational quality of the Russian original by inserting another Pushkin quote while reworking the text in English. Or was Pushkin's line, with its peculiar balance of melancholy and radiance, the original inspiration of Gritsman's Russian poem, now remembered by his American self? Of course, the Pushkin quote remains well-hidden within the English text of the poem. Only a bilingual reader steeped in the canon of Russian poetry can catch the allusion.

This observation raises another question: who is the implied addressee of the English text? Some indications point to a reader unfamiliar with Russian reality, someone who is in need of explanations and guidance (i.e., what we traditionally assume to be the typical reader of a translation). The title "Sheremet'evo," which may be meaningless to someone who has never been to Moscow, has been replaced in the English version with the generic "Moscow International Airport." The acronym VDNKh is spelled out (not quite correctly) as the "All-Union Fair of the Socialist Labor." The superfluous article before "Socialist Labor" marks the English version as a text "with a Russian accent." More importantly, the expression "Socialist Labor," which is not in the Russian original, seems calculated to evoke in the American reader stereotypical associations with the rhetoric of Soviet communism. This is Russia as seen by an American, rather than by a Russian.

Some of the differences between the Russian and English texts look rather arbitrary at first sight. For example, the "young British businessman" of the Russian poem becomes an "Englishman from Kent" of unknown profession encountered in an "Irish bar." Perhaps Gritsman's Russian persona was more struck by the occupation and youth of the British traveler, while his Anglophone self has become more discerning about the particularities of English geography and the branding of drinking establishments. An alternative explanation would be to read the word "Kent" as a bilingual pun. In Russian jargon, "kent" can mean something like "pal." In English, the word (which is absent, but perhaps implied in the Russian text) homophonically turns into the name of the British county. Again, only a reader attuned to the subtleties of Russian slang would be able to grasp this pun, which turns the English poem into a sort of double-coded text.[14]

A line that merits particular attention is "O, such a Russian custom!" which is present in the English version and absent in the Russian one. It is the only statement with an exclamation mark in either version of the poem. The idea expressed here could only have occurred to Gritsman while looking back at his Russian existence from the perspective of his present American alter ego. What appears as a normal and unreflected practice in the context of Russian culture becomes "exotic" when seen through American eyes. In that sense, "Moscow International Airport" functions as a comment on the translator's own feelings about returning to his Russian original poem while rewriting it in English.

A pertinent question when dealing with self-translation is not only "how," but also "why." I would argue that Gritsman was probably not motivated primarily by a desire to make his Russian poems accessible to a monolingual American audience. Rather, the process of self-translation serves as a way of exploring his own hybrid Russian-American identity. Printing the Russian and English versions of the poem on facing pages becomes a spatial enactment of the poet's own divided identity between competing linguistic and cultural codes. The ideal reader of this edition is a bilingual individual who, rather than being taken in by a translation's claim to total representation, shuttles back and forth between the two texts, uncovering their differences amidst their proclaimed similarities. In this sense, Gritsman's self-translational project can be associated with a postmodern understanding of translation as a practice bent on subverting textual authority. At the same time, producing a bilingual corpus of parallel texts can be seen as a way of stitching together a frayed bicultural identity, a way of coping with the experience of transnational dislocation by creating a space where the two sides of the author's linguistic self coexist and enter into dialogue. The traditional relation between "original" and "translation" gives way to a constellation where both texts coexist with equal authority and add new dimensions to each other.

THE HIDDEN SELF-TRANSLATIONS IN KATIA KAPOVICH'S *GOGOL IN ROME*

We will contrast Andrey Gritsman's practice of self-translation with that of another bilingual Russian-Jewish poet writing in Russian and English, Katia Kapovich (b. 1960). Born and raised in Kishinev, the capital of Moldavia, Kapovich left the Soviet Union for Israel in 1990 and immigrated to the United States in 1992. She resides in Cambridge, Massachusetts, where she coedits the literary journal *Fulcrum* together with her husband Philip Nikolayev. While Gritsman's oeuvre is more or less evenly split between Russian and English, the native language predominates in Kapovich's work. Of the ten volumes of poetry she has published thus far, eight are in Russian and two in English. Kapovich has a somewhat higher profile than Gritsman with regard to publication outlets and resonance. Her Russian volumes have appeared in Israel, the United States, and Russia, including an edition by the prestigious NLO publishing house in Moscow.[15] Her English poems have come out in such venues as the *London Review of Books*, *The New Republic*, *The Independent*, *Harvard Review*, and *Ploughshares*. Her two

English-language volumes, *Gogol in Rome* (2004) and *Cossacks and Bandits* (2007), both published by Salt Publishing in the United Kingdom, have reaped praise from prominent poets and critics. A blurb from the U.S. poet laureate Billy Collins printed on the back cover of both English-language volumes calls Kapovich "one of the freshest, most arresting poetic voices I have heard in a long time."

Unlike Gritsman, Kapovich does not foreground or showcase self-translation in her work. Only a small number of her English poems are self-translated from a Russian original. In a 2010 interview, Kapovich stated rather categorically, "I don't care about translation. Great poetry is untranslatable."[16] More recently, she doubled down on this statement in even stronger terms, which seem reminiscent of Nabokov's equation of self-translation with the inflicting of bodily harm. As she put it: "I cannot translate, I am completely unable to do this (not only myself, but others as well). It seems to me that it is tedious and frightful to perform open-heart surgery on oneself."[17]

Given this attitude, it may seem surprising that Kapovich would engage in self-translation at all. And yet, four of the poems in the collection *Gogol in Rome*, even though not marked as such, are English versions of poems that had appeared two years earlier in the Russian volume *Perekur* (*Smoke Break*) published in St. Petersburg. What prompted Kapovich to revisit and translate these four particular texts? Like many of her poems, they offer autobiographical vignettes of events from her Soviet past and American present. None of them deals directly with the topics of emigration, bilingualism, or transcultural identity, but a case can be made that these issues are present below the surface. One poem relates Kapovich's experience as a teacher in a Soviet school for deaf and mute children ("At the Kishinev School for Deaf and Mute Children").[18] The sounds produced by the pupils resemble a "foreign language" that is unknown to the teachers, and the theme explored in the poem is the challenge of establishing communication across a linguistic divide, which is accomplished by writing the letters of the alphabet on a blackboard. Another poem, "Apartment 75" (in Russian, "Kvartira Nomer 7-A"), presents the opposite case by highlighting a breakdown in communication.[19] The speaker of the poem intrudes into the apartment of an American neighbor who has committed suicide. The expectation of gaining a deeper understanding of the neighbor's personality from the expression on her dead face remains frustrated.

The other two of Kapovich's self-translated poems, which will be examined more closely here, concern themselves with questions of exile, displacement, and shifting identity. The poem "Prague" (in Russian, "Zamok") is dedicated to Alexei Tsvetkov, himself a bilingual Russian-American poet who was a longtime resident of the Czech capital. In this poem, Kapovich imagines herself living in Prague, a city that offers a Russian emigrant a more familiar habitat than the United States thanks to its Slavic identity. The poem can be read as an implied reflection of the author's own exilic condition:

ЗАМОК

А. Цветкову

Начинается день: от восточной стены
отделяется тень старика.
Я приду в этот город с другой стороны,
чем однажды пришел в него К.

Ветер рвет разноцветный туман на куски,
отпираются двери кафе,
и бросают на лавочки зеленщики
огурцы в огородной ботве.

Здесь бы жить, на простом языке говоря
«добри дэн» и «декуи» – и ключ
отмыкал бы певучий замок на дверях,
когда солнце выходит из туч,

когда свет шелушится меж грабель дождя
и, ногой оттолкнувшись от плит,
над рекой, над каштановой пеною дня
прямо к Пражскому замку летит.[20]

In a literal English translation:

Lock/Castle

For A. Tsvetkov

The day begins: from the eastern wall
escapes the shadow of an old man.
I will enter this city from the opposite side
than it was once entered by K.

The wind shreds the colored fog to pieces,
the doors of the cafés open,
and the greengrocers throw on the counters
cucumbers with leafy tops from the garden plot.

To live here, to say in an easy language
"dobrý den" and "děkuji"—and the key
would open the melodious lock on the doors,
when the sun comes out of the clouds,

when the light peels from the rake of the rain
and, pushing off with the foot from the flagstone,
over the river, over the chestnut foam of the day
flies directly to the Prague Castle.

In Kapovich's self-translation:

Prague

For Alexei Tsvetkov

The day starts as an old man's shadow splits away
from the eastern wall. I have entered the city
on the opposite side from Kafka's K.
Locks gnash their teeth behind my back,
low-lintel doors of cafés spring open, street vendors
lay out the first radishes and scallions
on newspapers by their feet. I can see myself
being from around here, speaking their easy language,
eyeing the same chestnut trees in the humpbacked
lane as I leave my house in the morning,
shutting a low-lintel door and bearing uphill
toward the dark castle all the way at the top.[21]

Taken on its own, the title of the original Russian poem, "Zamok," presents an unsolvable conundrum to an English translator, since the meaning of the word differs depending on stress: "zámok" means "castle," while "zamók" means "lock." Only the context, or, in the present case, the anapestic meter, indicates which of the two possibilities is intended. As it turns out, both meanings are operative in the poem: the third stanza mentions a key opening a "melodious lock," whereas the fourth and last stanza ends with an evocation of the Prague Castle. The title thus means both "Lock" and "Castle." In English it is impossible to achieve this effect, but it works well in Czech ("Zámek") or in German ("Das Schloss"). Not coincidentally, *Das Schloss* also happens to be the title of a novel by Franz Kafka, who emerges in the poem as Kapovich's alter ego. The character "K" in the poem (rhyming with "starika" [old man]) refers to Kafka's fictional hero Joseph K., while also evoking the initials KAtia KApovich.

Kapovich takes considerable liberties in her self-translation of this poem. The sixteen lines of the original, arranged into four "abab" quatrains, become a twelve-line poem without stanza breaks. Although written in free verse, the English text preserves one key rhyme: "away" in the first line rhymes with "Kafka's K" in the third line, thus explicitly naming the Prague novelist, who remains unnamed in the Russian original. Mixing rhymed with unrhymed lines is a general characteristic of Kapovich's English poetry (unlike her Russian poems, which are all strictly rhymed). The addition of anthropomorphic metaphors conveys to the English text a more disturbing and threatening tone. "Kliuch / otmykal by pevuchii zamok na dveriakh" ("The key would open a melodious lock on the doors") becomes "Locks gnash their teeth behind my back." Similarly, a "humpbacked lane" makes its appearance only in the English text. The English self-translation features other details that are absent in Russian, such as "low-lintel doors" (mentioned twice).

The greengrocers selling cucumbers in the Russian text become street vendors hawking radishes and scallions in the English self-translation. The omission of the cucumbers is probably intentional, since the sound play of "ogurtsy v ogorodnoi botve" would have been impossible to preserve, and the image of "botva" (green stalks), conveying the idea of fresh, first greenery, has no real English equivalent either. "Radishes and scallions" allow the poet to create an image of fresh spring vegetables while also adding some color to the poem. It is worth pointing out that an extraneous translator, as opposed to the author, would probably not have dared to make such a substitution.

The Czech language is also presented differently in the Russian and English versions. The Russian "Zdes' by zhit', na prostom iazyke govoria / 'dobri den' i 'dekui'" ("to live here, to say in an easy language 'good day' [dobrý den] and 'thank you' [děkuji]") is replaced by the shorter "I can see myself / being from around here, speaking their easy language." The Russian text demonstrates the "easiness" of Czech by rendering the greeting "dobrý den" in Cyrillic characters ("добри дэн"), which makes it look like a shortened and slightly comical version of the Russian "добрый день" pronounced by a speaker with a foreign accent. At the same time, the lyrical persona is more present in the English phrasing than in the impersonal Russian infinitive and gerund construction. The increased role of the speaker in the English version becomes particularly noticeable at the end of the poem. In the Russian text, sunlight breaks through the clouds and makes its way up to the Prague Castle. In the English translation, all references to the weather (wind, fog, sun, clouds, rain) have been eliminated. Instead of the sun rays, it is the first-person speaker who leaves her house to climb uphill to the Castle.

It is noteworthy, then, that the lyrical persona assumes a more active role in the self-translated English text. Living in Prague is presented as a real possibility, as opposed to the note of longing expressed in the Russian conditional ("by"). There is also a change in tense. The statement in the first stanza "Ia pridu v etot gorod" ("I will enter this city") becomes "I have entered the city." What is presented as an intention and potentiality in Russian, using the perfective future, is a fait accompli in English. This can be interpreted as a metacommentary resembling the glosses built into Gritsman's self-translations ("O, such a Russian custom!"). Like the speaker in the English version, Kapovich, in translating her earlier Russian poem, revisits a text and a place that she has already entered.

Overall, the poem sounds more subdued in English. The omission of the last quatrain, with its sweeping and surprising imagery of the anthropomorphized landscape, is particularly noteworthy. It is as if the emotional exuberance of the Russian text gives way to a calmer and more controlled discourse with somewhat more sinister overtones (remarkably, the Castle at the end of the poem becomes "dark" in English).

A similar gloominess in combination with an increased self-awareness can also be observed in Kapovich's English reworking of the poem "Avtonatiurmort v pizhame" ("Self-Still Life in Pajamas"):

АВТОНАТЮРМОРТ В ПИЖАМЕ

Кто это, заспанный, хмурый, лохматый,
утром на кухне сидит без еды,
и на обоях в листве виноградной –
тень от воды . . .

Это я с вечера кран не закрыла,
льется вода в оцинкованный таз.
Соевое растворяется мыло,
нить виноградная разорвалась.[22]

In a literal English translation:

Self-Still Life in Pajamas

Who is this, sleepy, gloomy, disheveled,
sitting in the morning in the kitchen without food,
and on the wallpaper in the foliage of grapes
the shadow of water . . .

It is I who have not shut the faucet off since last night,
the water pours into the zinc-coated basin.
The soy-soap is dissolving,
the thread of grapes is torn apart.

In Kapovich's self-translation:

> Self-Portrait in Pajamas
>
> Who is this sleepy, gloomy scarecrow
> in morning knots of her own red hair,
> who sits at the kitchen table
> without breakfast?
> Water shadows dance on the wall
> among grape leaves.
>
> Is she the same me
> that forgot to shut the faucet off
> before going to bed last night?
> Water drips into the kitchen sink,
> a vine breaks in the wallpaper vineyard,
> soy soap melts on zinc.[23]

Again, the tight form of the original (regular dactylic tetrameters arranged in AbAb quatrains, with a truncated line 4 in the first stanza to underline the ellipsis) is replaced by a loose free-verse structure in English, with just one rhyme ("sink"—"zinc"). The altered order of lines in the second stanza indicates that this final rhyme was a desired effect. The English version, slightly longer than the original, contains some information that is absent in the Russian version, such as the reference to the knotted red hair of the speaker (this being a self-translation, it is presumably permissible for Kapovich to insert "her own red hair" into the text).

The English title "Self-Portrait in Pajamas" flattens the effect of the Russian neologism "Avtonatiurmort," which confers on the lyrical subject the frozen immobility of a still life. Another effect lost in translation is the fact that, in the Russian text, the adjectives in the first line are given in the masculine form, while the verbal ending at the end of line 5 identifies the speaker as feminine. The person who is the solution to the riddle presented in the first stanza thus has a different gender than what the grammatical endings at the beginning of the poem suggest. The English version differs in one other major respect from the Russian source text. The Russian poem has the form of a straightforward riddle, with a question posed in the first stanza and the answer provided in the second stanza. In the English text, however, the answer to the riddle is itself a question: "Is she the same me . . . ?" This alteration makes the identity of the speaker more tentative and complex. It is a question that also applies to the situation of Kapovich producing an English self-translation of her earlier Russian poem. Is the speaker in the English text

really "the same me" as the speaker in the Russian text? The images of disin-
tegration and rupture seem to undermine the idea of an unwavering identity
surviving intact through the flux of time and shift of language. While the
Russian text features an inconsistency with grammatical gender, the English
version displays a more forceful mix-up of the third and first person. "Is
she the same *me*?"—similar to Arthur Rimbaud's iconic "je est un autre"—
illustrates the peculiar way in which self-translation makes the self both the
subject and object of displacement. As Kapovich's poem demonstrates, the
resulting alienation can lead to an uncanny encounter with one's own former
self in the form of a "gloomy scarecrow."

SELF-TRANSLATION AS SELF-EXPLORATION

For both Andrey Gritsman and Katia Kapovich, the practice of self-
translation becomes a form of self-exploration. Given the autobiographical
and confessional nature of much of Kapovich's poetic oeuvre, revisiting the
original texts of her poems and rendering them into English allows her to re-
evaluate instances of successful and failed communication, exilic alienation,
and multilingual identity, while Gritsman's "parallel poems" stage an encounter and dialogue between his former Russian and current American selves.

At the same time, there are important differences between Kapovich and Gritsman. In his introduction to *View from the Bridge*, as we have
seen, Gritsman claims to have "gone native" in his American poetry. Kapovich makes no such claim. The absence of different Russian and American
selves obviates the need for a sustained dialogue between the two via self-
translation. Kapovich's persona is that of a defiant outsider, both as a dissident
in the former Soviet Union and as a Russian immigrant in the United States.
The final poem of the volume *Gogol in Rome*, "Generation K," captures her
stance as a "stranger at home" with the lines: "We mumble in English with a
heavy accent, / dropping the articles like cigarette ashes."[24] Ironically, in spite
of occasional unidiomatic and even ungrammatical expressions, Kapovich's
written English has actually less of a Russian "accent" than Gritsman's. It is
Gritsman, rather than Kapovich, who tends to drop or misplace articles in
his English writings.

For Kapovich, writing and self-translating in English, as opposed to
writing in her native Russian, does not seem to involve a switch between
opposed selves. If there is a difference in personality, it concerns the discrepancy between chronological layers and levels of maturity. As she has pointed
out in a 2010 interview,

> everything is more placid when I write in English. I guess it's natural because
> English is the language of my adulthood. But it's only a poem in Russian that

cuts through all layers of my persona and shows me what a wonderful piece of dirt I am. I hope I will proceed till the final destination, but if I stop writing in Russian, I will probably stop writing poetry altogether.[25]

The two versions of Kapovich's Prague poem provide an apt illustration of the different emotional registers associated with Russian and English. At the same time, Kapovich acknowledges that writing in English has opened up new possibilities of artistic expression. As she noted in the same interview: "There are things that I'm unable to write in Russian. For example, I can't write free verse, somehow it doesn't come out well." While getting rid of the strictures of formal verse by crossing over into a new language may convey a sense of freedom to Kapovich, she embraces free verse in English more cautiously than Gritsman does. Many of her English poems remain at least partially rhymed or metered, and, as we have seen, occasional rhymes also crop up in her self-translations.

A significant difference between Kapovich and Gritsman concerns the way in which they present their poems. Kapovich's self-translations remain camouflaged as English originals. Nothing in the book *Gogol in Rome* indicates that these poems are translated from a Russian source. The acknowledgments page, which lists the previous publications of all the poems in the volume, remains silent about the fact that four of them originally came out in Russia. As Eva Gentes has shown, making self-translation invisible is the default practice of most publishers, who coax the reader into perceiving the text as a monolingual work written by a monolingual author.[26] Drawing attention to the translational process through a bilingual *en face* edition that forces the reader to compare the two texts and become aware of the gaps between them remains the exception rather than the rule. While Gritsman openly highlights and celebrates the practice of poetic self-translation in *View from the Bridge*, Kapovich does the opposite in *Gogol in Rome*, treating her self-translations almost like a sort of shameful secret that she tries to keep hidden from view. What is presented as a public spectacle in Gritsman's volume becomes in Kapovich's book a private maneuver performed behind the scenes.

The acts of self-translation—staged and performed differently by Kapovich and Gritsman—reveal not only different ways of self-exploration and creative life in the bilingual and bicultural context, but also different interpretations of poetry and the poetic. As we can see, the two poets have divergent opinions about conveying the form, the citations, and the poetic imagery of the original texts. Kapovich is reluctant to dispose entirely of a proclivity for meter and rhyme in her English verse. This is quite different from Gritsman, who, even in his Russian poetry, uses a looser form than Kapovich, and whose English poetry revels in what he refers to in his introduction to *View from the Bridge* as the American "breakthrough to freedom."[27] For Kapovich, who remains more rooted in her native idiom, self-translation is less a playful and liberating experience than an enterprise fraught with complications—an attempt to salvage in the new language something of the poetic essence residing in the form and sound of the Russian original.

For both Gritsman and Kapovich, the experience of shifting identity triggered by the process of self-translation turns into a poetics of displacement, making the recast version of the poem a metacommentary on its own production and existence. To be sure, any translation of a poetic text is always already different from the original, but, contrary to what one might expect from the coincidence of author and translator, for Gritsman and Kapovich this difference appears to grow in a self-translated poem.

Conclusion

IF WE INSIST on measuring the success of a work of litera-
ture by its critical or popular resonance, we probably would have to arrive at
the somewhat melancholy thought that the self-translated poems discussed
in this book were mostly failures. Even highly revered authors like Tsvetaeva,
Nabokov, and Brodsky had difficulties finding a receptive audience for their
self-translated poetry. The situation was worst for Tsvetaeva. To her great
frustration, she was unable to publish her French translation of *Mólodets*,
and when the book finally appeared in print half a century after the author's
death, it attracted little attention. Nabokov and Brodsky, unlike Tsvetaeva,
easily found a publisher for their self-translated poems, of course, given
that they had already become literary celebrities during their lifetime, but
their self-translations received at best a lukewarm reception. Even though
Tsvetaeva, Nabokov, and Brodsky have developed an international cult following and their works are the focus of major academic "industries," their
self-translated poetry has remained largely in the shadows. Only Brodsky's
self-translations have begun to attract scholarly scrutiny in recent years, but
the overall opinion of his achievements as a translingual poet seems not to
have improved much. In a generally laudatory review of Alexandra Berlina's
monograph on Brodsky's self-translations, Michael Eskin argues that the
book, in spite of its qualities, nevertheless fails to put Brodsky on the map of
American studies, given "the simple fact that Brodsky's English poems simply
do not make the cut *as* indigenous *poems in English*."[1] The double mentioning of "simple" and "simply" endows Eskin's statement with the seemingly
self-evident obviousness of a truism.

This apparent lack of success may validate the opinion that poetic self-
translation is an inherently doomed undertaking, given the doubly challenging task of writing poetry in a non-native tongue and reconstructing a text
with specific formal and aesthetic qualities in a different linguistic medium.
Personally, I do not find such an explanation particularly persuasive. In spite
of the assumed difficulty of poetic self-translation, a closer look reveals that
the practice is more widespread than one might think. The prejudice against
self-translated poems may stem less from an intrinsic weakness of the translations than from a monolingual bias of readers who assume that any translation of a poem—particularly one made by a non-native speaker of the target

171

language—is inevitably "worse" than the original, even when it comes with the cachet of authorial intention.

Interestingly, the Russian self-translating poet who has probably received the most positive response from Anglophone critics is Katia Kapovich. Paradoxically, she is someone who denies that poetry can be translated at all. Since Kapovich presents her self-translated poems as English-language originals, the American critics who praised her collection *Gogol in Rome* were unaware that some of the poems in that volume are self-translations of Russian source texts. The critical praise was based on the assumption that the poems in the book were all original English-language creations, albeit written by a non-native speaker of English.

The bias against poems composed directly in a non-native language seems to be weaker than the bias against self-translated poems. This becomes visible in the critical response to Nabokov's and Brodsky's Anglophone poetry. Richmond Lattimore, while denouncing Nabokov's "awkward" self-translations, claimed that "in most of the English-composed poems . . . the awkwardness vanishes."[2] Similarly, John Skow opined that Nabokov's self-translated poems were "generally flawed," but that "[a] few of the English poems are splendid, of the high quality of the long poem in *Pale Fire*."[3] As we have seen, Brodsky's poems written directly in English—at least some of them—have been praised as original and inspired contributions to Anglophone poetry, while his self-translations have found fewer defenders.

What seems to be at stake here is a romantic privileging of the original text and the original language, which makes translation—even when done by the author—a problematic enterprise. To be sure, ideas of translatability have fluctuated considerably over the years. The romantic cult of originality rooted in the individual genius of the mother tongue turned self-translation into a very marginal endeavor for much of the nineteenth century. Modernist and formalist theories, on the other hand, have made multilingual approaches to poetry viable again, even though the assumption of striving for "equivalence" between source and target text has been met with increased skepticism in the light of postmodern and deconstructionist approaches to translation.

Among the poets considered in this book, we find a wide spectrum of opinions concerning the translatability of poetry. The most optimistic position is taken by Tsvetaeva, who considered poetry itself a form of translation and thus by definition always translatable. Brodsky had a similar view. Like Tsvetaeva, he claimed that "poetry after all in itself is a translation; or, to put it another way, poetry is one of the aspects of the psyche rendered in language."[4] If we take the position that any poetic text is always already a translation, there is no reason to deny the theoretical feasibility of infinite further retranslations. Elizaveta Kul'man also assumed that the "spirit" of a poem survives its incarnation in different linguistic media. At the other end of the spectrum we find Katia Kapovich, who denies that poetry can be translated at all. Nabokov's rigid theory of literalism amounts to more or less the same position. Nabokov's characterization of translation as a form of physical violence is echoed by Kapovich's comparison of (self-)translation to open-heart surgery. Nevertheless, both Nabokov and Kapovich went against their own theory in their practice of self-translation—Nabokov by deviating from his literalist credo, and Kapovich by an (admittedly limited) engagement in an activity that she declared to be impossible in the first place.

The opposition between translatability and untranslatability is in reality somewhat of a false dichotomy. It is equally trivial to claim that nothing is translatable and that nothing is untranslatable. Lawrence Venuti has argued that the assumptions of translatability or untranslatability in fact represent two sides of the same coin, which he calls the "instrumental model" of translation. In this view, the task of translation is seen as the "reproduction or transfer of an invariant that is contained or caused by the source text, whether its form, meaning, or effect." Rather than the instrumental paradigm, Venuti champions what he calls the "hermeneutic model" of translation. In his definition, "translation is an interpretive act whereby the translated text comes to support meanings, values and functions specific to the receiving situation."[5]

Inevitably, this raises the question of the target audience. For whom are self-translations written? Walter Benjamin opened his famous essay on the task of the translator with the somewhat startling assertion that "no poem is intended for the reader, no picture for the beholder, no symphony for the listener."[6] By implication, Benjamin seems to be saying that no translation is intended for the hapless reader who is ignorant of the original language. Part of the negative reaction to the self-translations of Tsvetaeva, Nabokov, and Brodsky is probably due to the fact that none of them aimed to accommodate their respective target audience. In other words, they refrained from what Venuti would call a "domesticating" strategy. Tsvetaeva's and Brodsky's insistence on preserving meter and rhyme in translation was bound to appear outlandish to a public accustomed to free verse, while Nabokov's literalism flew in the face of received ideas of "poeticity." Rather than in an identifiable national tradition, these translations locate themselves in a transnational hybrid space. The risk one takes with such a position is to become unreadable to a monocultural audience. In the words of David Bethea:

Who is Tsvetaeva writing for *in this world* when late in life she translates her own *poema-skazka The Swain* (Molodets), a work already strangely inverted vis-à-vis the original, into French that, if grammatically correct, syntactically resembles Russian? Her voracious poetic appetite having exhausted the semantic, prosodic, and generic resources of her native speech, she moved into a linguistic no-man's land. By the same token, who is Brodsky writing for when he smuggles into his Russian verse extended scholastic arguments and elaborate English metaphysical conceits that can only be perceived as profoundly alien to the native tradition?[7]

Tellingly, the few positive appraisals of Tsvetaeva's and Brodsky's self-translations have generally come from bilingual native speakers of Russian, that is, readers who do not *need* a translation of the text. Perhaps self-translations serve a different function than the one traditionally imputed to translations. As we have seen, they can become a form of self-exploration, self-exegesis, or metacommentary. Rather than providing a simulacrum of the original text for readers who are ignorant of the source language, they can be described in terms of what Mikhail Epstein, drawing on the dialogical philosophy of Mikhail Bakhtin, has theorized as "interlation." In Epstein's words:

With the spread of multilingual competence, translation will come to serve not as a substitute but as a dialogical counterpart to the original text. Together they will comprise a multidimensional, multilingual, "culturally curved" discourse. Bilingual persons have no need of translation but they can enjoy an "interlation," a contrastive juxtaposition of two apparently identical texts running simultaneously in two different languages—for example, a poem by Joseph Brodsky in the Russian original and in English autotranslation. Interlation is a multilingual variation on the same theme, where the role of "source" and "target" languages are not established or are interchangeable, and one language allows the reader to perceive what another language misses or conceals.[8]

Typographically, the ideal presentation of an "interlation" is a bilingual *en face* edition showing the two versions of the text side by side. This is the solution adopted by Andrey Gritsman for his "parallel poems" published in his volume *View from the Bridge*. The only other self-translating Russian poet who resorted to this typographical layout was Nabokov in *Poems and Problems*. Nabokov's attitude was quite different from Gritsman's, however. Even though he published his self-translated poems in a bilingual edition, Nabokov's intent was hardly to achieve an Epsteinian "interlation." Rather, the juxtaposition between source and target text underlines the unbridgeable gap between the two versions, since, following Nabokov's own theory of translation, the Russian original can never be truly recovered in the English rendition. In its inevitable failure, the "ruined" English text validates the primacy and canonical sanctity of the Russian original. By contrast, Gritsman's approach does not privilege either variant. Both the Russian and the

English versions exist as "parallel poems" with equal rights. While Nabokov's bilingual edition reveals a frustrated quest for equivalence, in Gritsman's case the difference between original and translation is a fully intended and welcomed embodiment of transnational fluidity.

Aside from Gritsman's *View from the Bridge* and Nabokov's *Poems and Problems*, a bilingual edition showing the original and self-translated text on facing pages is also available for Tsvetaeva's *Mólodets/Le Gars* (Moscow: Ellis-Lak, 2005). The trilingual edition of Kul'man's poetry by the Russian Academy does not present the parallel versions facing each other (which would have been difficult to realize, given that three languages are involved), but at least the Russian, German, and Italian texts are included within the covers of the same book. By contrast, locating the parallel Russian and German versions of Kandinsky's self-translated poems is an extremely cumbersome task. A bilingual parallel edition of Brodsky's poems in Russian and English has never been realized either. But if we follow Epstein's thinking, it would probably be a good idea.

In the contemporary intellectual climate, "innocent" self-translation has become problematic in the same way that the concept of equivalence has been met with increasing suspicion by translation theorists. Nabokov's skepticism about translatability has become a widely accepted tenet of translation studies, albeit without Nabokov's gloomy conclusions. Rather than the impossible creation of a transparent simulacrum of an original text, translation is now understood as the creative rewriting and multiplying of potential meanings. In that sense, a self-translator is forced to grapple with his or her own multiple identities, which may not always be reducible to a common denominator. Mikhail Epstein explains the sea change in attitude toward language and translation as follows: "Translation as the search for equivalence has dominated the epoch of national cultures and monolinguistic communities, which needed bridges of understanding more than rainbows of cocreativity. . . . With the globalization of culture and the automatization of literal translation between languages, it is untranslatability (and nonequivalencies among languages: truly Bakhtinian polyglossia) that reach the foreground."[9]

Does an audience for such writings exist today? Over the past thirty years, we have witnessed an unprecedented global dispersion of Russian speakers over three continents, leading to the emergence of a new generation of bilingual or multilingual "diasporic" Russians dwelling in the countries of the "Near Abroad" as well as in Israel, Germany, the United States, and elsewhere. The "postmonolingual condition" that is affecting a growing number of today's global population and creative writers has ushered in an era of transnational mobility and linguistic mixing. In his 1979 interview with John Glad, Brodsky speculated that it was "entirely possible that in twenty or thirty years there will be people for whom [producing poetry in multiple languages] is completely natural."[10] We have now reached the age that Brodsky invoked in his prediction. Will the emergence of ever more deterritorialized communities lead to an increase in bilingual creativity? If so, the self-translating poets discussed in this book may provide a glimpse of a perhaps not too distant future.

Notes

INTRODUCTION

1. Frost's wording was actually somewhat different. In a 1959 conversation with Cleanth Brooks and Robert Penn Warren, Frost stated: "I like to say, guardedly, that I could define poetry this way: It is that which is lost out of both prose and verse in translation. That means something in the way the words are curved and all that—the way the words are taken, the way you take the words." *Interviews with Robert Frost*, ed. Edward Connery Lathem (New York: Holt, Rinehart and Winston, 1966), 203.

2. The Russian scholar V. V. Feshchenko makes this claim in his article "Avtoperevod poeticheskogo teksta kak raznovidnost' avtokommunikatsii," *Kritika i semiotika*, no. 1 (2015): 201.

3. Rainier Grutman, "A Sociological Glance at Self-Translation and Self-Translators," in *Self-Translation: Brokering Originality in Hybrid Culture*, ed. Anthony Cordingley (London: Bloomsbury, 2013), 70. As Grutman rightfully notes, "even if it proved to be the case that self-translators were overrepresented among Nobel Prize winners (but why should that be so?), this proportion invites us to revisit a number of preconceptions about the marginal nature of the practice."

4. Yasemin Yildiz, *Beyond the Mother Tongue: The Postmonolingual Condition* (New York: Fordham University Press, 2012), 2.

5. See Jahan Ramazani, *A Transnational Poetics* (Chicago: University of Chicago Press, 2009), 24.

6. See Brian James Baer, *Translation and the Making of Modern Russian Literature* (New York: Bloomsbury Academic, 2016), 7–9.

7. Friedrich Schleiermacher, "On the Different Methods of Translating," trans. Susan Bernofsky, in *The Translation Studies Reader*, 2nd ed., ed. Lawrence Venuti (New York: Routledge, 2004), 55, 58.

8. Cited in Yildiz, *Beyond the Mother Tongue*, 36.

9. Diana Abaeva-Maiers, "'My guliali s nim po nebesam . . .' (Beseda s Isaem Berlinom)," in *Iosif Brodskii: Trudy i dni*, ed. Lev Losev and Petr Vail' (Moscow:

Izdatel'stvo Nezavisimaia Gazeta, 1998), 100–101. Unless otherwise noted, all English translations of foreign language quotes in this book are my own.

10. Todorov, even though living in Paris for most of his life, confessed to Aneta Pavlenko that "he feels no affective ties to French poetry." Instead, he said that the poetry that touched him most deeply was Russian, the language in which he was schooled as an adolescent in a Bulgarian "Special School." See Aneta Pavlenko, *The Bilingual Mind and What It Tells Us about Language and Thought* (New York: Cambridge University Press, 2014), 244. Milosz, who spent decades in the United States and was fluent in multiple languages, told Joseph Brodsky that when he reads poetry in English he feels separated from it "as through a glass pane." He claimed that he was only able to appreciate Emily Dickinson's poems when he read them in Polish translation. See Brodsky's interview with Milosz in Iosif Brodskii, *Kniga interv'iu*, ed. V. Polukhina, 4th ed. (Moscow: Zakharov, 2007), 496.

11. David Ian Hanauer, *Poetry as Research: Exploring Second Language Poetry Writing* (Amsterdam: John Benjamins, 2010), 6.

12. Pavlenko, *The Bilingual Mind*, 283.

13. Ibid., 295.

14. T. S. Eliot, "Tradition and the Individual Talent" (1919), in *Selected Prose of T. S. Eliot*, ed. Frank Kermode (London: Faber and Faber, 1975), 43.

15. Hanauer, *Poetry as Research*, 34–35.

16. Leonard Forster, *The Poet's Tongues: Multilingualism in Literature* (London: Cambridge University Press, 1970), 19.

17. Viktor Shklovsky, *Theory of Prose*, trans. Benjamin Sher (Elmwood Park, Ill.: Dalkey Archive, 1990), 12.

18. Forster, *The Poet's Tongues*, 48.

19. Theodor Adorno, "Wörter aus der Fremde," cited in Yildiz, *Beyond the Mother Tongue*, 96.

20. The notion of fidelity has been met with increasing skepticism in contemporary translation theory. Wai-Ping Yau, for example, calls the term "sexist, moralistic, and dichotomous, with the implication, as in 'les belles infidèles,' that adaptations are either beautiful or faithful, but never both." The concept is criticized for assuming an impossible standard of complete correspondence between original and translation and a mistaken assumption of an extractable essence that disregards the instability of meaning inherent in all texts. See Wai-Ping Yau, "Translation and Film," in *A Companion to Translation Studies*, ed. Sandra Berman and Catherine Porter (Chichester, Eng.: Wiley Blackwell, 2014), 499.

21. Rainier Grutman, "Auto-Translation," in *Routledge Encyclopedia of Translation Studies*, ed. Mona Baker (London: Routledge, 1998), 17.

22. Rainier Grutman, "Self-Translation," in *Routledge Encyclopedia of Translation Studies*, 2nd ed., ed. Mona Baker and Gabriela Saldanha (London: Routledge, 2009), 257.

23. Jan Hokenson and Marcella Munson, *The Bilingual Text: History and Theory of Literary Self-Translation* (Manchester, Eng.: St. Jerome, 2007); Simona Anselmi, *On Self-Translation: An Exploration in Self-Translators' Teloi and Strategies* (Milan: LED, 2012); Sara Kippur, *Writing It Twice: Self-Translation and the Making of a World Literature in French* (Evanston, Ill.: Northwestern University Press, 2015).

24. *Self-Translation: Brokering Originality in Hybrid Culture*, ed. Cordingley; *L'Autotraduction littéraire: Perspectives théoriques*, ed. Alessandra Ferraro and Rainier Grutman (Paris: Classiques Garnier, 2016).

25. See the list provided in Ferraro and Grutman, *L'Autotraduction littéraire*, 8.

26. Anselmi, *On Self-Translation*, 11.

27. The bibliography can be downloaded at www.self-translation.blogspot.com.

28. Hokenson and Munson, *The Bilingual Text*, 161 (authors' emphasis).

29. Menakhem Perry, "Thematic and Structural Shifts in Autotranslations by Bilingual Hebrew-Yiddish Writers: The Case of Mendele Mokher Sforim," *Poetics Today* 2, no. 4 (1981): 181.

30. Kippur, *Writing It Twice*, 66.

31. Susan Bassnett, "Rejoinder," *Orbis Litterarum* 68, no. 3 (2013): 287.

32. As Rainier Grutman argued: "In examining a series of concrete cases, one would find perhaps as many self-translators who cling literally to their text as writers who use it as a springboard to rewrite themselves. It is not excluded either to find both cases represented with the same writer." Grutman, "L'Autotraduction: Dilemme social et entre-deux textuel," *Atelier de Traduction* 7 (2007): 225.

33. Rainier Grutman and Trish Van Bolderen, "Self-Translation," in *A Companion to Translation Studies*, ed. Berman and Porter, 329.

34. Gustavo Pérez Firmat, *Tongue Ties: Logo-Eroticism in Anglo-Hispanic Literature* (New York: Palgrave Macmillan, 2003), 6, 106 (author's emphasis).

35. Ilan Stavans, "On Self-Translation," *LA Review of Books*, August 23, 2016, https://lareviewofbooks.org/article/on-self-translation/.

36. Among 1,039 bilingual and multilingual individuals questioned by Aneta Pavlenko in 2001–03, 65 percent responded with "yes" to the question: "Do you feel like a different person sometimes when you use your different languages?" See "Bilingual Selves," in *Bilingual Minds: Emotional Experience, Expression and Representation*, ed. Aneta Pavlenko (Clevedon, Eng.: Multilingual Matters, 2006), 10.

37. Samuel Beckett and Alan Schneider, *No Author Better Served: The Correspondence of Samuel Beckett and Alan Schneider*, ed. Maurice Harmon (Cambridge, Mass.: Harvard University Press, 1998), 93.

38. Zinaida Shakhovskaia, *V poiskakh Nabokova: Otrazheniia* (Moscow: Kniga, 1991), 22.

39. Anthony Cordingley, "The Passion of Self-Translation: A Masocritical

Perspective," in *Self-Translation: Brokering Originality in Hybrid Culture*, ed. Cordingley, 81–94.

40. Costin Popescu, "Jocul de-a societatea / Jouer à la société," *Atelier de Traduction* 7 (2007): 29.

41. Steven G. Kellman, *The Translingual Imagination* (Lincoln: University of Nebraska Press, 2000), 12. Kellman's examples of "monolingual translinguals" include such writers as Adelbert von Chamisso (French to German), Joseph Conrad (Polish to English), Elena Poniatowska (French to Spanish), Michael Arlen (Armenian to English), Fazil Iskander (Abkhaz to Russian), Tristan Tzara (Romanian to French), Wole Soyinka (Yoruba to English), Nikolai Gogol (Ukrainian to Russian), Kazuo Ishiguro (Japanese to English), Salman Rushdie (Urdu to English), Léopold Senghor (Wolof to French), Elias Canetti (Ladino to German), and Tom Stoppard (Czech to English) (see ibid., 14). The most prominent "ambilinguals" are Nabokov and Beckett.

42. For a discussion of Ostashevsky's multilingual poetics and the presence of Russian elements in his English texts, see Miriam Finkelstein, "Die hässlichen Entlein: Russisch-amerikanische Gegenwartslyrik," in *Lyrik transkulturell*, ed. Eva Binder, Sieglinde Klettenhammer, and Birgit Mertz-Baumgartner (Würzburg: Verlag Königshausen & Neumann, 2016), 254–63. Ostashevsky himself states that he could have become a bilingual poet and self-translator in his younger years, but missed that opportunity, and would now have to invest too much time to catch up. See Iakov Klots, *Poety v N'iu-Iorke: O gorode, iazyke, diaspore* (Moscow: NLO, 2016), 543–44.

43. Mary Besemeres, *Translating One's Self: Language and Selfhood in Cross-Cultural Autobiography* (Oxford: Peter Lang, 2002).

44. Baer, *Translation and the Making of Modern Russian Literature*, 14.

45. Munavvarkhon Dadazhanova, "Obe—vedushchie: 'Perevod avtora'—tvorcheskoe peresozdanie," *Druzhba narodov* no. 3 (1984): 243–48. An English translation of this article appeared in *Soviet Studies in Literature* 20, no. 4 (1984): 67–79.

46. Rebecca L. Walkowitz, *Born Translated: The Contemporary Novel in an Age of World Literature* (New York: Columbia University Press, 2015), 11–13.

47. See the discussion of Imermanis and related cases in *Latyshskaia/Russkaia poeziia*, ed. Aleksandr Zapol' (Riga: Neputns, 2011), 69–70.

48. Christopher Whyte, "Against Self-Translation," *Translation and Literature* 11, no. 1 (spring 2002): 64–71.

49. For a discussion of Aigi's translingualism, see Tomas Glanc, "(Ino)strannyi iazyk poezii Aigi—problemy i posledstviia transnatsionalizma," *Russian Literature* 79–80 (2016): 13–27; and Natalia Azarova, "Mnogoiazychie Aigi i iazyki-posredniki," *Russian Literature* 79–80 (2016): 29–44.

50. Grutman, "A Sociological Glance at Self-Translation and Self-Translators," 72.

51. Rainier Grutman, "L'Écrivain bilingue et ses publics: Une perspective comparatiste," in *Écrivains multilingues et écritures métisses: L'Hospitalité des langues*, ed. Axel Gasquet and Modesta Suárez (Clermont-Ferrand, Fr.: Presses Universitaires Blaise Pascal, 2007), 35–39.

52. In accordance with current linguistic terminology, I am using the word "bilingual" as a term for non-monolingual individuals regardless of how many languages they have at their command. Kandinsky, Tsvetaeva, and Nabokov were trilingual, even though they self-translated only among two of their languages. Kul'man knew eleven languages and self-translated between three or four of them.

53. Natalya Rulyova, "Joseph Brodsky: Translating Oneself," Ph.D. diss., Cambridge University, 2002; Arina Volgina, "Avtoperevody Iosifa Brodskogo i ikh vospriatiie v SSHA i Velikobritanii." Ph.D. diss, Moscow State University, 2005; Zarema Kumakhova, "Joseph Brodsky as Self-Translator: Analysis of Lexical Changes in His Self-Translations." Ph.D. diss., Michigan State University, 2006; Zakhar Ishov, "'Post-Horse of Civilisation': Joseph Brodsky Translating Joseph Brodsky: Towards a New Theory of Russian-English Poetry Translation." Ph.D. diss, Free University of Berlin, 2008; Alexandra Berlina, *Brodsky Translating Brodsky: Poetry in Self-Translation* (London: Bloomsbury, 2014). A useful survey of the scholarship on Brodsky's Anglophone oeuvre can be found in Alexandra Berlina, "The American Brodsky: A Research Overview," *Resources for American Literary Study* 38 (2016): 195–211.

54. Mikhail Epstein, "The Unasked Question: What Would Bakhtin Say?" *Common Knowledge* 10, no. 1 (2004): 51.

55. Will Noonan, "Self-Translation, Self-Reflection, Self-Derision: Samuel Beckett's Bilingual Humor," in Cordingley, *Self-Translation*, 165.

56. Aurelia Klimkiewicz, "Self-Translation as Broken Narrativity: Towards an Understanding of the Self's Multilingual Dialogue," in Cordingley, *Self-Translation*, 190.

57. Grutman, "Self-Translation," *Routledge Encyclopedia of Translation Studies*, 2nd ed., 259.

58. See on this Günther Wytrzens, "Das Deutsche als Kunstmittel bei Marina Cvetaeva," *Wiener Slavistisches Jahrbuch* 15 (1969): 59–70; and L. V. Zubova, "Khudozhestvennyi bilingvizm v poezii M. Tsvetaevoi," *Vestnik Leningradskogo Universiteta*, Ser. 2, Iazykoznanie, no. 4 (1988): 40–45.

CHAPTER ONE

1. Quoted in Karl Friedrich von Großheinrich, "Vorrede," in *Sämmtliche Gedichte von Elisabeth Kulmann* (Leipzig: Verlag von Otto Wigand, 1847), 125. The tombstone does not seem to have been preserved. Kul'man's mortal remains were moved in the 1930s to the Aleksandr Nevsky Monastery in Leningrad. See

M. Sh. Fainshtein, "'Ee poeziia liubila . . .' (E. B. Kul'man)," in *Pisatel'nitsy pushkinskoi pory: Istoriko-literaturnye ocherki* (Leningrad: Nauka, 1989), 18.

2. See Schumann's "Mädchenlieder" for two soprano voices and piano, op. 103, and "Sieben Lieder von Elisabeth Kulmann" for one voice and piano, op. 104. Both works were composed in 1851.

3. See Großheinrich, "Vorrede"; and V. K. Grosgeinrikh, "Elizaveta Kul'man i ee stikhotvoreniia," *Biblioteka dlia chteniia* 94, no. 4 (1849): 69–117; 95, no. 5 (1849): 1–34 and no. 6 (1849): 61–96; 96, no. 6 (1849): 83–119.

4. A. Nikitenko, "Zhizneopisanie devitsy Elizavety Kul'man," in *Polnoe sobranie russkikh, nemetskikh i ital'ianskikh stikhotvorenii Elizavety Kul'man* (St. Petersburg: Tipografiia Imperatorskoi Rossiiskoi Akademii, 1839), I–XXV.

5. Hilde Hoogenboom, "Biographies of Elizaveta Kul'man and Representations of Female Poetic Genius," in *Models of Self*, ed. Marianne Liljeström, Arja Rosenholm, and Irina Savkina (Helsinki: Kikimora, 2001), 22.

6. See ibid., 26–27.

7. It has even been suggested that Grossheinrich himself wrote some of the poems attributed to Kul'man. This question remains difficult to resolve because of the strange fact that the extant manuscripts of Kul'man's works are partially in Grossheinrich's handwriting, which seems to be identical with Kul'man's (see on this Olga Lossewa, "Neues über Elisabeth Kulmann," in *Schumann und seine Dichter*, ed. Matthias Wendt [Mainz: Schott, 1993], 77–86). Nevertheless, even though he appears to have imitated Kul'man's handwriting, it is unlikely that Grossheinrich would have "faked" her complete works. Since Grossheinrich did not have a perfect command of Russian, it stands to reason that Kul'man's Russian poems were written by herself. In view of Kul'man's native command of German, it is certainly conceivable that the German poems are mostly her own as well. Italian was neither Grossheinrich's nor Kul'man's native language. My working assumption is that the poems quoted in this chapter were indeed written by Kul'man, although Grossheinrich may have edited them to some extent.

8. Kulmann, *Sämmtliche Gedichte*, 136.

9. See Grossheinrich's letter to Admiral A. S. Shishkov of the Russian Academy of Sciences, June 29, 1832, quoted in G. I. Ganzburg, "K istorii izdaniia i vospriiatiia sochinenii Elizavety Kul'man," *Russkaia literatura* 1 (1990): 151.

10. Großheinrich, "Vorrede," 6. Subsequent page references to this biography will be given directly in the text.

11. The German theologian and philosopher Christian Fürchtegott Gellert (1715–1769) and the Swiss painter and poet Salomon Gessner (1730–1788) were authors who both enjoyed immense popularity during their lifetime, but their reputation had suffered by the onset of romanticism, when many dismissed them as insipid mediocrities.

12. None of these poets is particularly well known today, but they were popular during the eighteenth century. The Swiss naturalist Albrecht von Haller

(1708–1777) is mainly known for his long poem "The Alps"; Friedrich Wilhelm Gotter (1746–1797) was a German poet and playwright; Ewald Christian von Kleist (1715–1795, not to be confused with the more famous Heinrich von Kleist), was a Prussian army officer and poet; Johann Wilhelm Ludwig Gleim (1719–1803), known as the "German Anacreon," was the mentor of the former; and Johann Georg Jacobi (1740–1814) was another German Anacreontic poet and protégé of Gleim.

13. The attribution to Anacreon of the odes that Kul'man translated is actually spurious, but these texts were still considered authentic in the nineteenth century. For a discussion of Kul'man's reception of Anacreon, see Angelika Fricke, "*Anakreon ljubeznyj*—zu Elizaveta Kul'man's Beschäftigung mit Anakreon," in *Festschrift für Hans-Bernd Harder zum 60. Geburtstag*, ed. Klaus Harer (Munich: Otto Sagner, 1995), 93–113.

14. See Hanspeter Bruppacher, "Erinnerung an Elisabeth Kulmann: Eine russische Dichterin aus dem frühen 19. Jahrhundert," *Neue Zürcher Zeitung*, no. 201 (August 31/September 1, 1991), 65.

15. Kulmann, *Sämmtliche Gedichte*, 261. The poem also exists in a Russian version: "Наверно б исцелилась / Я, по врача словам, / Пробыв две трети года / На теплом юге там." Cited in R. Iu. Danilevskii, "Nemetskie stikhotvoreniia russkikh poetov," in *Mnogoiazychie i literaturnoe tvorchestvo*, ed. M. P. Alekseev (Leningrad: Nauka, 1981), 40.

16. V. G. Belinskii, *Polnoe sobranie sochinenii*, vol. 4: *Stat'i i retsenzii 1840–1841* (Moscow: Izdatel'stvo Akademii Nauk SSSR, 1954), 570.

17. V. K. Kiukhel'beker, *Izbrannye proizvedeniia v dvukh tomakh*, ed. N. V. Koroleva (Moscow-Leningrad: Sovetskii pisatel', 1967), 1: 640.

18. "Elizaveta Kul'man," January 29–30, 1835. In Kiukhel'beker, *Izbrannye proizvedeniia v dvukh tomakh*, 281–84.

19. Quoted in Ulrich Mahlert, ". . . die Spuren einer himmlischen Erscheinung zurücklassend: Zu Schumanns Liedern nach Elisabeth Kulmann op. 104," in *Schumann in Düsseldorf: Werke, Texte, Interpretationen*, ed. Bernhard R. Appel (Mainz: Schott, 1993), 122.

20. Grossheinrich arranged these poems in two "Gemäldesammlungen" ("Collection of Paintings"), each divided into twenty "Säle" ("Galleries"). The first Gemäldesammlung contains 342 poems, and the second 268. See Kulmann, *Sämmtliche Gedichte*, 135–271 and 423–512.

21. See the article by Hoogenboom, "Biographies of Elizaveta Kul'man"; and also the Ph.D. thesis by Andrea Geffers, *Stimmen im Fluss: Wasserfrau-Entwürfe von Autorinnen: Literarische Beiträge zum Geschlechterdiskurs von 1800–2000* (Frankfurt am Main: Peter Lang, 2007), 59–102.

22. A sampling of representative quotes can be found in Mahlert, ". . . die Spuren einer himmlischen Erscheinung zurücklassend," 119–21.

23. S. Durylin, "Pushkin i Elizaveta Kul'man," *30 dnei* 2 (1937): 87–88.

24. E. S. Nekrasova, "Elizaveta Kul'man," quoted in Durylin, "Pushkin i Elizaveta Kul'man," 87.

25. Elisabeth Kulmann, "Göthe," in *Sämmtliche Gedichte*, 471.

26. In his notes to the German edition of Kul'man, Grossheinrich writes that "as a consequence of her very limited supply of books, and even that of her teacher, [Kul'man] knew only very few of Goethe's works." Kulmann, *Sämmtliche Gedichte*, 667.

27. Ganzburg, "K istorii izdaniia i vospriiatiia sochinenii Elizavety Kul'man," 150.

28. Danilevskii, "Nemetskie stikhotvoreniia russkikh poetov," 37.

29. See on this E. A. Leve, "Pervaia v Rossii neofilologichka," *Zapiski neofilologicheskogo obshchestva* 8 (1915): 218.

30. See Durylin, "Pushkin i Elizaveta Kul'man," 89–90.

31. As the son of a French mother and a German father, Grossheinrich grew up as a French-German bilingual. In spite of his command of multiple languages, he was not particularly well-traveled, however. He seems to have visited no country outside Germany, France, and Russia, where he moved immediately after graduation from Munich University. A short biography of Grossheinrich, written by his grand-nephew Franz Miltner in 1874, can be found in Elisabeth Kulmann, *Mond, meiner Seele Liebling: Eine Auswahl ihrer Gedichte*, ed. Hansotto Hatzig (Heidelberg: Meichsner & Schmidt, 1981), 23–25.

32. Wendy Rosslyn, *Feats of Agreeable Usefulness: Translations by Russian Women 1763–1825* (Fichtenwalde: Verlag F. K. Göpfert, 2000), 169.

33. Sherry Simon, *Gender in Translation: Cultural Identity and the Politics of Transmission* (London: Routledge, 1996), 1.

34. On pseudo-translation, see Gideon Toury, *Descriptive Translation Studies—and Beyond*, rev. ed. (Amsterdam: John Benjamins, 2012), 47–59.

35. For a discussion of how later Russian women writers addressed the gendered conception of translation in their fictional oeuvre, see the chapter "Refiguring Translation: Translator-Heroines in Russian Women's Writing" in Baer, *Translation and the Making of Modern Russian Literature*, 87–113.

36. Geffers, *Stimmen im Fluss*, 94.

37. Elizaveta Kul'man, *Polnoe sobranie russkikh, nemetskikh i ital'ianskikh stikhotvorenii Elizavety Kul'man* (St. Petersburg: Tipografiia Imperatorskoi Rossiiskoi Akademii, 1839), 11.

38. Rosslyn, *Feats of Agreeable Usefulness*, 96.

39. Danilevskii, "Nemetskie stikhotvoreniia russkikh poetov," 38.

40. An example of a rhymed self-translation can be found in Kul'man's French version of her poem "Homer and His Daughter." The German original, written in iambic trimeter with AbCb rhymes, is translated into fully rhymed AbAb French octosyllables. See "Homer und seine Tochter," in *Sämmtliche*

Gedichte, 189–90; and "Homère et sa fille," quoted in Leve, "Pervaia v Rossii neofilologichka," 237–38.

41. Kul'man, *Polnoe sobranie russkikh, nemetskikh i ital'ianskikh stikhotvorenii Elizavety Kul'man*, 5–9 (Russian section), 232–36 (German section), 126–42 (Italian section). The pagination begins anew with each language.

42. Kulmann, *Sämmtliche Gedichte*, 93.

43. Kul'man, *Polnoe sobranie*, 134 (Italian section).

44. Kulmann, *Sämmtliche Gedichte*, 653.

45. See Fricke, *"Anakreon ljubeznyj,"* 93.

46. Kulmann, *Sämmtliche Gedichte*, 653.

47. Kul'man, *Polnoe sobranie*, Russian section, 11–12. The spelling has been modernized, except for the word "polnyia," since the modern form "polnei" would disrupt the meter.

48. Ibid., German section, 238. Again, the spelling has been modernized (e.g., "teilst" instead of "theilst"), except for the archaic or dialectal "entgeusst" ("entgießt" in standard German).

49. Ibid., Italian section, 144. Given that the German and Italian versions follow the Russian text relatively closely, I will refrain from providing a separate English translation. Differences in wording will be addressed below.

50. In Kul'man's other German poems, the gender of the moon is handled inconsistently. While two texts from 1819, both entitled "An den Mond," present the personified moon as a woman, the later poems "Die Schöpfung des Himmels" (1823) and "Der Mond" (1824) conceive of it as a man. See Kulmann, *Sämmtliche Gedichte*, 144, 148, 242, 247.

51. Kul'man, *Polnoe sobranie*, German section, 1.

52. Ibid., Italian section, 1.

53. Ibid., 2.

54. For a discussion of Zhukovskii's German self-translations, see Dietrich Gerhardt, "Eigene und übersetzte deutsche Gedichte Žukovskijs," in *Gorski Vijenac: A Garland of Essays Offered to Professor E. M. Hill* (Cambridge: Cambridge University Press, 1970), 118–54; and Natalia Nikonova and Yulia Tikhomirova, "The Father of Russian Romanticism's Literary Translingualism: Vasilii Zhukovskii's German Compositions and Self-Translations," *Translation Studies* 11, no. 2 (2018): 139–57. Baratynskii's self-translations are discussed in L. G. Frizman, "Prozaicheskie avtoperevody Baratynskogo," *Masterstvo perevoda* 6, 1969 (Moscow: Sovetskii pisatel', 1970), 201–16; and Igor A. Pilshchikov, "Baratynsky's Russian-French Self-Translations (On the Problem of Invariant Reconstruction)," *Essays in Poetics* 17, no. 2 (1992): 15–22. Pilshchikov offers the interesting argument that Baratynskii *thought* in French even when he wrote in Russian, which makes the French versions of his poems less a translation into a foreign language than a manifestation of an initial "proto-text."

55. See the poem "Na serebrianuiu svad'bu E. P. Shchukinoi" (February 4, 1874) and its German self-translation in A. A. Fet, *Polnoe sobranie stikhotvorenii* (Leningrad: Sovetskii pisatel', 1959), 356–57, 785–86.

CHAPTER TWO

1. Wassily Kandinsky, *Complete Writings on Art*, ed. Kenneth C. Lindsay and Peter Vergo (Boston: G. K. Hall, 1982), 817.

2. E. A. Khal'-Kokh [Jelena Hahl-Koch], "Zametki o poezii i dramaturgii Kandinskogo," in *Mnogogrannyi mir Kandinskogo*, ed. N. B. Avtonomova (Moscow: Nauka, 1998), 124.

3. *Kandinskii: Put' khudozhnika: Khudozhnik i vremia*, ed. D. V. Sarab'ianov and N. B. Avtonomova (Moscow: Galart, 1994), 164–72. Boris Sokolov published a few additional Russian poems related to this album in the late 1990s ("Vozvrashchenie" and "Vecher" in *Nashe nasledie* vol. 37 [1996]: 87, and "Vzor," "Vesna," and "Pesnia" in *Znamia* no. 2 [1999], http://magazines.russ.ru/znamia /1999/2/kandin.html). Jelena Hahl-Koch included an undated Russian poem, "Kaplia padala so zvonom," and two prose poems, "Vecher" and "Peizazh," in her 1998 article cited above.

4. Sokolov gives the complete text of 11 of the extant 13 Russian prose poems from this cycle. See "'Otdelit' tsveta ot veshchei': Poisk bepredmetnosti v poeticheskom tsikle V. V. Kandinskogo 'Tsvety bez zapakha,'" in *Bespredmetnost' i abstraktsiia*, ed. G. F. Kovalenko et al. (Moscow: Nauka, 2011), 166–82.

5. See "Unveröffentlichte Gedichte" ("Unpublished Poems") in Wassily Kandinsky, *Gesammelte Schriften 1889–1916: Farbensprache, Kompositionslehre und andere unveröffentlichte Texte*, ed. Helmut Friedel (Munich: Prestel, 2007), 510–46. This volume also contains three early poetic works in Russian. Some of the texts are accompanied by a facsimile reproduction of Kandinsky's manuscript. In a few instances, but by far not in all, the Russian variant is published together with the German version.

6. Wassily Kandinsky, *Vergessenes Oval: Gedichte aus dem Nachlass*, ed. Alexander Graeff and Alexander Filyuta (Berlin: Verlagshaus Berlin, 2016).

7. On the neglect of Kandinsky's Russian writings, see Zhan-Klod Markade [Jean-Claude Marcadé], "V. V. Kandinskii—russkii pisatel'," in *Na rubezhe dvukh stoletii: Sbornik v chest' 60-letiia Aleksandra Vasil'evicha Lavrova*, ed. Vsevolod Bagno et al. (Moscow: NLO, 2009), 388–98.

8. An example can be found in the prose poem "Und" (in German), or "I" (in Russian), which is printed both in German and Russian together with a facsimile reproduction of the two manuscripts in Kandinsky, *Gesammelte Schriften*, 526–27. The German editors misread the word "ungeschmolzen" (not melted) as "angeschmolzen" (meaning something like "fused by melting together"). In the German manuscript the letter "u" is written in such a minuscule size that it

could easily be mistaken for an "a." However, "on ne taial" ("it did not melt") in the Russian variant indicates that the correct reading of the German word must be "ungeschmolzen." Conversely, in transcribing the Russian manuscript, the word "levyi" (left) was misread as "lenivyi" (lazy), a mistake that could easily have been avoided by glancing at the German variant. A similar error occurred to Boris Sokolov when he transcribed the manuscript of the Russian poem "Tainyi smysl" ("Secret Meaning") quoted in "Otdelit' tsveta ot veshchei," 179. The expression "k sharu" ("to the sphere"), which Sokolov himself flags with a question mark, clearly needs to be amended to "k shagu" ("to the step") in view of the wording "zum Schritt" in the German variant of the text published in *Gesammelte Schriften*, 525.

9. On Kandinsky's gradual shift from Russian to German, see Jean-Claude Marcadé, "L'Écriture de Kandinsky," in *Kandinsky: Collections du Centre Georges Pompidou* (Paris: Musée National d'Art Moderne, 1998), 150–51.

10. See Nadia Podzemskaia, "L'Écriture théorique de Vassily Kandinsky et le problème du multilinguisme," in *Multilinguisme et créativité littéraire*, ed. Olga Anokhina (Louvain-la-Neuve: Harmattan, 2012), 159.

11. On the genesis of *On the Spiritual in Art* and its different linguistic incarnations, see Nadia Podzemskaia, "Note sur la genèse et l'histoire de l'édition de *Du Spirituel dans l'art* de V. Kandinsky," *Histoire de l'Art* 39 (October 1997): 107–16.

12. Wassily Kandinsky, *Die gesammelten Schriften*, ed. Hans K. Roethel and Jelena Hahl-Koch, vol. 1 (Bern: Benteli Verlag, 1980), 33. Interestingly, Kandinsky omitted this passage in the Russian self-translation, which appeared in 1918 in Moscow.

13. See "Vologodskaia zapisnaia knizhka" in Kandinsky, *Gesammelte Schriften 1889–1916*, 30–76, with the poems "Pechalnyi zvon" (38) and "Ty— moia teper' na veki" (42).

14. "Molchanie," "Poeziia," "Pozdniaia osen,'" in Kandinsky, *Gesammelte Schriften*, 510.

15. On the parallels between Kandinsky and the Russian symbolists, see John Bowlt, "Vasilii Kandinsky: The Russian Connection," in *The Life of Vasilii Kandinsky in Russian Art: A Study of "On the Spiritual in Art,"* ed. John Bowlt and Rose-Carol Washton Long (Newtonville, Mass.: Oriental Research Partners, 1980), 1–41; D. V. Sarab'ianov, "Kandinskii i russkii simvolizm," *Izvestiia Akademii Nauk: Seriia literatury i iazyka* 53, no. 4 (1994): 16–26; and V. Turchin, "'Klänge' V. V. Kandinskogo i poeticheskaia kul'tura nachala XX veka," *Iskusstvoznanie* 2 (1998): 428–54.

16. Wassily Kandinsky, *Über das Theater/Du théâtre/O teatre*, ed. Jessica Boissel (Paris: Éditions Adam Biro, 1998), 56, 58.

17. Naoko Kobayashi-Bredenstein, *Wassily Kandinskys frühe Bühnenkompositionen: Über Körperlichkeit und Bewegung* (Berlin: De Gruyter, 2012), 117.

18. *Wassily Kandinsky und Gabriele Münter in Murnau und Kochel 1902–1914: Briefe und Erinnerungen*, ed. Annegret Hoberg (Munich: Prestel Verlag, 1994), 42. This poem has never been published.

19. Cited in Gisela Kleine, *Gabriele Münter und Wassily Kandinsky: Biographie eines Paares* (Frankfurt am Main: Insel Verlag, 1990), 181.

20. See Peg Weiss, "Kandinsky, Wolfskehl und Stefan George," *Castrum Peregrini* 138 (1979): 31. Unfortunately, Weiss provides no direct quotation or date.

21. Kleine, *Gabriele Münter und Wassily Kandinsky*, 181.

22. *Weisse Wolke* is part of the permanent collection of the Kreeger Museum in Washington, D.C. A reproduction can be found at https://www.kreeger museum.org/about-us/collection/works-on-paper/Wassily-Kandinsky_White -Cloud-Weisse-Wolke.

23. Kleine, *Gabriele Münter und Wassily Kandinsky*, 180–81.

24. Another one of these "songs," with the title "Der Wind" ("The Wind"), is quoted in Jelena Hahl-Koch, *Kandinsky* (Stuttgart: Verlag Gerd Hatje, 1993), 404, fn. 69. Hahl-Koch speculates that Münter, who was taking lessons in singing and composition at that time, put these texts to music (ibid., 84).

25. "Abend" has been published in Kandinsky, *Über das Theater*, 22–27.

26. "As a child I spoke a lot of German (my maternal grandmother was from the Baltics" [in the Russian version: "nemka" ("German")]. Kandinsky, *Die gesammelten Schriften*, 28. Kandinsky made the same claim in a letter to Alois Schardt on December 28, 1933, on the occasion of his emigration to Paris: "Since my maternal grandmother was German, I spoke German already as a small boy" (quoted in Kleine, *Gabriele Münter und Wassily Kandinsky*, 138).

27. See Kleine, *Gabriele Münter und Wassily Kandinsky*, 125.

28. Ibid., 191.

29. Ibid., 184.

30. Ibid., 220. Münter's roots were in fact not entirely German. Her parents were German-Americans who fled from the United States to their ancestral homeland during the Civil War. Her American-born mother, a native speaker of English who never learned perfect German, retained nostalgic feelings for the American South for the rest of her life. Münter herself spent the years 1898–1900 in the United States, with extended stays in New York, the Midwest, and Texas.

31. Letter to Münter from Odessa, August 12, 1910, published in Hoberg, *Wassily Kandinsky und Gabriele Münter*, 95–96.

32. B. M. Sokolov, "Poeticheskii al'bom V. V. Kandinskogo 'Zvuki'/'Klänge' i problema kul'turnogo dvuiazychiia," in *Rossiia-Germania: Kul'turnye sviazy v pervoi polovine XX veka*, Vipperovskie chteniia 1996, vol. 19 (Moscow: Gosudarstvennyi muzei izobrazitel'nykh iskusstv im. A. S. Pushkina, 2000),

209. Sokolov draws a contrast between the theoretical writings and Kandinsky's correspondence, in which he used a more "natural" Russian.

33. Quoted in Marcadé, "V. V. Kandinskii—russkii pisatel'," 391.

34. "Auch so," in Kandinsky, *Gesammelte Schriften*, 553.

35. A facsimile of the first page of the manuscript of "Auch so" is reproduced in Kandinsky, *Gesammelte Schriften*, 534.

36. Sokolov, "Otdelit' tsveta ot veshchei," 177.

37. Kandinsky, *Die Gesammelten Schriften*, 146.

38. The most recent and extensive study of Kandinsky's theatrical pieces is Kobayashi-Bredenstein's *Wassily Kandinskys frühe Bühnenkompositionen*, which interprets his four early stage compositions as a Christian tetralogy covering both the Old and New Testament. Earlier monographs include Claudia Emmert, *Bühnenkompositionen und Gedichte von Wassily Kandinsky im Kontext eschatologischer Lehren seiner Zeit 1896–1914* (Frankfurt am Main: Peter Lang, 1998); and Ulrike-Maria Eller-Rüter, *Kandinsky: Bühnenkomposition und Dichtung als Realisation seines Synthese-Konzepts* (Hildesheim: Georg Olms Verlag, 1990).

39. The text of *Zheltyi zvuk*, based on a manuscript kept at the RGALI archive in Moscow, was first published by V. Turchin in 1993. See "'Zheltyi zvuk—sinezteicheskaia kompozitsiia V. V. Kandinskogo," *Dekorativnoe iskusstvo* 1–2 (1993): 24–27.

40. The development from *Riesen* to *Der gelbe Klang* was first discussed by Susan Alyson Stein in "Kandinsky and Abstract Stage Composition: Practice and Theory, 1909–12," *Art Journal* 43, no. 1 (spring 1983): 61–66. There is no mention, however, of the Russian *Zheltyi zvuk* as a crucial link in this chain.

41. The Russian and German variants of the stage compositions (together with a French translation) can be found in Kandinsky, *Über das Theater/Du théâtre/O teatre*. See *Gelber Klang* (53–87), *Stimmen oder Grüner Klang* (89–96), *Schwarz und Weiss* (99–107), *Schwarze Figur* (109–17), and *Violett* (213–79).

42. Kobayashi-Bredenstein's assertion that Kandinsky's stage compositions contain "only unrhymed verse" (fn. 2, 1–2) is clearly erroneous. Both the Russian and German lyrics are mostly rhymed.

43. Kandinsky, *Über das Theater*, 57.

44. See Eller-Rüter, *Kandinsky*, 72; and Emmert, *Bühnenkompositionen*, 90–91.

45. See Jutta Göricke, "Kandinsky's Lautmalerei *Der gelbe Klang*: Ein Interpretationsversuch," in *Besichtigung der Moderne: Bildende Kunst, Architektur, Musik, Literatur, Religion. Aspekte und Perspektiven*, ed. Hans Holländer and Christian W. Thomsen (Cologne: DuMont Buchverlag, 1987), 122.

46. Kandinsky, *Über das Theater*, 70.

47. Kandinsky, *Complete Writings*, 269.

48. Emmert, *Bühnenkompositionen*, 94.

49. The Russian and German texts can be found in Kandinsky, *Über das Theater*, 93–94, 96.

50. Kandinsky, *Über das Theater*, 105–6. I have modernized the spelling.

51. Even with its reduced syllable count, "Fernländer" doesn't scan correctly. The same is true for several of the other compound words ("Berggipfel," "wildrasende," "Stillschweigen"). In order to fit in the metrical scheme, they would have to be accented on the second rather than the first syllable.

52. For a brief discussion of the "Lied" translation, see Feshchenko, "Avtoperevod poeticheskogo teksta," 206–8. Feshchenko erroneously claims that Kandinsky self-translated no more than five poems (207). In reality there are sixteen Russian-German doublettes among the *Klänge* texts alone, and at least eleven more among the prose poems not included in the volume.

53. Wassily Kandinsky, *Sounds*, trans. Elizabeth R. Napier (New Haven, Conn.: Yale University Press, 1981), 126–27.

54. A metrical and partially rhymed English translation of this poem by Elizabeth R. Napier can be found ibid., 88.

55. Sarab'ianov and Avtonomova, *Kandinskii*, 169.

56. See Eller-Rütter, *Kandinsky*, 165.

57. The rhyme makes a final appearance in the scenic composition *Violett* (1914), where the chorus screams: "Ei! Der Wall! Der Knall! Der Fluß! Der Guß! Der Wald! Ei! Bald! Bald! Bald!" (Kandinsky, *Über das Theater*, 246). One wonders whether Kandinsky engages here in a self-parody. In general, *Violett* is different from the earlier scenic compositions. It seems more "Dadaist" than symbolist-expressionist and contains more dialogue, much of it of an absurdist nature.

58. "Für mich sind diese Sachen schon ziemlich veraltet, besonders manche Gedichte darin. Ich würde es auffrischen." Quoted in Kandinsky, *Über das Theater*, 53 (emphasis added).

59. For a history of the prose poem in Russia, see Adrian Wanner, *Russian Minimalism: From the Prose Poem to the Anti-Story* (Evanston, Ill.: Northwestern University Press, 2003). I discuss Kandinsky's *Klänge* on pp. 114–22.

60. The exact date of publication is unclear. Kandinsky himself, in "Mes gravures sur bois," claims that *Klänge* appeared in 1913. However, the records of the publisher seem to indicate that it came out in the fall of 1912. An English translation of the prose poems can be found in Kandinsky, *Sounds*, trans. Napier. The German text is provided in an appendix of this edition. For an alternative, more literal English translation by Kenneth C. Lindsay and Peter Vergo, see Kandinsky, *Complete Writings on Art*, 291–339. Both of these editions also contain black-and-white reproductions of the woodcuts.

61. Kandinsky, *Complete Writings on Art*, 155 (Kandinsky's italics).

62. Richard Sheppard, in "Kandinsky's *Klänge*: An Interpretation," *German Life and Letters* 33, no. 2 (January 1980): 135–46, argues that the woodcuts form a sequence that roughly parallels the development of the prose poems, moving from violent conflict and centripetality towards pattern and spirituality. The most thorough analysis of the relation between the individual prose poems and woodcuts in *Klänge* can be found in Patrick McGrady's Ph.D. thesis, "An Interpretation of Wassily Kandinsky's *Klänge*" (State University of New York at Binghamton, 1989). The fact that the originally planned Russian edition of the album had an entirely different layout from the German version has not been taken into account by any of the scholars interpreting the sequence of *Klänge*.

63. The history and structure of the planned Russian edition are discussed in Boris Sokolov, "Kandinskii: Zvuki 1911: Istoriia i zamysel neosushchestvennogo poeticheskogo al'boma," *Literaturnoe obozrenie* 4, no. 258 (1996): 3–41. A maquette reproducing the order of the texts and images has been preserved in Kandinsky's Munich estate and was partially published in facsimile in 2007 (Kandinsky, *Gesammelte Schriften*, 389–97). Additional manuscripts of prose poems intended for the Russian volume exist in Kandinsky's Munich and Paris archives. Sixteen of the Russian texts kept at the Centre Pompidou in Paris were published in 1994 in the appendix to a Moscow edition of Kandinsky's memoirs (Sarab'ianov and Avtonomova, *Kandinskii: Put' khudozhnika: Khudozhnik i vremia*, 164–71).

64. For an example, see the Russian and German manuscripts of the prose poem "I"/"Und" reproduced in Kandinsky, *Gesammelte Schriften*, 526–27.

65. Sokolov, "Kandinskii: Zvuki 1911," 11.

66. In at least one case, the French scholar Jean-Claude Marcadé has come to the opposite conclusion from Sokolov's. In discussing the German and Russian versions of the prose poem "Pestryi lug"/"Bunte Wiese," Marcadé argues that the Russian version came first, since the expression "v nitochku" (meaning "in a straight line") is more idiomatic than the German "in gerader Linie," and because of the Russian play with verbal prefixes which has no easy equivalent in German (see Marcadé, "Kandinsky, citoyen du monde: L'Écrivain russe et allemand et ses liaisons avec l'Italie et la France," April 30, 2015, http://www.vania-marcade.com/kandinsky-citoyen-du-monde-lecrivain-russe-et-allemand-et-ses-liaisons-avec-litalie-et-la-france/). Sokolov assigns "Bunte Wiese" to the category of likely German originals without providing a justification.

67. Kandinsky, *Complete Writings on Art*, 178.

68. *Kandinskii: Put' khudozhnika*, 166.

69. Both the Moscow futurists and the Zurich Dadaists, somewhat misguidedly, welcomed Kandinsky's prose poems as an illustration of their own aesthetic revolution. For more on this, see Wanner, *Russian Minimalism*, 116 and 120.

70. Sokolov, "'Otdelit' tsveta ot veshchei.'" Sokolov provides the complete Russian text of eleven of these prose poems. The corresponding German ver-

sion of seven of them can be found in the collection of "unpublished poems" in *Gesammelte Schriften*.

71. For the Russian text, see Sokolov, "Kandinskii: Zvuki 1911," 20; for the German text, see Kandinsky, *Gesammelte Schriften*, 513.

72. Kandinsky, *Complete Writings on Art*, 311–12.

73. A more detailed discussion of this text can be found in Emmert, *Bühnenkompositionen*, 184–86.

74. The Russian version has been published in Sokolov, "Otdelit' tsveta ot veshchei," 176, the German one in Kandinsky, *Gesammelte Schriften*, 543.

75. See "Sonet," one of Kharms's "mini-stories" written in the 1930s. I discuss this text in *Russian Minimalism*, 133–34.

76. In *On the Spiritual in Art*, Kandinsky comments on how the figure of a red horse differs from a red dress or a red tree: "The very sound of the words creates an altogether different atmosphere. The natural impossibility of a red horse necessarily demands a likewise unnatural milieu in which this horse is placed." *Complete Writings on Art*, 201.

77. For the text of "Karawane," see https://de.wikisource.org/wiki/Karawane. Hugo Ball greatly admired Kandinsky's prose poems and recited them at the Cabaret Voltaire in Zurich.

78. There is a slight difference in spelling between the two versions. The Russian text, as transcribed by Boris Sokolov, reads "Lavrentii, naudandra, limuzukha, direkeka! Diri—keka! Di—ri—ke—ka!" However, Kandinsky's handwriting allows for various interpretations. In the German manuscript, the word transcribed as "nandamdra" might very well be "naudandra." Of course, in spite of the identical sounds, the neologisms could still be perceived differently by German and Russian recipients. For a Russian, for example, the "a"-ending might signal a feminine noun. (I am indebted to Miriam Finkelstein for this observation.)

79. Christopher Short, "Between Text and Image in Kandinsky's Oeuvre: A Consideration of the Album *Sounds*," *Tate Papers*, no. 6 (autumn 2006), http://www.tate.org.uk/research/publications/tate-papers/06/between-text-and-image-in-kandinskys-oeuvre-a-consideration-of-the-album-sounds.

80. Kandinsky, *Complete Writings on Art*, 541.

81. The poem has been republished in Kandinsky, *Vergessenes Oval*, 69. For an English translation, see Kandinsky, *Complete Writings*, 510.

82. "Ergo," "S," "Erinnerungen," "Immer Zusammen" (English translation, with the German original of "S," in Kandinsky, *Complete Writings*, 810–12).

83. "Salongespräch," Testimonium Paupertatis," "Weiss-Horn" (English translation in Kandinsky, *Complete Writings*, 837–39).

84. The album *Kandinsky: 11 Tableaux et 7 poèmes* (Amsterdam: Editions Duwaer, 1945) contains the first publication of one German and three French poems ("Viribus Unitis," "Midi," "Les Promenades," "Lyrique") together with the three texts originally published in *Plastique*. These poems appear along-

side reproductions of oil and gouache paintings dating from 1935 to 1943. Max Bill's book contains two German poems written in 1936, "Von-Zu," and "Und das Ende?" and a French poem from 1938, "Le Fond," together with the prose poem "Bunte Wiese" from *Klänge*. See Max Bill, ed., *Kandinsky* (Paris: Maeght, 1951), 91–93.

85. Wassily Kandinsky, "Le Sourd qui entend," in Philippe Sers, "Le Clocher d'Ivan Veliky: Poésie, théâtre et peinture chez Wassily Kandinsky," *Courier du Centre International d'Études Poétiques*, vol. 193–94 (1992): 46–47.

86. See Marcadé, "Kandinsky, citoyen du monde."

87. Kandinsky, *Complete Writings*, 811.

88. Bill, *Kandinsky*, 92.

89. The word "Kurbe" is attested in Johann Christoph Adelung's dictionary from 1793–1801 as a variant of "Kurbel" (see http://de.academic.ru/dic.nsf /grammatisch/28824/Kurbe%2C_die), but it has long disappeared from German usage.

90. *Dominant Curve* is on display at the Guggenheim Museum in New York. For a reproduction, see https://www.guggenheim.org/artwork/1972.

91. A horse walking on its own without a rider is a rare occurrence in Kandinsky's oeuvre. It could be a reminiscence of the poem "Bassoon" in *Klänge*, where a white horse is wandering alone through deserted streets.

92. "Lyrique" is the final poem in the posthumously published album *Kandinsky: 11 Tableaux et 7 poèmes*. The entire album can be accessed online at https://archive.org/details/kandin00kand.

93. I am indebted to Natasha Lvovich for this observation.

94. A reproduction of the *Klänge* woodcut can be found at https://www .moma.org/s/ge/collection_ge/object/object_objid-26604.html.

95. Kandinsky, *Complete Writings on Art*, 183.

96. Sers, "Le Clocher d'Ivan Veliky," 46–47.

97. Letter to Münter from October 2, 1912, quoted in Hahl-Koch, *Kandinsky*, 179.

98. Kandinsky, *Complete Writings on Art*, 160.

99. Forster, *The Poet's Tongues*, 28–29.

100. Feshchenko, "Avtoperevod poeticheskogo teksta," 208.

101. Kandinsky, *Complete Writings on Art*, 191.

102. Ibid. As in the title *Klänge*, the word "sounds" does not necessarily refer to actual acoustic phenomena here, or the signifier of the verbal sign, but rather the "inner vibration" of the soul generated by a work of art.

CHAPTER THREE

1. Tsvetaeva also published a French self-translation of her poem "Kamennogrudyi," which appeared in the Belgian journal *Lumière* in 1922 together with her translation of poems by Vladimir Mayakovsky, Osip Mandelstam, and Ilya

Ehrenburg. Unlike the French version of *Mólodets*, these are literal prose translations with no attempt to reproduce the formal features of the original. See Wim Coudenys, "'Te poslednie vy mozhete ispravliat' s tochki zreniia stilistiki': Chetyre zabytykh frantsuzskikh perevoda Mariny Tsvetaevoi." *Revue des Études Slaves* 66, no. 2 (1994): 411.

2. Marina Tsvetaeva, *Le Gars*, preface by Efim Etkind (Paris: Des Femmes, 1992), 15.

3. Efim Etkind, "Marina Cvetaeva, poète français," in *Un chant de vie: Marina Tsvétaeva: Actes du Colloque International de l'Université Paris IV* (Paris: YMCA, 1996), 239.

4. Marina Tsvetaeva, *Sobranie sochinenii v semi tomakh*, vol. 5: *Avtobiograficheskaia proza, stat'i, esse, perevody* (Moscow: Ellis Lak, 1994), 295–96.

5. Michael Makin, "Text and Violence in Tsvetaeva's *Mólodets*," in *Discontinuous Discourses in Modern Russian Literature*, ed. Catriona Kelly, Michael Makin, and David Shepherd (London: Macmillan, 1989), 115–35. See also Makin's book *Marina Tsvetaeva: Poetics of Appropriation* (Oxford: Clarendon, 1993), 135–54.

6. Simon Karlinsky, *Marina Tsvetaeva: The Woman, Her World and Her Poetry* (Cambridge: Cambridge University Press, 1985), 143–44.

7. Vladislav Khodasevich, "Zametki o stikhakh: M. Tsvetaeva: 'Mólodets'" (first published in *Poslednie novosti*, June 11, 1925). In *Marina Cvetaeva: Studien und Materialien*, ed. Horst Lampl and Aage Hansen-Löve, *Wiener Slawistischer Almanach*, special volume 3 (1981): 265.

8. Marina Tsvetaeva, *Sobranie sochinenii v semi tomakh*, vol. 6: *Pis'ma* (Moscow: Ellis Lak, 1995), 236.

9. See Tsvetaeva's letters to Pasternak of May 22 and July 10, 1926 (ibid., 249 and 264). An English translation can be found in *Letters: Summer 1926: Boris Pasternak, Marina Tsvetayeva, Rainer Maria Rilke*, ed. Yevgeny Pasternak, Yelena Pasternak, and Konstantin M. Azadovsky, trans. Margaret Wettlin, Walter Arndt, and Jamey Gambrell (New York: New York Review of Books, 2001), 137, 232.

10. See Karlinsky, *Marina Tsvetaeva*, 207. To this day, *Mólodets* is unavailable in English. Aside from Tsvetaeva's French version, the poem has also been translated into German. See Marina Cvetaeva, *Mólodets: Skazka / Mólodec: Ein Märchen*, ed. and trans. Christiane Hauschild (Göttingen: Wallstein Verlag, 2004). The Russian text of *Mólodets* will be cited from Hauschild's bilingual edition by indicating the line numbers.

11. "V gost'iakh u M. I. Tsvetaevoi," in Marina Tsvetaeva, *Sobranie sochinenii v semi tomakh*, vol. 4: *Vospominaniia o sovremennikakh, dnevikovaia proza* (Moscow: Ellis Lak, 1994), 627.

12. Karlinsky, *Marina Tsvetaeva*, 207. The same assertion is repeated by Elizabeth Beaujour, who calls *Le Gars* a poem written "directly in French"

and "loosely based on the original text." See Elizabeth Klosty Beaujour, *Alien Tongues: Bilingual Russian Writers of the "First" Emigration* (Ithaca, N.Y.: Cornell University Press, 1989), 131.

13. "V gost'iakh u M. I. Tsvetaevoi," 626.

14. Letter to S. N. Andronnikova-Gal'perin, March 19, 1930, in Marina Tsvetaeva, *Sobranie sochinenii v semi tomakh*, vol. 7: *Pis'ma* (Moscow: Ellis Lak, 1995), 127.

15. See Marina Tsvetaeva, "Poet o kritike," in *Sobranie sochinenii*, 5: 287; and her letter to Anna Teskova, February 25, 1931, in *Sobranie sochinenii*, 6: 391.

16. Cited in Marina Tsvetaeva, *Mólodets/Le Gars*, illustrations by Natalia Goncharova (Moscow: Ellis Lak, 2005), 297.

17. Letter to Nanny Wunderli-Volkart, March 6, 1931, in Tsvetaeva, *Sobranie sochinenii*, 7: 361.

18. Since Tsvetaeva did not name the poem's source, Efim Etkind speculated in 1981 that "La Neige" was probably a pseudo-translation written directly in French (see "Marina Cvetaeva: Französische Texte," *Wiener Slawistischer Almanach*, special volume 3 [1981]: 201). He later corrected this error in his article "'Mólodets': Original i avtoperevod," *Slavia* 61 (1992): 283–84. However, the editors of Tsvetaeva's collected works published in Moscow in the mid-1990s still claim that a Russian original for "La Neige" has never been found (see *Sobranie sochinenii*, 7: 639). They provide a Russian (re)translation of "La Neige" (first published in Iu. P. Kliukin, "Inoiazychnye proizvedeniia Mariny Tsvetaevoi," *Nauchnye doklady vysshei shkoly* 4 [1986]: 70–71), which makes for rather interesting reading compared with Tsvetaeva's original Russian text.

19. The French text appeared in two different editions: Marina Tsvetaeva, *Le Gars* (Sauve: Clémence Hiver, 1991), and Marina Tsvetaeva, *Le Gars*, preface by Efim Etkind (Paris: Des Femmes, 1992). Citations will refer to the latter edition, with page numbers given in the text.

20. Marina Tsvetaeva, *Molodets*, ed. Natal'ia Teletova (St. Petersburg: DORN, 2003); Marina Tsvetaeva, *Mólodets/Le Gars* (Moscow: Ellis Lak, 2005).

21. Neither of the two existing monographs on *Mólodets* discusses the French version of the poem: see Christiane Hauschild, *Häretische Transgressionen: Das Märchenpoem "Molodec" von Marina Cvetaeva* (Göttingen: Wallstein Verlag, 2004); and Tora Lane, *Rendering the Sublime: A Reading of Marina Tsvetaeva's Fairy-Tale Poem "The Swain"* (Stockholm: Acta Universitatis Stockholmiensis, 2009). The most extensive comments on *Le Gars* are provided by Efim Etkind's two articles (see note 18 above). A brief discussion (based on only a partial knowledge of *Le Gars*, which was then still unpublished) can also be found in Michael Makin's *Marina Tsvetaeva: Poetics of Appropriation*, 309–15. Mikhail Gasparov discusses Tsvetaeva's Franco-Russian metrical experiments in his article "Russkii Mólodets i frantsuzskii Mólodets: Dva stikhovykh eksperimenta,"

in Gasparov, *Izbrannye trudy.* vol. 3: *O stikhe* (Moscow: Iazyki russkoi kul'tury, 1997), 267–78. French Slavists have shown no interest in *Le Gars.* The only exception seems to be the paper by the Russian-born Anna Lushenkova Foscolo, "L'Autotraduction dans la poésie de Marina Tsvetaeva," in *Plurilinguisme et autotraduction,* ed. Anna Lushenova Foscolo and Malgorzata Smorag-Goldberg (Paris: Éditions EUR'ORBEM, 2019), 137–58.

22. Vladimir Nabokov, *Strong Opinions* (New York: McGraw-Hill, 1973), 43.

23. Marina Tsvetaeva, "Avtobiografiia," in Tsvetaeva, *Sobranie sochinenii,* 5: 6.

24. Karlinsky, *Marina Tsvetaeva,* 10.

25. Ibid., 14.

26. Marina Tsvetaeva, "Otvet na anketu" (1926), in Tsvetaeva, *Sobranie sochinenii,* 4: 622.

27. Tsvetaeva, "Avtobiografiia," 5: 6–7.

28. *Rainer Maria Rilke und Marina Zwetajewa: Ein Gespräch in Briefen,* ed. Konstantin M. Asadowski (Frankfurt am Main: Insel Verlag, 1992), 76 (English translation in *Letters: Summer 1926,* 221). The quote imputed to Goethe is nowhere to be found in Goethe's works. Perhaps Tsvetaeva is referring to an entry in Goethe's diary in 1770: "Wer in einer fremden Sprache schreibt oder dichtet, ist wie einer, der in einem fremden Haus wohnt" ("He who writes or composes poetry in a foreign language is like someone who lives in a house not his own"). See *Rainer Maria Rilke und Marina Zwetajewa,* 235, fn. 134.

29. "Neskol'ko pisem Rainer Mariia Ril'ke," in Tsvetaeva, *Sobranie sochinenii,* 4: 322 (English translation in *Letters: Summer 1926,* 359).

30. Cited in Etkind, "Marina Cvetaeva, poète français," 237.

31. I am indebted to David Bethea for this observation.

32. July 6, 1926. *Letters: Summer 1926,* 221.

33. Ibid.

34. The online *Dictionnaire du moyen français* defines "rouble" as an "instrument en fer, servant à creuser ou à aplanir."

35. For example, the adjective "lointe" (103, 110), a variant of "lointaine" (far), seems to be Tsvetaeva's own invention. Sometimes one wonders whether Tsvetaeva simply made a mistake that she probably would have corrected in the final page proofs, such as the expression "ma m'amie" (31), which is a contamination of "mon amie" in standard French and "ma mie" in folksy ballad style.

36. Etkind, "'Mólodets': Original i avtoperevod," 274.

37. Quoted in Tsvetaeva, *Mólodets/Le Gars,* 280.

38. The word "tutolki," apparently a mutation of "pritolki" (lintels), seems to be Tsvetaeva's invention. Christiane Hauschild translates the word into German as "Schwellen" (thresholds), but I have not been able to find support for this in any Russian dictionary.

39. For a discussion of Tsvetaeva's use of syllabotonic meters in *Le Gars*, see Gasparov, "Russkii Mólodets i frantsuzskii Mólodets." Gasparov argues that a sort of convergence between Russian and French prosody happens in *Mólodets*. While the Russian original contains frequent metrical deviations and inversions that make it drift away from the syllabotonic toward a syllabic principle, the opposite phenomenon can be observed in Tsvetaeva's French verse, which gravitates toward a syllabotonic system (273).

40. L. V. Zubova, *Iazyk poezii Mariny Tsvetaevoi (fonetika, slovoobrazovanie, frazeologiia)* (St. Petersburg: Izdatel'stvo S.-Peterburgskogo Universiteta, 1999), 204, fn. 16.

41. The two types of vampire are contaminated both in Afanasiev's tale and in Tsvetaeva's poem, but the French version makes this contamination more visible. It is evident that folkloric accuracy was as unimportant to Tsvetaeva as semantic accuracy in translation. She also conveys features of a werewolf in her character, which would be impossible in traditional folk belief, given that vampires are "undead" and werewolves are alive. See Hauschild, *Häretische Transgressionen*, 55.

42. E. V. Khvorostianova calls "love" the major taboo word in *Mólodets*. See "'Zhest smysla' (invariantnye struktury ritma kak semanticheskii printsip poemy M. Tsvetaevoi 'Mólodets')," *Wiener Slawistischer Almanach* 37 (1996): 53. This is not entirely accurate: the nobleman does use the word "love" in his marriage proposal ("Khochesh' zhit' so mnoi v liubovi?" v. 1174), but it is true that this is the only time the word occurs in the Russian text. It is never used between Marusia and the vampire.

43. Etkind, "'Mólodets': Original i avtoperevod," 278.

44. For the sake of convenience, I will keep referring to the nameless male protagonist as "the vampire," even though his identity is in fact more complex. In the second half of the poem, he seems to turn into a force of nature with elemental powers. For a discussion of the polymorphous nature of this character, see the chapter "Der Widerspruch in Gestalt des Mólodec" in Hauschild, *Häretische Transgressionen*, 53–58.

45. The neologism "serd'" combines "serdtse" (heart) with "seredina" (middle). For a discussion of this word, see Zubova, *Iazyk poezii Mariny Tsvetaevoi*, 163.

46. The noun "nourisse" does not seem to exist in French. My translation is based on the assumption that Tsvetaeva meant "nourrice."

47. There are several *stolbik* constructions in the Russian version of *Mólodets*. For a discussion, see Lane, *Rendering the Sublime*, 97.

48. May 22, 1926. *Letters: Summer 1926*, 137.

49. Hauschild, *Häretische Transgressionen*, 146.

50. Ibid., 121.

51. N. M. Gerasimova, "Energetika tsveta v Tsvetaevskom 'Molodtse,'" in *Imia-siuzhet-mif: Mezhvuzovskii sbornik* (St. Petersburg: Izdatel'stvo S.-Peterburgskogo Universiteta, 1995), 159–78.

52. Hauschild, *Häretische Transgressionen*, 52, 61–62.

53. Only half of the chapter titles remain the same in the French translation. They include three chapters in Part One, I. 2 ("Lesenka" / "L'Échelle" [The Ladder], I. 5 ("Pod porogom" / "Sous le seuil" [Under the Threshold], II. 1 ("Barin" / "Le Barine"), and two chapters in Part Two, II. 2 ("Mramorá" / "Marmoréa") and II. 5 ("Kheruvimskaia," with the expanded French title "Le Chant des anges (Priére dite 'des Chérubins'" [The Chant of Angels: The Prayer Called "Of the Cherubs")]. The other five titles are completely different in French: I. 1, "Mólodets" becomes "Accordailles" (an archaic French term for "betrothal"), I. 3, "V vorotákh" (At the Gate) becomes "Soeur et frère" (Brother and Sister), I. 4, "Vtorye vorotá" (The Second Gate) becomes "Mère et fille" (Mother and Daughter), II. 3, "Syn" (The Son) becomes "L'Épousée" (The Married Woman), and II. 4, "Pirovan'itse" (The Feast) becomes "Les Compères" (The Partners, or Accomplices).

54. Hauschild, *Häretische Transgressionen*, 62.

55. Karlinsky, *Marina Tsvetaeva*, 41.

56. Etkind, "'Mólodets': Original i avtoperevod," 271.

57. Lushenkova Foscolo, "L'Autotraduction dans la poésie de Marina Tsvetaeva," 150.

58. This passage is omitted in the French version.

59. See the chapter "Der Mólodec als männliche Muse" in Hauschild, *Häretische Transgressionen*, 200–211.

60. Sibelan Forrester, "Marina Cvetaeva and Folklore," in *A Companion to Marina Cvetaeva: Approaches to a Major Russian Poet*, ed. Sibela E. S. Forrester (Leiden: Brill, 2017), 87.

61. See Caroline Bérenger, "Écrits français de Marina Tsvetaeva," in *Multilinguisme et créativité littéraire*, ed. Olga Anokhina (Louvain-la-Neuve: Harmattan, 2012), 27.

62. See Tsvetaeva, "Trois poèmes écrits en français: Publication, présentation et commentaire de H. B. Korkina et V. Lossky," in *Un chant de vie*, 388–96.

63. The poem "Ce noir et blanc," for example, is written in regular décasyllabes with the traditional grouping of 4 plus 6 syllables in each line. See ibid., 392.

64. About the circumstances of Tsvetaeva's translations of Pushkin, see Iu. Kliukin, "Pushkin po-frantsuzski v perevode Mariny Tsvetaevoi (K istorii sozdaniia)," *Wiener Slawistischer Almanach*, special volume 32 (1992): 63–84.

65. Letter to Iu. Ivask, November 23, 1936, in Tsvetaeva, *Sobranie sochinenii*, 7: 403.

66. Tsvetaeva's French translation of "Besy" came out in a special publica-

tion devoted to the Pushkin jubilee in February 1937, while two more translations ("Pesnia predsedatelia" from *Pir vo vremia chumy* and "Niane") appeared
in *La Vie intellectuelle* in the same year. See Kliukin, "Pushkin po-frantsuzski,"
77, 79.

67. These translations can all be found in Marina Tsvétaïéva, *Tentative de jalousie et autres poèmes* (Paris: La Découverte, 1986), 188–202. Perhaps there are more poems by Pushkin in Tsvetaeva's translation. According to Alexandra Smith, Tsvetaeva "translated at least 14 of Pushkin's poems into French." See *The Song of the Mocking Bird: Puškin in the Works of Marina Tsvetaeva* (Bern: Peter Lang, 1994), 152. An even higher number is given by Kliukin, who mentions that there may be as many as twenty-two translations ("Pushkin po-frantsuzski," 74).

68. Tsvétaïéva, *Tentative de jalousie et autres poèmes*, 204–16.

69. Marina Tsvetaeva, *"I zvezda s zvezdoiu govorit": Stikhotvoreniia Mikhaila Lermontova vo frantsuzskikh perevodakh Mariny Tsvetaevoi* (Moscow: Dom-muzei Mariny Tsvetaevoi, 2014).

70. On this, see the study by Robin Kemball, "Puškin en français: Les Poèmes traduits par Marina Cvetaeva: Essai d'analyse métrique." *Cahiers du Monde Russe et Soviétique* 32, no. 2 (1991): 217–35.

71. Studies of Tsvetaeva's Pushkin translations, in addition to the ones already mentioned, include V. V. Ivanov, "O Tsvetaevskikh perevodakh pesni iz 'Pira vo vremia chumy' i 'Besov' Pushkina" (1968), in *Izbrannye trudy po semiotike i istorii kul'tury*, vol. 2: *Stat'i o russkoi literature* (Moscow: Iazyki russkoi kul'tury, 2000), 664–84; Jean-Claude Lanne, "M. Cvetaeva traductrice de Puškin," in *Marina Cvetaeva: Trudy 1-go mezhdunarodnogo simpoziuma, Lausanne, 1982* (Bern: Peter Lang, 1991), 436–44; Etkind, "Marina Tsvétaeva, poète français," 240–50; the chapter "An Endeavor of Fidelity? Tsvetaeva's French Translations of Pushkin's Poems in the Light of Her Poetics" in Smith, *The Song of the Mocking Bird*, 151–81; and E. D. Bogatyreva, "Perevod ili perelozhenie? (A. S. Pushkin v perevode Mariny Tsvetaevoi)," in *Liki Mariny Tsvetaevoi: XIII Mezhdunarodnaia nauchno-tematicheskaia konferentsiia, 2005* (Moscow: Dom-muzei Mariny Tsvetaevoi, 2006), 77–85. Tsvetaeva's translations of Lermontov have remained largely unexplored.

72. Tsvetaeva, *"I zvezda s zvezdoiu govorit,"* 18–19.

73. Ibid., 79.

74. The only known verse lines by Tsvetaeva written in German can be found in a letter to Pasternak on May 23, 1926, where, commenting on her relationship with Rilke, she included the following distich: "Durch alle Welten, durch alle Gegenden, an allen Weg-Enden / Das ewige Paar der sich-Nie-Begegnenden" ("Across all worlds, all landscapes, on all ends of the road / the eternal couple of those-who-never-meet"). Tsvetaeva adds that "this couplet came of itself, as all of it does," constituting "a kind of sigh" (*Letters: Summer 1926*, 152). With

their ingenious sound play and composite rhyme, the two lines offer a tantalizing glimpse of what Tsvetaeva might have sounded like as a German poet.

75. Beaujour, *Alien Tongues*, 129.

76. See ibid., 53–54.

77. Ibid., 132 (Beaujour's emphasis).

78. Makin, *Marina Tsvetaeva: Poetics of Appropriation*, 318.

79. This is the verdict of Olga Anokhina on Tsvetaeva's French oeuvre expressed in the "Avant-propos" to the volume *Multilinguisme et créativité littéraire*, 8.

80. Mikhail Gasparov raises the interesting point that while the French public of the 1930s may have been put off by the syllabotonic meter of Tsvetaeva's translations, today's French readers are so used to free verse that they have forgotten their own syllabic tradition. In consequence, they may have become more tolerant of syllabotonic elements in French. See Gasparov, "Russkii Mólodets i frantsuzskii Mólodets," 278.

81. Vladimir Weidle, "O poetakh i poezii," quoted in Gasparov, "Russkii Mólodets i frantsuzskii Mólodets," 278.

CHAPTER FOUR

1. For a useful survey of Nabokov's poetic work, see Barry P. Scherr, "Poetry," in *The Garland Companion to Vladimir Nabokov*, ed. Vladimir E. Alexandrov (New York: Garland, 1995), 608–25. The first monograph devoted to Nabokov's poetry is Paul D. Morris, *Vladimir Nabokov: Poetry and the Lyric Voice* (Toronto: University of Toronto Press, 2010).

2. Vladimir Nabokov, *Poems and Problems* (New York: McGraw-Hill, 1970), 13. Page numbers given in the text will refer to this edition.

3. These texts are all available in Vladimir Nabokov, *Selected Poems* (New York: Alfred A. Knopf, 2012). Of course, a more complete collection of Nabokov's English poetry would also have to include the poems written by his fictional heroes, such as John Shade's "Pale Fire" and Humbert Humbert's poems quoted in *Lolita*. However, as I will argue later, Nabokov's practice of self-translation reveals an essential difference between the poems that he published under his own name (or the pen name Sirin) and those attributed to his invented characters.

4. Nabokov's self-translated fiction and memoirs have been discussed by a number of scholars, including Jane Grayson, *Nabokov Translated: A Comparison of Nabokov's Russian and English Prose* (Oxford: Oxford University Press, 1977), Elizabeth Beaujour, "Translation and Self-Translation," in *The Garland Companion to Vladimir Nabokov*, 714–24; and, most recently, Inés García de la Puente, "Bilingual Nabokov: Memories and Memoirs in Self-Translation," *Slavic and East European Journal* 59, no. 4 (2015): 585–608. None of these critics addresses Nabokov's poetic self-translations. Morris's monograph on Nabokov's

poetry completely bypasses this issue. Citing the self-translated poems in English without providing the Russian original (as he does with the poems originally composed in Russian), Morris treats the self-translated text as a perfect substitute for the original. The question of how the English version might differ from the Russian source text is not addressed. Thomas Eekman's article "Vladimir Nabokov's Poetry," in *The Language and Verse of Russia*, ed. Henrik Birnbaum and Michael S. Flier (Moscow: Vostochnaia literatura, 1995), 88–100, devotes one paragraph (97) to Nabokov's self-translated poems. Eekman does not go beyond generalities ("the translations are more or less literal," "the meter of each line is usually identical with or close to that of the original, although sometimes there is no meter at all," "here and there a rhyme is maintained"). Barry Scherr is somewhat more specific, naming concrete examples of Nabokov's varying translational approaches, and observing that Nabokov "clearly makes great efforts to maintain the sense of the original, even if it must come at the expense of a certain smoothness or elegance in the English" ("Poetry," 621).

5. Alexander Sergeevich Pushkin, *Eugene Onegin: A Novel in Verse*, translated from the Russian, with a commentary, by Vladimir Nabokov, rev. ed. (Princeton, N.J.: Princeton University Press, 1975), vii.

6. Ibid., viii.

7. David Bethea, "Brodsky's and Nabokov's Bilingualism(s): Translation, American Poetry, and the Muttersprache," *Russian Literature* 37, nos. 2–3 (1995): 159.

8. The word "rugged" seems to have potential semantic connotations with the "robust" style that Nabokov described as the hallmark of his mature poetry, characterized by a "sudden liberation from self-imposed shackles" (*Poems and Problems*, 14).

9. Vladimir Nabokov, "Problems of Translation: *Onegin* in English" (*Partisan Review*, 1955). Republished in *Theories of Translation: An Anthology of Essays from Dryden to Derrida*, ed. Rainer Schulte and John Biguenet (Chicago: University of Chicago Press, 1992), 143.

10. Nabokov, *Poems and Problems*, 14.

11. Richmond Lattimore, "Poetry Chronicle," *Hudson Review* 24, no. 3 (1971): 506–7.

12. Kostantin Bazarov, "Poet's Problems," *Books and Bookmen*, October 1972, xii.

13. John Skow, "Drinker of Words," *Time*, June 14, 1971, 66–68.

14. Bazarov, "Poet's Problems," xii.

15. See Gerald S. Smith, "Nabokov and Russian Verse Form," *Russian Literature TriQuarterly* 24 (1991): 286.

16. See Vladimir Nabokov, *Notes on Prosody* (New York: Pantheon Books, 1964), 9.

17. For a discussion of this issue, see Roman Jakobson's essay "Ob

odnoslozhnykh slovakh v russkom stikhe" in his *Selected Writings*, vol. 5: *On Verse, Its Masters and Explorers*, ed. Stephen Rudy and Martha Taylor (The Hague: Mouton, 1979), 201–14.

18. In his *Notes on Prosody*, Nabokov writes that "on the whole the iambic tetrameter has fared better in Russia than in England," given that the English version of the meter has become, in his opinion, "a hesitating, loose, capricious form" (52).

19. Omri Ronen observes a comparable technique in Nabokov's rendering of Tiutchev's poem "Uspokoenie," where the sound reiteration of the Slavic thunder god's name Perun in the word "pernatye" (the "feathered ones") is represented anagrammatically by distributing the two halves of the name of Perun's Germanic equivalent, Thor, to the ornithological species "<u>th</u>rush" and "<u>or</u>iole." See Ronen, "The Triple Anniversary of World Literature: Goethe, Pushkin, Nabokov," in *Nabokov at Cornell*, ed. Gabriel Shapiro (Ithaca, N.Y.: Cornell University Press, 2003), 180. Ronen claims that Nabokov eventually "abandoned such attempts to create equivalent substitutes in English for Russian lyric texts." As the present example demonstrates, this may not entirely be the case.

20. In a teasing footnote, Nabokov confirms the connection with *Lolita* by denying it, stating that "intelligent readers will abstain from examining this impersonal fantasy for any links with my later fiction" (*Poems and Problems*, 55).

21. See Scherr, "Poetry," 610; and Morris, *Vladimir Nabokov: Poetry and the Lyric Voice*, 160.

22. Pushkin's poem "Rifma" ("Rhyme," 1830), which is written in unrhymed elegiac distichs, may have provided a model of a poem about rhymes that does not rhyme.

23. Metrically speaking, line 7 is not imperfect, of course. The Russian version, with omitted stress on the third foot, is an example of what Nabokov, in his *Notes on Prosody*, calls "that facile and dangerous thing, the third-foot scudder," presenting "the commonest line in Russian poetry, the pastime of the cruising genius and the last refuge of the poetaster" (71). As R. Dyche Mullins has shown, Nabokov uses a preponderance of omitted stresses on the penultimate foot to create an atmosphere of "Russianness" in the poems "An Evening of Russian Poetry" and "Pale Fire" ("Conjuring in Two Tongues: The Russian and English Prosodies of Nabokov's 'Pale Fire,'" *Nabokov Online Journal* 10–11 [2016/2017]: 58, 69–70). He does nothing of the sort in *Poems and Problems*, though. In the present example, to keep with Nabokov's terminology, line 7 becomes a more rarefied "fourth-foot scudder" in English.

24. In his painstaking metrical analysis of all 999 lines of the poem "Pale Fire," Mullins notes the "ruthless correctness of Nabokov's English prosody" ("Conjuring in Two Tongues," 15). He comes to the conclusion that while Nabokov may occasionally stretch the rules of English versification, he never

breaks them. This is emphatically not the case here, or elsewhere in *Poems and Problems*.

25. I am indebted to Alexandra Shapiro for this observation.

26. Morris, *Vladimir Nabokov: Poetry and the Lyric Voice*, 163.

27. Nabokov, *Selected Poems*, 158.

28. Morris, *Vladimir Nabokov: Poetry and the Lyric Voice*, 22.

29. Fedor Tiutchev's poem "Den' i noch'" ("Day and Night," 1839), for example, displays a similar polar contrast between the diurnal and nocturnal world, with the night becoming the gateway for the experience of primordial chaos.

30. See Scherr, "Poetry," 613–14.

31. Ibid., 613. The English self-translation of the poem, mostly unrhymed except for the unusual identical rhyme words at the beginning, renders the striking truncated rhyme "sumerki-umer" in the final punchline as "recognize-died."

32. Smith, "Nabokov and Russian Verse Form," 295.

33. Stanislav Shvabrin has pointed out that while Nabokov may have spurned unconventional metric forms in his own work, he was attentive to the prosodic innovations brought to Russian poetry by Tiutchev and the symbolists. See "'. . . A Sob That Alters the Entire History of Russian Letters . . .': Cincinnatus's Plight, Tyutchev's 'Last Love,' and Nabokov's Metaphysics of Poetic Form," *Slavic and East European Journal* 58, no. 3 (2014): 460. In that sense, the English self-translations offered Nabokov the chance to conduct his own experiments with "broken rhythms."

34. Julia Trubikhina, *The Translator's Doubts: Vladimir Nabokov and the Ambiguity of Translation* (Boston: Academic Studies, 2015), 23.

35. Douglas Robinson, *The Translator's Turn* (Baltimore, Md.: Johns Hopkins University Press, 1991), xvi.

36. Nabokov, "Problems of Translation: *Onegin* in English," 143.

37. On this, see the chapters "Selbstironie im Kommentar" and "Der Kommentar als parodistische Textform" in Michael Eskin, *Zwischen Version und Fiktion: Nabokovs Version von Puškins Evgenij Onegin: Eine Übersetzungs- und fiktionstheoretische Untersuchung* (Munich: Otto Sagner, 1994), 105–16.

38. To some extent, Nabokov does display his poems as canonical texts, as Richmond Lattimore has pointed out in his review of *Poems and Problems*: "The book is presented in the manner of a 'classic,' with line numbers for the Russian poems, introduction, some notes, and a 'bibliography,' which is not really that but a full record of previous publication" (Lattimore, "Poetry Chronicle," 506).

39. Trubikhina, *The Translator's Doubts*, 107.

40. Zinaida Shakhovskaia, *V poiskakh Nabokova: Otrazheniia* (Moscow: Kniga, 1991), 22.

41. Vladimir Nabokov, "Reply to My Critics" (*Encounter*, 1966). Republished in *Strong Opinions* (New York: McGraw-Hill, 1973), 243.

42. Alexander Dolinin has argued that Nabokov did something similar in *Eugene Onegin* with occasional perfect "iambic clones." These "repeated flashes of Pushkinian harmony," according to Dolinin, "stick out of the surrounding jumble like the actual fragments of the virtual ideal translation never to be attained" ("Eugene Onegin," in *The Garland Companion to Vladimir Nabokov*, 124). In reality, though, such perfect clones are quite rare in *Eugene Onegin* (see Trubikhina, *The Translator's Doubts*, 127–28, citing a study by Liuba Tarvi).

43. Joseph Schlegel, "The Shapes of Poetry: Andrey Bely's Poetics in Vladimir Nabokov's *The Gift*," *Slavic and East European Journal* 59, no. 4 (2015): 573.

44. Vladimir Nabokov, *The Annotated Lolita*, ed. Alfred Appel, Jr. (New York: Vintage Books, 1991), 256; Vladimir Nabokov, *Lolita: Roman*, perevod s angliiskogo avtora (Moscow: Izvestiia, 1989), 292.

45. Interestingly, Nabokov included these texts in the posthumously published collection of his Russian poetry, where they are printed with line breaks. See Vladimir Nabokov, *Stikhi* (Ann Arbor, Mich.: Ardis, 1979), 314–15, 317. For a discussion of the Onegin stanza in *Dar*, see Michael Wachtel, *The Development of Russian Verse: Meter and Its Meaning* (Cambridge: Cambridge University Press, 1998), 165–68. Wachtel's observation that "Russia's most celebrated apologist for literal translation was forced to reassess his position when the question arose in regard to his own poetry" (168) can be generalized beyond the specific example of the Onegin stanza in *Dar*.

46. Vladimir Nabokov, "Pounding the Clavichord" (*New York Review of Books*, 1964). Republished in *Strong Opinions*, 239.

47. Nabokov, *The Annotated Lolita*, 316–17.

48. As Stanislav Shvabrin shows in his recent monograph on Nabokov's evolution as a translator, Nabokov continued to produce occasional "poetic" translations of other poets as well, in spite of his official adherence to literalism. They include his rendering of *The Song of Igor* and rhymed verse translations of poems by Rémy Belleau, Henri de Régnier, Pushkin, Lermontov, and the Soviet bard Bulat Okudzhava. See the chapter "Beyond *Eugene Onegin* (1965–1977)" in Stanislav Shvabrin, *Between Rhyme and Reason: Vladimir Nabokov, Translation, and Dialogue* (Toronto: University of Toronto Press, 2019), 311–38.

49. Brian Boyd, *Vladimir Nabokov: The American Years* (Princeton, N.J.: Princeton University Press, 1991), 440.

CHAPTER FIVE

1. According to Arina Volgina's count, Brodsky wrote a total of 540 poems in Russian and 46 in English. See Volgina, "Iosif Brodskii and Joseph Brodsky," *Russian Studies in Literature* 42, no. 3 (summer 2006): 18. Nabokov published a few hundred poems in Russian (out of possibly thousands that he wrote) and

composed 23 poems directly in English (excluding the poems attributed to literary characters). In addition, he translated 39 of his Russian poems into English.

2. Brodsky's poems written directly in English or self-translated into English, either alone or in collaboration with others, can all be found in Joseph Brodsky, *Collected Poems in English*, ed. Ann Kjellberg (New York: Farrar, Straus and Giroux, 2000).

3. For a comparison between Nabokov's and Brodsky's poetry, see David Bethea, "Brodsky's and Nabokov's Bilingualism(s): Translation, American Poetry and the Muttersprache," *Russian Literature* 37, no. 2–3 (February-April 1995): 157–84. This article is also included in Bethea's *Joseph Brodsky and the Creation of Exile* (Princeton, N.J.: Princeton University Press, 1994). Brodsky valued Nabokov as a novelist but had a low opinion of his poetry, a stance reciprocated by Nabokov's own condescending attitude toward Brodsky's work. See Bethea, "Brodsky's and Nabokov's Bilingualism(s)," 177, n. 3; and Lev Loseff, *Joseph Brodsky: A Literary Life*, trans. Jane Ann Miller (New Haven, Conn.: Yale University Press, 2011), 199–201.

4. Joseph Brodsky, "Learning English," unpublished manuscript, Beinecke Library, Yale University. Quoted in Zakhar Ishov, "'Post-Horse of Civilisation': Joseph Brodsky Translating Joseph Brodsky: Towards a New Theory of Russian-English Poetry Translation." Ph.D. diss., Freie Universität Berlin, 2008, 61.

5. See Ishov, "Post-Horse of Civilisation," 62.

6. On this, see the interesting study by Nila Friedberg, *English Rhythms in Russian Verse: On the Experiment of Joseph Brodsky* (Berlin: De Gruyter Mouton, 2011).

7. Quoted in Ishov, "Post-Horse of Civilisation," 61.

8. "Naglaia propoved' idealizma" (Interview with David Bethea on March 28–29, 1991), in Brodskii, *Kniga interv'iu*, ed. Polukhina, 589. Even though the interview was conducted in English, the full transcript seems to be available only in Russian translation.

9. "Real'nost' absoliutno nekontroliruema," *Den' za dnem*, Tallinn, September 8, 1995, in Brodskii, *Kniga interv'iu*, ed. Polukhina, 730.

10. Solomon Volkov, *Conversations with Joseph Brodsky: A Poet's Journey through the Twentieth Century*, trans. Marian Schwartz (New York: Free Press, 1998), 185–86.

11. Library of Congress, Manuscript Division, cited in Ishov, "Post-Horse of Civilisation," 67.

12. The translation is kept at the Beinecke Library at Yale University. See ibid.

13. Joseph Brodsky, *Less Than One: Selected Essays* (New York: Farrar, Straus and Giroux, 1986), 357.

14. See Bethea, "Brodsky's and Nabokov's Bilingualism," 174–75.

15. Ibid., 176.

16. Joseph Brodsky, "Elegy: For Robert Lowell" (1977), in Brodsky, *Collected Poems in English*, 147.

17. "Nastignut' utrachennoe vremia," *Vremia i my*, no. 97 (1979), in Brodskii, *Kniga interv'iu*, ed. Polukhina, 123.

18. Eugenia Kelbert, "Joseph Brodsky's Supralingual Evolution," in *Das literarische Leben der Mehrsprachigkeit: Methodische Erkundungen*, ed. Till Dembeck and Anne Uhrmacher (Heidelberg: Universitätsverlag Winter, 2016), 146.

19. The 2000 edition of Brodsky's *Collected Poems in English* makes a clear editorial choice in that regard: all poems, whether they were written directly in English, self-translated by Brodsky, translated in collaboration with someone else, or translated by an extraneous translator with little or no input from Brodsky, are presented on an equal footing. A reader interested in these distinctions has to resort to the endnotes to find out. Even so, the nature and scope of Brodsky's individual contribution to the collaborative translations or those edited by him remain unclear.

20. Joseph Brodsky, *Elegy for John Donne and Other Poems*, selected, trans., and intro. Nicholas William Bethell (London: Longman, 1967).

21. Letter to George Kline, Easter 1969, Beinecke Library, cited in Ishov, "Post-Horse of Civilisation," 81.

22. Brodsky, *Collected Poems in English*, 507.

23. For an account of this conflict from the point of view of a translator, see Daniel Weissbort's memoir, *From Russian with Love: Joseph Brodsky in English: Pages from a Journal 1996–97* (London: Anvil Press Poetry, 2004).

24. "Joseph Brodsky: The Poet and the Poem," in *Joseph Brodsky: Conversations*, ed. Cynthia L. Haven (Jackson: University Press of Mississippi, 2002), 144.

25. "The Art of Poetry XXVIII: Joseph Brodsky," in *Joseph Brodsky: Conversations*, ed. Haven, 74.

26. "Joseph Brodsky: An Interview," Mike Hammer and Christina Daub (1991), in *Joseph Brodsky: Conversations*, ed. Haven, 163.

27. Brodsky, *Collected Poems in English*, 517, 525.

28. George L. Kline, "Revising Brodsky," in *Translating Poetry: The Double Labyrinth*, ed. Daniel Weissbort (Iowa City: University of Iowa Press, 1989), 96.

29. Ibid., 104.

30. Ibid., 106.

31. Daniel Weissbort, "Translating Brodsky: A Postscript," in *Translating Poetry: The Double Labyrinth*, ed. Weissbort, 221.

32. See the chapter "A Second Christmas by the Shore" in Ishov, "Post-Horse of Civilisation," 136–80.

33. Weissbort, *From Russian with Love*, 226, 36.

34. Joseph Brodsky, "Translating Akhmatova," *New York Review of Books* 20, no. 13 (August 9, 1973), http://www.nybooks.com/articles/9770.

35. Joseph Brodsky, "Beyond Consolation," *New York Review of Books* 21, no. 1 (February 7, 1974), http://www.nybooks.com/articles/9613.

36. Pushkin, *Eugene Onegin*, trans. Nabokov, x.

37. Valentina Polukhina, "Angliiskii Brodskii," in *Iosif Brodskii: Tvorchestvo, lichnost', sud'ba: Itogi trekh konferentsii* (St. Petersburg: Zhurnal "Zvezda," 1998), 52.

38. See the testimony by Irma Kudrova, "'Eto osheshomliaet . . .': Iosif Brodskii o Marine Tsvetaevoi," in *Iosif Brodskii: Tvorchestvo, lichnost'*, 154. Of course, Brodsky would not have been able to appraise Tsvetaeva's French (self-) translations since he didn't know French.

39. Brodsky, *Collected Poems in English*, 130–32. For a detailed discussion of this self-translation, see Alexandra Berlina, *Brodsky Translating Brodsky: Poetry in Self-Translation* (New York: Bloomsbury, 2014), 9–45.

40. Brodsky, *Collected Poems in English*, 414–16.

41. Natalia E. Rulyova, "Joseph Brodsky: Translating Oneself," Ph.D. thesis, Cambridge University, 2002, 112–17. A discussion of Brodsky's self-translation of "Portrait of Tragedy" can also be found in Anton Nesterov, "Avtoperevod kak avtokommentarii," *Inostrannaia literatura* 7 (2001): 251–53.

42. *Sochineniia Iosifa Brodskogo* (St. Petersburg: Pushkinskii fond, 1992), 2: 275.

43. Brodsky, *Collected Poems in English*, 213.

44. The average word length in prose is 1.4 syllables in English and 3.0 syllables in Russian. See Jiri Levy, *The Art of Translation*, trans. Patrick Corness (Amsterdam: John Benjamins, 2011), 196.

45. See the discussion of this line in Liudmila Zubova, "Prilagatel'nye Brodskogo," in *Poeticheskii iazyk Iosifa Brodskogo: Stat'i* (St. Petersburg: LEMA, 2015), 154.

46. Berlina, *Brodsky Translating Brodsky*, 192.

47. Ibid., 197.

48. As Eugenia Kelbert has noted, a large number of Brodsky's poems written in English bear titles like "Song," "Blues," or "Tune," or are composed in a song-like style. Kelbert interprets this decision as a consequence of Brodsky's insistence on using rhyme. Since he was aware of the association of rhyme with comedy and popular song in modern English usage, Brodsky may have resorted to a conscious strategy: "Indeed, if your audience perceives the form that comes naturally to you as obsolete and song-like, why not use this perception to your own advantage and exaggerate its relevant aspects?" Kelbert, "Joseph Brodsky's Supralingual Evolution," 148.

49. Berlina, *Brodsky Translating Brodsky*, 194.

50. Cynthia Haven, "The Book That's Rocking Russia: Ellendea Proffer's *Brodsky Among Us* Is a Bestseller," The Book Haven, April 20, 2015, http://bookhaven.stanford.edu/2015/04/to-russia-with-love-ellendea-proffers -brodsky-among-us-is-a-russian-bestseller/.

51. "His English: Ann Kjellberg on Brodsky's Self-Translations," The Book Haven, April 29, 2015, http://bookhaven.stanford.edu/2015/04/his-english-ann -kjellberg-on-brodskys-self-translations/.

52. Christopher Reid, "Great American Disaster" (review of *To Urania* by Joseph Brodsky), *London Review of Books*, December 8, 1988, 17–18; Craig Raine, "A Reputation Subject to Inflation," *Financial Times*, November 16, 1996, 19.

53. See Denise Levertov's irate denunciation of Brodsky in her letter to the editors of the *American Poetry Review* in 1973, discussed in Ishov, "Post-Horse of Civilisation," 88–90.

54. See Bethea's analysis of Brodsky's English-language poem "To My Daughter" in *Joseph Brodsky: The Art of a Poem*, ed. Lev Loseff and Valentina Polukhina (Houndmills, Eng.: Macmillan, 1999), 240–57.

55. Bethea, *Joseph Brodsky and the Creation of Exile*, 13.

56. Charles Simic, "Working for the Dictionary," *New York Review of Books*, October 19, 2000, http://www.nybooks.com/articles/2000/10/19/working-for-the -dictionary/; Valentina Polukhina, "Literaturnoe vospriiatie Brodskogo v Anglii," *Storony Sveta* 9 (2007), http://www.stosvet.net/9/polukhina/.

57. See Weissbort, *From Russian with Love*, 41–53, 60–62, 67–73, 85–86, 107–10, 210–23, 233–34; and Alexandra Berlina, "Self-Creation in Self-Translation: Joseph Brodsky's 'May 24, 1980,'" *Translation Review* 89, no. 1 (2014): 35–48.

58. Not all Russian-English bilinguals have a high opinion of Brodsky's self-translations, however. See, for example, the comments by the Russian-American poet Alexei Tsvetkov, who states that Brodsky "simply entered the cage of the beast and began to force his own rules on that beast." Iakov Klots, *Poety v N'iu-Iorke: O gorode, iazyke, diaspore* (Moscow: NLO, 2016), 113.

59. Rulyova, "Joseph Brodsky: Translating Oneself," 144.

60. See the discussion of "interlation" and bilingual vs. monolingual editions in the conclusion of this book.

61. Seamus Heaney, "Brodsky's Nobel: What the Applause Was About," *New York Times Book Review*, November 8, 1987, 65.

CHAPTER SIX

1. I have discussed this phenomenon in my book *Out of Russia: Fictions of a New Translingual Diaspora* (Evanston, Ill.: Northwestern University Press, 2011), which deals with Russian emigrant novelists in France, Germany, Israel, and the United States.

2. A useful survey of the Anglophone Russian-American poetry scene in the first decade of the twenty-first century can be found in Matvei Yankelevich, "The Russians Are Coming! The Russians Are Coming! Field Notes on Russian-

American Poets," *Octopus Magazine* 5, http://www.octopusmagazine.com/Issue 05/essays/Matvei_Yankelevich.htm; *Octopus Magazine* 7, http://octopusmagazine.com/Issue07/html/matvei_yankelevich.htm. An example of a trilingual poet is Alexander Stessin. His volume *Point of Reference / Точка отсчета / Le Point de la référence* (New York: Slovo-Word, 2002) contains poems written in Russian, English, and French (but no self-translations).

3. Steven G. Kellman, *The Translingual Imagination* (Lincoln: University of Nebraska Press, 2000), 12.

4. See Adrian Wanner, "*Lolita* and *Kofemolka*: Vladimir Nabokov's and Michael Idov's Self-Translations from English into Russian," *Slavic and East European Journal* 57, no. 3 (2013): 450–64.

5. Other contemporary Russian-American poets who have engaged in self-translation, at least occasionally, include Irina Mashinski, Alexei Tsvetkov, and Anna Halberstadt. A self-translated poem by Mashinski in English and Russian can be found at http://www.radiuslit.org/2011/03/21/poem-english-translation-russian-by-irina-mashinski/. Tsvetkov's volume *Edem* contains an equimetrical and rhymed English self-translation of his poem "Oskudevaet vremeni ruda." See Aleksei Tsvetkov, *Edem* (Ann Arbor, Mich.: Ardis, 1985), 79. The Russian original has been republished in Aleksei Tsvetkov, *Vse eto, ili Eto vse: Sobranie stikhotvorenii v dvukh tomakh*, vol. 2 (New York: Ailuros, 2015), 400. Anna Halberstadt's volume *Transit* contains a number of Russian self-translations of poems originally published in English in her *Vilnius Diary*. See Anna Gal'bershtadt, *Transit: Stikhotvoreniia* (Moscow: Vest-Konsalting, 2016) and Anna Halberstadt, *Vilnius Diary* (New York: Box Turtle, 2014).

6. Andrey Gritsman, Roger Weingarten, Kurt Brown, and Carmen Firan, eds., *Stranger at Home: American Poetry with an Accent: An Anthology of Contemporary Poetry by American Poets of Foreign Origin* (New York: Interpoezia, 2008).

7. Andrey Gritsman, *Vid s mosta / View from the Bridge* (New York: Slovo-Word, 1998), 18.

8. Ibid., 20.

9. Ibid., 25.

10. Ibid., 25–26.

11. Ibid., 50.

12. The acronym VDNKh stands for Vystavka Dostizhenii Narodnogo Khoziaistva (Exhibit of the Achievements of the National Economy), the name of a large fairground in northern Moscow that opened in 1939.

13. Gritsman, *Vid s mosta*, 51.

14. I am indebted to Gasan Guseinov for this observation.

15. Katia Kapovich, *Veselyi distsiplinarii* (Moscow: NLO, 2005).

16. Marc Vincenz, "A Cloud of Voices: A Conversation and Twenty Cigarettes with Katia Kapovich," *Open Letters Monthly*, July 1, 2010, http://www.openlettersmonthly.com/voices-before-and-after-the-storm/.

17. Iakov Klots, *Poety v N'iu-Iorke: O gorode, iazyke, diaspore* (Moscow: NLO, 2016), 306.

18. Katia Kapovich, *Gogol in Rome* (Cambridge, Eng.: Salt, 2004), 14.

19. Ibid., 27.

20. Katia Kapovich, *Perekur* (St. Petersburg: Pushkinskii fond, 2002). Available online at http://www.vavilon.ru/texts/kapovich1.html.

21. Kapovich, *Gogol in Rome*, 15.

22. Kapovich, *Perekur*.

23. Kapovich, *Gogol in Rome*, 18.

24. Ibid., 96.

25. Vincenz, "A Cloud of Voices."

26. Eva Gentes, "Potentials and Pitfalls of Publishing Self-Translations as Bilingual Editions," *Orbis Litterarum* 68, no. 3 (2013): 267.

27. Gritsman, *Vid s mosta*, 21.

CONCLUSION

1. Michael Eskin, review of *Brodsky Translating Brodsky: Poetry in Self-Translation*, by Alexandra Berlina, *The Russian Review* 74, no. 2 (2015): 313 (author's italics).

2. Lattimore, "Poetry Chronicle," 507.

3. Skow, "Drinker of Words," 68.

4. Joseph Brodsky, "In the Shadow of Dante," in *Less Than One* (New York: Farrar, Straus and Giroux, 1986), 104.

5. Lawrence Venuti, "Introduction: Translation, Interpretation, and the Humanities," in *Teaching Translation: Programs, Courses, Pedagogies*, ed. Lawrence Venuti (London: Routledge, 2017), 6–7.

6. Walter Benjamin, "The Task of the Translator" (1923), trans. Harry Zohn, in *Theories of Translation: An Anthology of Essays from Dryden to Derrida*, ed. Rainer Schulte and John Biguenet (Chicago: University of Chicago Press, 1992), 71.

7. Bethea, *Joseph Brodsky and the Creation of Exile*, 290–91 (Bethea's italics). Tsvetaeva's self-translation of *Mólodets* was not really "late in life," but a similar argument could perhaps be made for her French translations of Mikhail Lermontov's poems written in 1941 shortly before her death.

8. Mikhail Epstein, "The Unasked Question: What Would Bakhtin Say?" *Common Knowledge* 10, no. 1 (2004): 50.

9. Ibid., 51.

10. Brodskii, *Kniga interv'iu*, ed. Polukhina, 123.

Bibliography

Abaeva-Maiers, Diana. "'My guliali s nim po nebesam . . .' (Beseda s Isaem Berlinom)." In *Iosif Brodskii: Trudy i dni*, ed. Lev Losev and Petr Vail', 90–110.
Moscow: Izdatel'stvo Nezavisimaia Gazeta, 1998.

Anokhina, Olga. "Avant-propos: Le Multilinguisme et le processus de création."
In *Multilinguisme et créativité littéraire*, ed. Olga Anokhina, 5–11. Louvain-
la-Neuve: Harmattan, 2012.

Anselmi, Simona. *On Self-Translation: An Exploration in Self-Translators' Teloi
and Strategies*. Milan: LED, 2012.

Asadowski, Konstantin M., ed. *Rainer Maria Rilke und Marina Zwetajewa: Ein
Gespräch in Briefen*. Frankfurt am Main: Insel Verlag, 1992.

Azarova, Natalia. "Mnogoiazychie Aigi i iazyki-posredniki." *Russian Literature*
79–80 (2016): 29–44.

Baer, Brian James. *Translation and the Making of Modern Russian Literature*.
New York: Bloomsbury Academic, 2016.

Bassnett, Susan. "Rejoinder." *Orbis Litterarum* 68, no. 3 (2013): 282–89.

Bazarov, Kostantin. "Poet's Problems." *Books and Bookmen*, October 1972,
xi–xii.

Beaujour, Elizabeth Klosty. *Alien Tongues: Bilingual Russian Writers of the
"First" Emigration*. Ithaca, N.Y.: Cornell University Press, 1989.

———. "Translation and Self-Translation." In *The Garland Companion to Vladimir Nabokov*, ed. Vladimir E. Alexandrov, 714–24. New York: Garland,
1995.

Beckett, Samuel, and Alan Schneider. *No Author Better Served: The Correspondence of Samuel Beckett and Alan Schneider*, ed. Maurice Harmon. Cambridge, Mass.: Harvard University Press, 1998.

Belinskii, V. G. *Polnoe sobranie sochinenii*, vol. 4: *Stat'i i retsenzii 1840–1841*.
Moscow: Izdatel'stvo Akademii Nauk SSSR, 1954.

Benjamin, Walter. "The Task of the Translator" (1923). Trans. Harry Zohn. In
Theories of Translation: An Anthology of Essays from Dryden to Derrida,
ed. Rainer Schulte and John Biguenet, 71–82. Chicago: University of Chicago Press, 1992.

Bérenger, Caroline. "Écrits français de Marina Tsvetaeva." In *Multilinguisme et créativité littéraire*, ed. Olga Anokhina, 27–39. Louvain-la-Neuve: Harmattan, 2012.

Berlina, Alexandra. "The American Brodsky: A Research Overview." *Resources for American Literary Study* 38 (2016): 195–211.

———. *Brodsky Translating Brodsky: Poetry in Self-Translation*. New York: Bloomsbury, 2014.

———. "Self-Creation in Self-Translation: Joseph Brodsky's 'May 24, 1980.'" *Translation Review* 89, no. 1 (2014): 35–48.

Besemeres, Mary. *Translating One's Self: Language and Selfhood in Cross-Cultural Autobiography*. Oxford: Peter Lang, 2002.

Bethea, David. "Brodsky's and Nabokov's Bilingualism(s): Translation, American Poetry, and the Muttersprache." *Russian Literature* 37, nos. 2–3 (1995): 157–84.

———. *Joseph Brodsky and the Creation of Exile*. Princeton, N.J.: Princeton University Press, 1994.

———. "To My Daughter." In *Joseph Brodsky: The Art of a Poem*, ed. Lev Loseff and Valentina Polukhina, 240–57. Houndmills, Eng.: Macmillan, 1999.

Bill, Max, ed. *Kandinsky*. Paris: Maeght, 1951.

Bogatyreva, E. D. "Perevod ili perelozhenie? (A. S. Pushkin v perevode Mariny Tsvetaevoi)." In *Liki Mariny Tsvetaevoi: XIII Mezhdunarodnaia nauchno-tematicheskaia konferentsiia, 2005*, 77–85. Moscow: Dom-muzei Mariny Tsvetaevoi, 2006.

Bowlt, John. "Vasilii Kandinsky: The Russian Connection." In *The Life of Vasilii Kandinsky in Russian Art: A Study of "On the Spiritual in Art,"* ed. John Bowlt and Rose-Carol Washton Long, 1–41. Newtonville, Mass.: Oriental Research Partners, 1980.

Boyd, Brian. *Vladimir Nabokov: The American Years*. Princeton, N.J.: Princeton University Press, 1991.

Brodskii, Iosif. *Kniga interv'iu*, ed. V. Polukhina. 4th ed. Moscow: Zakharov, 2007.

———. *Sochineniia Iosifa Brodskogo*. 4 vols. St. Petersburg: Pushkinskii fond, 1992.

Brodsky, Joseph. "Beyond Consolation." *New York Review of Books*, vol. 21, no. 1 (February 7, 1974). http://www.nybooks.com/articles/9613.

———. *Collected Poems in English*, ed. Ann Kjellberg. New York: Farrar, Straus and Giroux, 2000.

———. *Elegy for John Donne and Other Poems*, selected, trans., and intro. Nicholas William Bethell. London: Longman, 1967.

———. *Joseph Brodsky: Conversations*, ed. Cynthia L. Haven. Jackson: University Press of Mississippi, 2002.

———. *Less Than One: Selected Essays*. New York: Farrar, Straus and Giroux, 1986.

———. "Translating Akhmatova." *New York Review of Books* 20, no. 13 (August 9, 1973). http://www.nybooks.com/articles/9770.

Bruppacher, Hanspeter. "Erinnerung an Elisabeth Kulmann: Eine russische Dichterin aus dem frühen 19. Jahrhundert." *Neue Zürcher Zeitung*, no. 201 (August 31/September 1, 1991): 65–66.

Cordingley, Anthony. "The Passion of Self-Translation: A Masocritical Perspective." In *Self-Translation: Brokering Originality in Hybrid Culture*, ed. Anthony Cordingley, 81–94. London: Bloomsbury, 2013.

———, ed. *Self-Translation: Brokering Originality in Hybrid Culture*. London: Bloomsbury, 2013.

Coudenys, Wim. "'Te poslednie vy mozhete ispravliat' s tochki zreniia stilistiki': Chetyre zabytykh frantsuzskikh perevoda Mariny Tsvetaevoi." *Revue des Études Slaves* 66, no. 2 (1994): 401–11.

Dadazhanova, Munavvarkhon. "Obe—vedushchie: 'Perevod avtora'—tvorcheskoe peresozdanie." *Druzhba narodov*, no. 3 (1984): 243–48. English translation in *Soviet Studies in Literature* 20, no. 4 (1984): 67–79.

Danilevskiii, R. Iu. "Nemetskie stikhotvoreniia russkikh poetov." In *Mnogoiazychie i literaturnoe tvorchestvo*, ed. M. P. Alekseev, 18–65. Leningrad: Nauka, 1981.

Dolinin, Alexander. "Eugene Onegin." In *The Garland Companion to Vladimir Nabokov*, ed. Vladimir E. Alexandrov, 117–29. New York: Garland, 1995.

Durylin, S. "Pushkin i Elizaveta Kul'man." *30 dnei* 2 (1937): 87–91.

Eekman, Thomas. "Vladimir Nabokov's Poetry." In *The Language and Verse of Russia: In Honor of Dean S. Worth on His Sixty-Fifth Birthday*, ed. Henrik Birnbaum and Michael S. Flier, 88–100. Moscow: Vostochnaia literatura, 1995.

Eliot, T. S. "Tradition and the Individual Talent" (1919). In *Selected Prose of T. S. Eliot*, ed. Frank Kermode, 37–44. London: Faber and Faber, 1975.

Eller-Rüter, Ulrike-Maria. *Kandinsky: Bühnenkomposition und Dichtung als Realisation seines Synthese-Konzepts*. Hildesheim: Georg Olms Verlag, 1990.

Emmert, Claudia. *Bühnenkompositionen und Gedichte von Wassily Kandinsky im Kontext eschatologischer Lehren seiner Zeit 1896–1914*. Frankfurt am Main: Peter Lang, 1998.

Epstein, Mikhail. "The Unasked Question: What Would Bakhtin Say?" *Common Knowledge* 10, no. 1 (2004): 42–60.

Eskin, Michael. Review of *Brodsky Translating Brodsky: Poetry in Self-Translation*, by Alexandra Berlina. *Russian Review* 74, no. 2 (2015): 313–14.

———. *Zwischen Version und Fiktion: Nabokovs Version von Puškins Evgenij*

Onegin: Eine Übersetzungs- und fiktionstheoretische Untersuchung. Munich: Otto Sagner, 1994.

Etkind, Efim. "Marina Cvetaeva: Französische Texte." *Wiener Slawistischer Almanach*, special volume 3 (1981): 195–205.

———. "Marina Cvetaeva, poète français." In *Un chant de vie: Marina Tsvétaeva. Actes du Colloque International de l'Université Paris IV*, 237–62. Paris: YMCA, 1996.

———. "Molodets' Tsvetaevoi: Original i avtoperevod." *Slavia* 61 (1992): 265–84. Republished in *Tam, vnutri: Stat'i o russkoi poezii XX v. Ocherki*, 422–45. St. Petersburg: Maksima, 1997.

Fainshtein, M. Sh. "'Ee poeziia liubila . . .' (E. B. Kul'man)." In *Pisatel'nitsy pushkinskoi pory: Istoriko-literaturnye ocherki*, 6–24. Leningrad: Nauka, 1989.

Ferraro, Alessandra, and Rainier Grutman, eds. *L'Autotraduction littéraire: Perspectives théoriques*. Paris: Classiques Garnier, 2016.

Feshchenko, V. V. "Avtoperevod poeticheskogo teksta kak raznovidnost' avtokommunikatsii." *Kritika i semiotika* 1 (2015): 199–218.

Fet, A. A. *Polnoe sobranie stikhotvorenii*. Leningrad: Sovetskii pisatel', 1959.

Finkelstein, Miriam. "Die hässlichen Entlein: Russisch-amerikanische Gegenwartslyrik." In *Lyrik transkulturell*, ed. Eva Binder, Sieglinde Klettenhammer, and Birgit Mertz-Baumgartner, 251–70. Würzburg: Verlag Königshausen & Neumann, 2016.

Forrester, Sibelan. "Marina Cvetaeva and Folklore." In *A Companion to Marina Cvetaeva: Approaches to a Major Russian Poet*, ed. Sibela E. S. Forrester, 66–91. Leiden: Brill, 2017.

Forster, Leonard. *The Poet's Tongues: Multilingualism in Literature*. London: Cambridge University Press, 1970.

Fricke, Angelika. "*Anakreon ljubeznyj*—zu Elizaveta Kul'man's Beschäftigung mit Anakreon." In *Festschrift für Hans-Bernd Harder zum 60. Geburtstag*, ed. Klaus Harer, 93–113. Munich: Otto Sagner, 1995.

Friedberg, Nila. *English Rhythms in Russian Verse: On the Experiment of Joseph Brodsky*. Berlin: De Gruyter Mouton, 2011.

Frizman, L. G. "Prozaicheskie avtoperevody Baratynskogo." *Masterstvo perevoda* 6, 1969 (Moscow: Sovetskii pisatel', 1970), 201–16.

Frost, Robert. *Interviews with Robert Frost*, ed. Edward Connery Lathem. New York: Holt, Rinehart and Winston, 1966.

Ganzburg, G. I. "K istorii izdaniia i vospriiatiia sochinenii Elizavety Kul'man." *Russkaia literatura* 1 (1990): 148–55.

García de la Puente, Inés. "Bilingual Nabokov: Memories and Memoirs in Self-Translation." *Slavic and East European Journal* 59, no. 4 (2015): 585–608.

Gasparov, M. L. "Russkii Mólodets i frantsuzskii Mólodets: Dva stikhovykh eksperimenta." In *Izbrannye trudy*, vol. 3: *O stikhe*, by M. L. Gasparov, 267–78. Moscow: Iazyki russkoi kul'tury, 1997.

Geffers, Andrea. *Stimmen im Fluss: Wasserfrau-Entwürfe von Autorinnen. Literarische Beiträge zum Geschlechterdiskurs von 1800–2000*. Frankfurt am Main: Peter Lang, 2007.

Gentes, Eva, ed. *Bibliography Autotraduzione / Autotraducción / Self-Translation: XXXVII Edition: July 2019*. www.self-translation.blogspot.com.

———. "Potentials and Pitfalls of Publishing Self-Translations as Bilingual Editions." *Orbis Litterarum* 68, no. 3 (2013): 266–81.

Gerasimova, N. M. "Energetika tsveta v Tsvetaevskom 'Molodtse.'" In *Imiasiuzhet-mif: Mezhvuzovskii sbornik*, 159–78. St. Petersburg: Izdatel'stvo S.-Peterburgskogo Universiteta, 1995.

Gerhardt, Dietrich. "Eigene und übersetzte deutsche Gedichte Žukovskijs." In *Gorski Vijenac: A Garland of Essays Offered to Professor E. M. Hill*, 118–54. Cambridge: Cambridge University Press, 1970.

Glanc, Tomas. "(Ino)strannyi iazyk poezii Aigi—problemy i posledstviia transnatsionalizma." *Russian Literature* 79–80 (2016): 13–27.

Göricke, Jutta. "Kandinsky's Lautmalerei *Der gelbe Klang*: Ein Interpretationsversuch." In *Besichtigung der Moderne: Bildende Kunst, Architektur, Musik, Literatur, Religion: Aspekte und Perspektiven*, ed. Hans Holländer and Christian W. Thomsen, 121–31. Cologne: DuMont Buchverlag, 1987.

Grayson, Jane. *Nabokov Translated: A Comparison of Nabokov's Russian and English Prose*. Oxford: Oxford University Press, 1977.

Gritsman, Andrei. *Dvoinik: Stikhi*. Tenafly, N.J.: Hermitage, 2002.

———. *Nicheinaia zemlia*. St. Petersburg: Al'manakh Petropol', 1995.

———. *Peresadka*. Moscow: Arion, 2003.

Gritsman, Andrey. *In Transit*. Craiova, Romania: Scrisul Romanesc, 2004.

———. *Vid s mosta / View from the Bridge*. New York: Slovo-Word, 1998.

Gritsman, Andrey, Roger Weingarten, Kurt Brown, and Carmen Firan, eds. *Stranger at Home: American Poetry with an Accent: An Anthology of Contemporary Poetry by American Poets of Foreign Origin*. New York: Interpoezia, 2008.

Großheinrich, Karl Friedrich. "Vorrede." In *Sämmtliche Gedichte von Elisabeth Kulmann*, 3–132. Leipzig: Verlag von Otto Wigand, 1847. Russian translation: V. K. Grosgeinrikh, "Elizaveta Kul'man i ee stikhotvoreniia." *Biblioteka dlia chteniia* 94, no. 4 (1849): 69–117; 95, no. 5 (1849): 1–34 and no. 6 (1849): 61–96; 96, no. 6 (1849): 83–119.

Grutman, Rainier. "Auto-Translation." In *Routledge Encyclopedia of Translation Studies*, ed. Mona Baker, 17–20. London: Routledge, 1998.

———. "L'Autotraduction: Dilemme social et entre-deux textuel." *Atelier de Traduction* 7 (2007): 219–29.

————. "L'Écrivain bilingue et ses publics: Une perspective comparatiste." In *Écrivains multilingues et écritures métisses: L'Hospitalité des langues*, ed. Axel Gasquet and Modesta Suárez, 31–50. Clermont-Ferrand, Fr.: Presses Universitaires Blaise Pascal, 2007.

————. "Self-Translation." In *Routledge Encyclopedia of Translation Studies*, 2nd ed., ed. Mona Baker and Gabriela Saldanha, 257–60. London: Routledge, 2009.

————. "A Sociological Glance at Self-Translation and Self-Translators." In *Self-Translation: Brokering Originality in Hybrid Culture*, ed. Anthony Cordingley, 63–80. London: Bloomsbury, 2013.

Grutman, Rainier, and Trish Van Bolderen. "Self-Translation." In *A Companion to Translation Studies*, ed. Sandra Berman and Catherine Porter, 323–32. Chichester, Eng.: Wiley Blackwell, 2014.

Hahl-Koch, Jelena. *Kandinsky*. Stuttgart: Verlag Gerd Hatje, 1993.

[Hahl-Koch, Jelena]. E. A. Khal'-Kokh. "Zametki o poezii i dramaturgii Kandinskogo." In *Mnogogrannyi mir Kandinskogo*, ed. N. B. Avtonomova, 124–30. Moscow: Nauka, 1998.

Halberstadt, Anna. *Vilnius Diary*. New York: Box Turtle, 2014.

[Halberstadt, Anna] Anna Gal'bershtadt. *Transit: Stikhotvoreniia*. Moscow: Vest-Konsalting, 2016.

Hanauer, David Ian. *Poetry as Research: Exploring Second Language Poetry Writing*. Amsterdam: John Benjamins, 2010.

Hauschild, Christiane. *Häretische Transgressionen: Das Märchenpoem "Molodec" von Marina Cvetaeva*. Göttingen: Wallstein Verlag, 2004.

Haven, Cynthia. "The Book That's Rocking Russia: Ellendea Proffer's *Brodsky Among Us* Is a Bestseller." The Book Haven, April 20, 2015. http://book haven.stanford.edu/2015/04/to-russia-with-love-ellendea-proffers-brodsky -among-us-is-a-russian-bestseller/.

Heaney, Seamus. "Brodsky's Nobel: What the Applause Was About." *New York Times Book Review*, November 8, 1987, 65.

Hoberg, Annegret, ed. *Wassily Kandinsky und Gabriele Münter in Murnau und Kochel 1902–1914: Briefe und Erinnerungen*. Munich: Prestel Verlag, 1994.

Hokenson, Jan, and Marcella Munson. *The Bilingual Text: History and Theory of Literary Self-Translation*. Manchester, Eng.: St. Jerome, 2007.

Hoogenboom, Hilde. "Biographies of Elizaveta Kul'man and Representations of Female Poetic Genius." In *Models of Self*, ed. Marianne Liljeström, Arja Rosenholm, and Irina Savkina, 17–32. Helsinki: Kikimora, 2001.

Ishov, Zakhar. "'Post-Horse of Civilisation': Joseph Brodsky Translating Joseph Brodsky: Towards a New Theory of Russian-English Poetry Translation." Ph.D. diss., Free University of Berlin, 2008.

Ivanov, V. V. "O Tsvetaevskikh perevodakh pesni iz 'Pira vo vremia chumy' i 'Besov' Pushkina" (1968). In *Izbrannye trudy po semiotike i istorii kul'tury*, vol. 2: *Stat'i o russkoi literature*, 664–84. Moscow: Iazyki russkoi kul'tury, 2000.

Jakobson, Roman. "Ob odnoslozhnykh slovakh v russkom stikhe." In *Selected Writings*, vol. 5: *On Verse, Its Masters and Explorers*, ed. Stephen Rudy and Martha Taylor, 201–14. The Hague: Mouton, 1979.

Kandinskii, Vasilii. *Kandinskii: Put' khudozhnika: Khudozhnik i vremia*, ed. D. V. Sarab'ianov and N. B. Avtonomova. Moscow: Galart, 1994.

———. "Kuda idet 'novoe' iskusstvo: Teksty 1910–1915 godov," ed. Boris Sokolov. *Nashe nasledie* 37 (1996): 81–96.

———. "O ponimanii iskusstva: Stikhotvoreniia i stat'i 1910—1920-kh godov," ed. Boris Sokolov. *Znamia* 2 (1999). http://magazines.russ.ru/znamia/1999/2/kandin.html.

———. "Zheltyi zvuk—sinezteicheskaia kompozitsiia V. V. Kandinskogo," ed. V. Turchin. *Dekorativnoe iskusstvo* 1–2 (1993): 24–27.

Kandinsky, Wassily. *Complete Writings on Art*, ed. Kenneth C. Lindsay and Peter Vergo. Boston: G. K. Hall, 1982.

———. *Die gesammelten Schriften*, ed. Hans K. Roethel and Jelena Hahl-Koch. Vol. 1. Bern: Benteli Verlag, 1980.

———. *11 Tableaux et 7 poèmes*. Amsterdam: Editions Duwaer, 1945.

———. *Gesammelte Schriften 1889–1916: Farbensprache, Kompositionslehre und andere unveröffentlichte Texte*, ed. Helmut Friedel. Munich: Prestel, 2007.

———. *Sounds*, trans. Elizabeth R. Napier. New Haven, Conn.: Yale University Press, 1981.

———. *Über das Theater/Du théâtre/O teatre*, ed. Jessica Boissel. Paris: Éditions Adam Biro, 1998.

———. *Vergessenes Oval: Gedichte aus dem Nachlass*, ed. Alexander Graeff and Alexander Filyuta. Berlin: Verlagshaus Berlin, 2016.

Kapovich, Katia. *Cossacks and Bandits: Poems 2003–2006*. Cambridge, Eng.: Salt, 2007.

———. *Gogol in Rome*. Cambridge, Eng.: Salt, 2004.

———. *Perekur*. St. Petersburg: Pushkinskii fond, 2002. http://www.vavilon.ru/texts/kapovich1.html.

———. *Veselyi distsiplinarii*. Moscow: NLO, 2005.

Karlinsky, Simon. *Marina Tsvetaeva: The Woman, Her World and Her Poetry*. Cambridge: Cambridge University Press, 1985.

Kelbert, Eugenia. "Joseph Brodsky's Supralingual Evolution." In *Das literarische Leben der Mehrsprachigkeit: Methodische Erkundungen*, ed. Till Dembeck and Anne Uhrmacher, 143–63. Heidelberg: Universitätsverlag Winter, 2016.

Kellman, Steven G. *The Translingual Imagination*. Lincoln: University of Nebraska Press, 2000.

Kemball, Robin. "Puškin en français: Les Poèmes traduits par Marina Cvetaeva: Essai d'analyse métrique." *Cahiers du Monde Russe et Soviétique* 32, no. 2 (1991): 217–35.

Khodasevich, Vladislav. "Zametki o stikhakh: M. Tsvetaeva: 'Mólodets'" (*Poslednie novosti*, June 11, 1925). In *Marina Cvetaeva: Studien und Materialien*, ed. Horst Lampl and Aage Hansen-Löve, *Wiener Slawistischer Almanach*, special volume 3 (1981): 262–66.

Khvorostianova, E. V. "'Zhest smysla' (invariantnye struktury ritma kak semanticheskii printsip poemy M. Tsvetaevoi 'Mólodets')." *Wiener Slawistischer Almanach* 37 (1996): 27–65.

Kippur, Sara. *Writing It Twice: Self-Translation and the Making of a World Literature in French*. Evanston, Ill.: Northwestern University Press, 2015.

Kiukhel'beker, V. K. *Izbrannye proizvedeniia v dvukh tomakh*, ed. N. V. Koroleva. Moscow-Leningrad: Sovetskii pisatel, 1967.

Kjellberg, Ann. "His English: Ann Kjellberg on Brodsky's Self-Translations." The Book Haven, April 29, 2015. http://bookhaven.stanford.edu/2015/04/his-english-ann-kjellberg-on-brodskys-self-translations/.

Kleine, Gisela. *Gabriele Münter und Wassily Kandinsky: Biographie eines Paares*. Frankfurt am Main: Insel Verlag, 1990.

Klimkiewicz, Aurelia. "Self-Translation as Broken Narrativity: Towards an Understanding of the Self's Multilingual Dialogue." In *Self-Translation: Brokering Originality in Hybrid Culture*, ed. Anthony Cordingley, 189–201. London: Bloomsbury, 2013.

Kline, George L. "Revising Brodsky." In *Translating Poetry: The Double Labyrinth*, ed. Daniel Weissbort, 95–106. Iowa City: University of Iowa Press, 1989.

Kliukin, Iu. P. "Inoiazychnye proizvedeniia Mariny Tsvetaevoi." *Nauchnye doklady vysshei shkoly*, "Filologicheskie nauki," no. 4 (1986): 66–73.

———. "Pushkin po-frantsuzski v perevode Mariny Tsvetaevoi (K istorii sozdaniia)." *Wiener Slawistischer Almanach*, special volume 32 (1992): 63–84.

Klots, Iakov. *Poety v N'iu-Iorke: O gorode, iazyke, diaspore*. Moscow: NLO, 2016.

Kobayashi-Bredenstein, Naoko. *Wassily Kandinskys frühe Bühnenkompositionen: Über Körperlichkeit und Bewegung*. Berlin: De Gruyter, 2012.

Kudrova, Irma. "'Eto oshelomliaet . . .': Iosif Brodskii o Marine Tsvetaevoi." In *Iosif Brodskii: Tvorchestvo, lichnost', sud'ba: Itogi trekh konferentsii*, 154–60. St. Petersburg: Zhurnal "Zvezda," 1998.

Kul'man, Elizaveta. *Polnoe sobranie russkikh, nemetskikh i ital'ianskikh stikhotvorenii Elizavety Kul'man*. St. Petersburg: Tipografiia Imperatorskoi Rossiiskoi Akademii, 1839.

Kulmann, Elisabeth. *Mond, meiner Seele Liebling: Eine Auswahl ihrer Gedichte,* ed. Hansotto Hatzig. Heidelberg: Meichsner & Schmidt, 1981.

———. *Sämmtliche Gedichte von Elisabeth Kulmann.* Leipzig: Verlag von Otto Wigand, 1847.

Kumakhova, Zarema. "Joseph Brodsky as Self-Translator: Analysis of Lexical Changes in His Self-Translations." Ph.D. diss., Michigan State University, 2006.

Lane, Tora. *Rendering the Sublime: A Reading of Marina Tsvetaeva's Fairy-Tale Poem "The Swain."* Stockholm: Acta Universitatis Stockholmiensis, 2009.

Lanne, Jean-Claude. "M. Cvetaeva traductrice de Puškin." In *Marina Tsvetaeva: Trudy 1-go mezhdunarodnogo simpoziuma, Lausanne, 1982,* 436–44. Bern: Peter Lang, 1991.

Lattimore, Richmond. "Poetry Chronicle." *Hudson Review* 24, no. 3 (1971): 499–510.

Letters: Summer 1926: Boris Pasternak, Marina Tsvetayeva, Rainer Maria Rilke, ed. Yevgeny Pasternak, Yelena Pasternak, and Konstantin M. Azadovsky, trans. Margaret Wettlin, Walter Arndt, and Jamey Gambrell. New York: New York Review of Books, 2001.

Leve, E. A. "Pervaia v Rossii neofilologichka." *Zapiski neo-filologicheskogo obshchestva* 8 (1915): 211–57.

Levy, Jiri. *The Art of Translation,* trans. Patrick Corness. Amsterdam: John Benjamins, 2011.

Loseff, Lev, and Valentina Polukhina, eds. *Joseph Brodsky: The Art of a Poem.* New York: St. Martin's, 1999.

Lossewa, Olga. "Neues über Elisabeth Kulmann." In *Schumann und seine Dichter,* ed. Matthias Wendt, 77–86. Mainz: Schott, 1993.

Lushenkova Foscolo, Anna. "L'Autotraduction dans la poésie de Marina Tsvetaeva." In *Plurilinguisme et autotraduction,* ed. Anna Lushenkova Foscolo and Malgorzata Smorag-Goldberg, 137–58. Paris: Éditions EUR'ORBEM, 2019.

Mahlert, Ulrich. ". . . die Spuren einer himmlischen Erscheinung zurücklassend: Zu Schumanns Liedern nach Elisabeth Kulmann op. 104." In *Schumann in Düsseldorf: Werke, Texte, Interpretationen,* ed. Bernhard R. Appel, 119–26. Mainz: Schott, 1993.

Makin, Michael. *Marina Tsvetaeva: Poetics of Appropriation.* Oxford: Clarendon, 1993.

———. "Text and Violence in Tsvetaeva's *Mólodets.*" In *Discontinuous Discourses in Modern Russian Literature,* ed. Catriona Kelly, Michael Makin, and David Shepherd, 115–35. London: Macmillan, 1989.

Marcadé, Jean-Claude. "Kandinsky, citoyen du monde: L'Écrivain russe et allemand et ses liaisons avec l'Italie et la France." April 30, 2015. http://www

.vania-marcade.com/kandinsky-citoyen-du-monde-lecrivain-russe-et-allem and-et-ses-liaisons-avec-litalie-et-la-france/.

———. "L'Écriture de Kandinsky." In *Kandinsky: Collections du Centre Georges Pompidou,* 148–60. Paris: Musée National d'Art Moderne, 1998.

[Marcadé, Jean-Claude] Zhan-Klod Markade. "V. V. Kandinskii—russkii pisatel'." In *Na rubezhe dvukh stoletii: Sbornik v chest' 60-letiia Aleksandra Vasil'evicha Lavrova,* ed. Vsevolod Bagno et al., 388–98. Moscow: NLO, 2009.

Mashinski, Irina. "The Letter. It's Just . . ." / "Otvet." *Radius,* March 21, 2011. http://www.radiuslit.org/2011/03/21/poem-english-translation-russian-by -irina-mashinski/.

McGrady, Patrick. "An Interpretation of Wassily Kandinsky's *Klänge.*" Ph.D. diss., State University of New York at Binghamton, 1989.

Morris, Paul D. *Vladimir Nabokov: Poetry and the Lyric Voice.* Toronto: University of Toronto Press, 2010.

Mullins, R. Dyche. "Conjuring in Two Tongues: The Russian and English Prosodies of Nabokov's 'Pale Fire.'" *Nabokov Online Journal* 10–11 (2016/2017): 1–85.

Nabokov, Vladimir. *The Annotated Lolita,* ed. Alfred Appel, Jr. New York: Vintage Books, 1991.

———. *Lolita: Roman.* Perevod s angliiskogo avtora. Moscow: Izvestiia, 1989.

———. *Notes on Prosody.* New York: Pantheon Books, 1964.

———. *Poems and Problems.* New York: McGraw-Hill, 1970.

———. "Problems of Translation: *Onegin* in English" (*Partisan Review,* 1955). Republished in *Theories of Translation: An Anthology of Essays from Dryden to Derrida,* ed. Rainer Schulte and John Biguenet, 127–43. Chicago: University of Chicago Press, 1992.

———. "Pounding the Clavichord" (*New York Review of Books,* 1964). Republished in *Strong Opinions,* 231–40. New York: McGraw-Hill, 1973.

———. "Reply to My Critics" (*Encounter,* 1966). Republished in *Strong Opinions,* 241–67. New York: McGraw-Hill, 1973.

———. *Selected Poems.* New York: Alfred A. Knopf, 2012.

———. *Stikhi.* Ann Arbor, Mich.: Ardis, 1979.

Nesterov, Anton. "Avtoperevod kak avtokommentarii." *Inostrannaia literatura* 7 (2001): 249–55.

Nikitenko, A. "Zhizneopisanie devitsy Elizavety Kul'man." In *Polnoe sobranie russkikh, nemetskikh i ital'ianskikh stikhotvorenii Elizavety Kul'man,* by Elizaveta Kul'man, I–XXV. St. Petersburg: Tipografiia Imperatorskoi Rossiiskoi Akademii, 1839.

Nikonova, Natalia, and Yulia Tikhomirova. "The Father of Russian Romanticism's Literary Translingualism: Vasilii Zhukovskii's German Compositions and Self-Translations." *Translation Studies* 11, no. 2 (2018): 139–57.

Noonan, Will. "Self-Translation, Self-Reflection, Self-Derision: Samuel

Beckett's Bilingual Humor." In *Self-Translation: Brokering Originality in Hybrid Culture*, ed. Anthony Cordingley, 159–76. London: Bloomsbury, 2013.

Pavlenko, Aneta. *The Bilingual Mind and What It Tells Us about Language and Thought*. New York: Cambridge University Press, 2014.

———. "Bilingual Selves." In *Bilingual Minds: Emotional Experience, Expression and Representation*, ed. Aneta Pavlenko, 1–33. Clevedon, Eng.: Multilingual Matters, 2006.

Pérez Firmat, Gustavo. *Tongue Ties: Logo-Eroticism in Anglo-Hispanic Literature*. New York: Palgrave Macmillan, 2003.

Perry, Menakhem. "Thematic and Structural Shifts in Autotranslations by Bilingual Hebrew-Yiddish Writers: The Case of Mendele Mokher Sforim." *Poetics Today* 2, no. 4 (1981): 181–92.

Pilshchikov, Igor A. "Baratynsky's Russian-French Self-Translations (On the Problem of Invariant Reconstruction)." *Essays in Poetics* 17, no. 2 (1992): 15–22.

Podzemskaia, Nadia. "L'Écriture théorique de Vassily Kandinsky et le problème du multilinguisme." In *Multilinguisme et créativité littéraire*, ed. Olga Anokhina, 157–74. Louvain-la-Neuve: Harmattan, 2012.

———. "Note sur la genèse et l'histoire de l'édition de *Du Spirituel dans l'art* de V. Kandinsky." *Histoire de l'Art* 39 (October 1997): 107–16.

Polukhina, Valentina. "Angliiskii Brodskii." In *Iosif Brodskii: Tvorchestvo, lichnost', sud'ba: Itogi trekh konferentsii,* 49–59. St. Petersburg: Zhurnal "Zvezda," 1998.

Popescu, Costin. "Jocul de-a societatea / Jouer à la société." *Atelier de Traduction* (Suceava, Romania), no. 7 (2007): 27–40.

Pushkin, Alexander Sergeevich. *Eugene Onegin: A Novel in Verse*. Translated from the Russian, with a commentary, by Vladimir Nabokov. Revised edition. Princeton, N.J.: Princeton University Press, 1975.

Raine, Craig. "A Reputation Subject to Inflation." *Financial Times*, November 16, 1996, 19.

Reid, Christopher. "Great American Disaster" (review of *To Urania*, by Joseph Brodsky). *London Review of Books*, December 8, 1988, 17–18.

Robinson, Douglas. *The Translator's Turn*. Baltimore, Md.: Johns Hopkins University Press, 1991.

Ronen, Omri. "The Triple Anniversary of World Literature: Goethe, Pushkin, Nabokov." In *Nabokov at Cornell*, ed. Gabriel Shapiro, 172–81. Ithaca, N.Y.: Cornell University Press, 2003.

Rosslyn, Wendy. *Feats of Agreeable Usefulness: Translations by Russian Women 1763–1825*. Fichtenwalde: Verlag F. K. Göpfert, 2000.

Rulyova, Natalya. "Joseph Brodsky: Translating Oneself." Ph.D. diss., Cambridge University, 2002.

Sarab'ianov, D. V. "Kandinskii i russkii simvolizm." *Izvestiia Akademii Nauk. Seriia literatury i iazyka* 53, no. 4 (1994): 16–26.

Scherr, Barry P. "Poetry." In *The Garland Companion to Vladimir Nabokov*, ed. Vladimir E. Alexandrov, 608–25. New York: Garland, 1995.

Schlegel, Joseph. "The Shapes of Poetry: Andrey Bely's Poetics in Vladimir Nabokov's *The Gift*." *Slavic and East European Journal* 59, no. 4 (2015): 565–84.

Schleiermacher, Friedrich. "On the Different Methods of Translating" (1813). Trans. Susan Bernofsky. In *The Translation Studies Reader*, 2nd ed., ed. Lawrence Venuti, 43–63. New York: Routledge, 2004.

Sers, Philippe. "Le Clocher d'Ivan Veliky: Poésie, théâtre et peinture chez Wassily Kandinsky." *Courier du Centre International d'Études Poétiques*, vol. 193–94 (1992): 31–70.

Shakhovskaia, Zinaida. *V poiskakh Nabokova: Otrazheniia*. Moscow: Kniga, 1991.

Sheppard, Richard. "Kandinsky's *Klänge*: An Interpretation," *German Life and Letters* 33, no. 2 (1980): 135–46.

Shklovsky, Viktor. *Theory of Prose*, trans. Benjamin Sher. Elmwood Park, Ill.: Dalkey Archive, 1990.

Short, Christopher. "Between Text and Image in Kandinsky's Oeuvre: A Consideration of the Album *Sounds*." *Tate Papers*, no. 6 (autumn 2006). http://www.tate.org.uk/research/publications/tate-papers/06/between-text-and-image-in-kandinskys-oeuvre-a-consideration-of-the-album-sounds.

Shvabrin, Stanislav. "'. . . A Sob That Alters the Entire History of Russian Letters . . .': Cincinnatus's Plight, Tyutchev's 'Last Love,' and Nabokov's Metaphysics of Poetic Form." *Slavic and East European Journal* 58, no. 3 (2014): 437–64.

———. *Between Rhyme and Reason. Vladimir Nabokov, Translation, and Dialogue*. Toronto: University of Toronto Press, 2019.

Simic, Charles. "Working for the Dictionary." *New York Review of Books*, October 19, 2000. http://www.nybooks.com/articles/2000/10/19/working-for-the-dictionary/.

Simon, Sherry. *Gender in Translation: Cultural Identity and the Politics of Transmission*. London: Routledge, 1996.

Skow, John. "Drinker of Words." *Time*, June 14, 1971, 66–68.

Smith, Alexandra. *The Song of the Mocking Bird: Puškin in the Works of Marina Tsvetaeva*. Bern: Peter Lang, 1994.

Smith, Gerald S. "Nabokov and Russian Verse Form." *Russian Literature Tri-Quarterly* 24 (1991): 271–306.

Sokolov, Boris. "Kandinskii: Zvuki 1911: Istoriia i zamysel neosushchestvennogo poeticheskogo al'boma." *Literaturnoe obozrenie* 4, no. 258 (1996): 3–41.

———. "'Otdelit' tsveta ot veshchei': Poisk bepredmetnosti v poeticheskom tsikle V. V. Kandinskogo 'Tsvety bez zapakha.'" In *Bespredmetnost' i abstraktsiia*, ed. G. F. Kovalenko et al., 166–82. Moscow: Nauka, 2011.

———. "Poeticheskii al'bom V.V. Kandinskogo 'Zvuki'/'Klänge' i problema kul'turnogo dvuiazychiia." In *Rossiia-Germania: Kul'turnye sviazy v pervoi polovine XX veka*. Vipperovskie chteniia 1996, vol. 19 (Moscow: Gosudarstvennyi muzei izobrazitel'nykh iskusstv im. A. S. Pushkina, 2000), 208–42.

Stavans, Ilan. "On Self-Translation." *LA Review of Books*, August 23, 2016. https://lareviewofbooks.org/article/on-self-translation/.

Stein, Susan Alyson. "Kandinsky and Abstract Stage Composition: Practice and Theory, 1909–12." *Art Journal* 43, no. 1 (1983): 61–66.

Steiner, George. *After Babel: Aspects of Language and Translation*. 3rd ed. Oxford: Oxford University Press, 1998.

Stessin, Alexander. *Point of Reference / Tochka otscheta / Le Point de la référence*. New York: Slovo-Word, 2002.

Toury, Gideon. *Descriptive Translation Studies—and Beyond*. Rev. ed. Amsterdam: John Benjamins, 2012.

Trubikhina, Julia. *The Translator's Doubts: Vladimir Nabokov and the Ambiguity of Translation*. Boston: Academic Studies, 2015.

Tsvetaeva, Marina. *"I zvezda s zvezdoiu govorit": Stikhotvoreniia Mikhaila Lermontova vo frantsuzskikh perevodakh Mariny Tsvetaevoi*. Moscow: Dom-muzei Mariny Tsvetaevoi, 2014.

———. *Le Gars*. Sauve: Clémence Hiver, 1991.

———. *Le Gars*. Preface by Efim Etkind. Paris: Des Femmes, 1992.

———. *Molodets*, ed. Natal'ia Teletova. St. Petersburg: DORN, 2003.

———. *Mólodets/Le Gars*. Illustrations by Natalia Goncharova. Moscow: Ellis Lak, 2005.

———. *Sobranie sochinenii v semi tomakh*. Moscow: Ellis Lak, 1994–95.

———. *Tentative de jalousie et autres poèmes*. Paris: La Découverte, 1986.

———. "Trois poèmes écrits en français." Publication, presentation, and commentary by H. B. Korkina and V. Lossky. In *Un chant de vie: Marina Tsvétaeva: Actes du Colloque International de l'Université Paris IV*, 388–96. Paris: YMCA, 1996.

[Tsvetaeva, Marina] Marina Cvetaeva. *Mólodets. Skazka / Mólodec: Ein Märchen*, ed. and trans. Christiane Hauschild. Göttingen: Wallstein Verlag, 2004.

Tsvetkov, Aleksei. *Edem*. Ann Arbor, Mich.: Ardis, 1985.

———. *Vse eto, ili Eto vse: Sobranie stikhotvorenii v dvukh tomakh*. New York: Ailuros, 2015.

Turchin, V. "'Klänge' V. V. Kandinskogo i poeticheskaia kul'tura nachala XX veka." *Iskusstvoznanie* 2 (1998): 414–54.

Venuti, Lawrence. "Introduction: Translation, Interpretation, and the Humanities." In *Teaching Translation: Programs, Courses, Pedagogies*, ed. Lawrence Venuti, 1–14. London: Routledge, 2017.

Vincenz, Marc. "A Cloud of Voices: A Conversation and Twenty Cigarettes with Katia Kapovich." *Open Letters Monthly*, July 1, 2010. http://www.openlettersmonthly.com/voices-before-and-after-the-storm/.

Volgina, Arina. "Avtoperevody Iosifa Brodskogo i ikh vospriatiie v SSHA i Velikobritanii." Ph.D. diss, Moscow State University, 2005.

———. "Iosif Brodskii and Joseph Brodsky." *Russian Studies in Literature* 42, no. 3 (2006): 7–20.

Volkov, Solomon. *Conversations with Joseph Brodsky: A Poet's Journey through the Twentieth Century*, trans. Marian Schwartz. New York: Free Press, 1998.

Wachtel, Michael. *The Development of Russian Verse: Meter and Its Meaning.* Cambridge: Cambridge University Press, 1998.

Walkowitz, Rebecca L. *Born Translated: The Contemporary Novel in an Age of World Literature.* New York: Columbia University Press, 2015.

Wanner, Adrian. "*Lolita* and *Kofemolka*: Vladimir Nabokov's and Michael Idov's Self-Translations from English into Russian." *Slavic and East European Journal* 57, no. 3 (2013): 450–64.

———. *Out of Russia: Fictions of a New Translingual Diaspora.* Evanston, Ill.: Northwestern University Press, 2011.

———. *Russian Minimalism: From the Prose Poem to the Anti-Story.* Evanston, Ill.: Northwestern University Press, 2003.

Weiss, Peg. "Kandinsky, Wolfskehl und Stefan George." *Castrum Peregrini* 138 (1979): 26–51.

Weissbort, Daniel. *From Russian with Love: Joseph Brodsky in English: Pages from a Journal 1996–97.* London: Anvil Press Poetry, 2004.

———. "Translating Brodsky: A Postscript." In *Translating Poetry: The Double Labyrinth*, ed. Daniel Weissbort, 221–27. Iowa City: University of Iowa Press, 1989.

Whyte, Christopher. "Against Self-Translation." *Translation and Literature* 11, no. 1 (spring 2002): 64–71.

Wytrzens, Günther. "Das Deutsche als Kunstmittel bei Marina Cvetaeva." *Wiener Slavistisches Jahrbuch* 15 (1969): 59–70.

Yankelevich, Matvei. "The Russians Are Coming! The Russians Are Coming! Field Notes on Russian-American Poets." *Octopus Magazine* 5. http://www.octopusmagazine.com/Issue05/essays/Matvei_Yankelevich.htm; *Octopus Magazine* 7. http://octopusmagazine.com/Issue07/html/matvei_yankelevich.htm.

Yau, Wai-Ping. "Translation and Film: Dubbing, Subtitling, Adaptation, and Remaking." In *A Companion to Translation Studies*, ed. Sandra Berman and Catherine Porter, 492–503. Chichester, Eng.: Wiley Blackwell, 2014.

Yildiz, Yasemin. *Beyond the Mother Tongue: The Postmonolingual Condition.* New York: Fordham University Press, 2012.

Zapol', Aleksandr, ed. *Latyshskaia/Russkaia poeziia.* Riga: Neputns, 2011.

Zubova, Liudmila. *Iazyk poezii Mariny Tsvetaevoi (fonetika, slovoobrazovanie, frazeologiia).* St. Petersburg: Izdatel'stvo S.-Peterburgskogo Universiteta, 1999.

———. "Khudozhestvennyi bilingvizm v poezii M. Tsvetaevoi." *Vestnik Leningradskogo Universiteta,* Ser. 2, Iazykoznanie, no. 4 (1988): 40–45.

———. "Prilagatel'nye Brodskogo." In *Poeticheskii iazyk Iosifa Brodskogo: Stat'i,* 141–61. St. Petersburg: LEMA, 2015.

Index

Index

Turgenev, Ivan, 59
Tzara, Tristan, 180n41

Ufliand, Vladimir, 138
universal poetic idiom, 11, 66, 73, 111
USSR. *See* Soviet Union

Valéry, Paul, 82
Van Bolderen, Trish, 8
Venuti, Lawrence, 173
Vergo, Peter, 53, 62, 67–68
versification (syllabic vs. syllabotonic), 87,
    110–11, 197n39, 200n80
Villon, François, 83
Vivier, Robert, 84
Volgina, Arina, 204n1
Volkov, Solomon, 138
Voss, Johann Heinrich, 26

Wachtel, Michael, 204n45
Wagner, Richard, 2, 51
Walcott, Derek, 141
Walkowitz, Rebecca, 10–11
Warren, Robert Penn, 177n1
Weidlé, Vladimir, 110
Weissbort, Daniel, 143–44, 152–53
Whyte, Christopher, 11
Wilbur, Richard, 141
women and translation, 30–31

Yau, Wai-Ping, 178n20
Yildiz, Yasemin, 1–2

zaum' (transmental language), 64, 78
Zhukovskii, Vasilii, 42
Zubova, Liudmila, 88, 207n45
Zweiklang (two-sound), 65–66, 72–75